iPad® 2 For Seniors

FOR

DUMMIES®

3RD EDITION

by Nancy Muir

WILEY

John Wiley & Sons, Inc.

iPad® 2 For Seniors For Dummies®

Published by
John Wiley & Sons, Inc.
111 River Street
Hoboken, NJ 07030-5774

www.wiley.com

WILEY

About the Author

Nancy Muir is the author of over 60 books on technology and business topics. In addition to her writing work, Nancy runs a website on technology for seniors called TechSmartSenior.com and a companion website for her iPad books in the For Dummies series, iPadMadeClear.com. She writes a regular column on computers and the Internet on Retirenet.com. Prior to her writing career Nancy was a manager at several publishing companies, and a training manager at Symantec.

Dedication

To Edward and Lindy Carder who have provided a great example of seniors who have become great iPad enthusiasts, as well as being my dearest friends and wonderful people.

Author's Acknowledgments

I was lucky enough to have Blair Pottenger, the absolute best editor in the world, assigned to lead the team on this book. Blair, I couldn't have gotten through this rush schedule without you; you went way above and beyond on this one! Thanks also to Dennis Cohen for his able work as technical editor, and to Barry Childs-Helton, the book's copy editor. Last but never least, thanks to Kyle Looper, Acquisitions Editor, for hiring me to write this book.

Publisher's Acknowledgments

We're proud of this book; please send us your comments at http://dummies.custhelp.com. For other comments, please contact our Customer Care Department within the U.S. at 877-762-2974, outside the U.S. at 317-572-3993, or fax 317-572-4002.

Some of the people who helped bring this book to market include the following:

Acquisitions and Editorial

Project Editor: Blair J. Pottenger

Acquisitions Editor: Kyle Looper

Senior Copy Editor: Barry Childs-Helton

Technical Editor: Dennis Cohen

Editorial Manager: Kevin Kirschner

Editorial Assistant: Amanda Graham

Sr. Editorial Assistant: Cherie Case

Cover Photo: © GETTY IMAGES / Douglas Waters

Cartoons: Rich Tennant (www.the5thwave.com)

Composition Services

Project Coordinator: Sheree Montgomery

Layout and Graphics: Corrie Socolovitch

Proofreader: Susan Hobbs

Indexer: Potomac Indexing, LLC

Publishing and Editorial for Technology Dummies

Richard Swadley, Vice President and Executive Group Publisher

Andy Cummings, Vice President and Publisher

Mary Bednarek, Executive Acquisitions Director

Mary C. Corder, Editorial Director

Publishing for Consumer Dummies

Kathleen Nebenhaus, Vice President and Executive Publisher

Composition Services

Debbie Stailey, Director of Composition Services

Table of Contents

*I*f you bought this book (or are even thinking about buying it), you've probably already made the decision to buy an iPad. The iPad is set up to be simple to use, but still, you can spend hours exploring the preinstalled apps, finding how to change settings, and syncing the device to your computer or through iCloud. I've invested those hours so that you don't have to — and I've added advice and tips for getting the most out of your iPad.

This book helps you get going with the iPad quickly and painlessly so that you can move directly to the fun part.

About This Book

This book is specifically written for mature people like you, folks who may be relatively new to using computing gadgets and want to discover the basics of buying an iPad, working with its pre-installed apps, and getting on the Internet. In writing this book, I've tried to consider the types of activities that might interest someone who is 50 years old or older and picking up an iPad for the first time.

Conventions Used in This Book

This book uses certain conventions to help you find your way around, including

⟶ Text you type in a text box is in **bold**. Figure references, such as "see **Figure 1-1**," are also in bold, to help you find them.

⟶ Whenever I mention a website address, or *URL*, I put it in a different font, like this.

⟶ Figure callouts draw your attention to actions you need to perform. In some cases, points of interest in a figure might be indicated. The text tells you what to look for; the callout line makes it easy to find.

Tip icons point out insights or helpful suggestions related to tasks in the step lists.

New icons highlight what features of iPad 2 or iOS 5 are new and exciting, in case you're moving up from earlier versions.

Foolish Assumptions

This book is organized by sets of tasks. These tasks start from the beginning, assuming that you've never laid your hands on an iPad, and guide you through basic steps provided in nontechnical language.

This book covers both Wi-Fi and Wi-Fi/3G iPad features. I'm also assuming that you'll want to download and use the iBooks e-reader app, so I tell you how to do that in Chapter 9 and cover its features in Chapter 10.

Why You Need This Book

The iPad is cool and perfect for many seniors because it provides a simple, intuitive interface for activities such as checking e-mail and playing music. But why should you stumble around, trying to figure out its features? Using the simple step-by-step approach in this book, you can get up to speed with the iPad right away and overcome any technophobia you might have.

How This Book Is Organized

This book is conveniently divided into several handy parts to help you find what you need:

➡ **Part I: Making the iPad Your Pad:** If you're about to buy your iPad or are ready to get started with the basics of using it, this part is for you. These chapters highlight the newest features in iPad 2 and iOS 5 and help you explore the different specifications, styles, and price ranges for all iPad models. You find out how to set up your iPad out of the box, including

  • Opening an iCloud account to register and push content to all your Apple devices automatically.

- Opening an iTunes account to buy entertainment content and additional apps.

These chapters also provide information for exploring the iPad Home screen when you first turn it on, and useful accessibility features to help out if you have hearing or vision challenges.

➠ **Part II: Taking the Leap Online:** In Part II, you find out how to connect to the Internet and use the built-in Safari browser. You putter with the preinstalled Mail app and set up your iPad to access e-mail from your existing e-mail accounts. In this part, you also get to shop online for multimedia content, such as movies and music, and additional fun iPad apps. You explore the exciting FaceTime feature, used for making video calls to other people who use the iPad 2, a Mac, the iPhone 4 or 4S, or the iPod touch.

➠ **Part III: Having Fun and Consuming Media:** The iPad has been touted by some as a device for consuming media such as music, podcasts, and movies. Built into the iPad are a Music app for playing music and the Videos and YouTube apps for watching video content. In addition, in Part III I explain how to use iBooks, the free e-reader app from Apple. You also explore playing games on your iPad, which — trust me — is a lot of fun. Finally, explore playing around with the Maps app to find your favorite restaurant or bookstore with ease. You also discover the wonderful possibilities for using still and video cameras on iPad 2, and the amazingly fun things you can do with Photo Booth and videos in Chapters 12 and 13, respectively.

In this part you also explore the new Newsstand app for subscribing to and reading magazines.

⟱➡ **Part IV: Managing Your Life and Your iPad:** For the organizational part of your brain, the iPad makes available Calendar, Contacts, and Notes apps, all of which are covered in this part. I also offer advice about keeping your iPad safe and troubleshooting common problems that you might encounter, including using the Find My iPad feature to deal with a lost or stolen iPad. You can also use the new iCloud service to back up your content or restore your iPad.

 The new Reminders app and Notification Center feature in iOS 5 are great for keeping you on schedule. Reminders is a great to-do list feature that allow you enter tasks and details about them, and can also display tasks from your online calendars. Notification Center sends you alerts for apps and items you select to be notified about.

Where to Go from Here

You can work through this book from beginning to end or simply open a chapter to solve a problem or acquire a specific new skill whenever you need it. The steps in every task quickly get you to where you want to go, without a lot of technical explanation.

Note: At the time I wrote this book, all the information it contained was accurate for the Wi-Fi and Wi-Fi + 3G iPads and iPad 2s, version 5 of the iOS (operating system) used by the iPad, and version 10.5 of iTunes. Apple is likely to introduce new iPad models and new versions of iOS and iTunes between book editions. If you've bought a new iPad and its hardware, user interface, or the version of iTunes on your computer looks a little different, be sure to check out what Apple has to say at www.apple.com/ipad. You'll no doubt find updates on the company's latest releases. When a change is very substantial, we may add an update or bonus information that you can download at this book's companion web site, www.dummies.com/go/ipadforseniors.

Part I
Making the iPad Your Pad

The 5th Wave   By Rich Tennant

"Other than this little glitch with the landscape view, I really love my iPad."

Buying Your iPad

*Y*ou've read about it. You've seen on the news the lines at Apple Stores on the day it was released. You're so intrigued that you've decided to get your own iPad to have fun, explore the online world, read e-books, organize your photos, and more.

Trust me: You've made a good decision, because the iPad redefines the computing experience in an exciting, new way. It's also an absolutely perfect fit for many seniors.

In this chapter, you discover the different types of iPad models and their advantages, as well as where to buy this little gem. After you have one in your hands, I help you explore what's in the box and get an overview of the little buttons and slots you'll encounter — luckily, the iPad has very few of them.

Discover What's New in iPad 2 and iOS 5

Apple's iPad gets its features from a combination of hardware and its software operating system (called *iOS;* the term is short for iPhone Operating System, in case you need to know that to impress your friends). The most current operating system is iOS 5. If you've seen the first-generation iPad in action or you own one, it's helpful to understand which new features the iPad 2 device brings to the table (all of which are covered in more detail in this book). In addition to features on the first-generation iPad device, the second-generation iPad offers

⟶ **A thinner, lighter design:** You also now get to choose between a black or white model.

⟶ **A dual-core A5 chip:** This chip gives your iPad much faster performance.

⟶ **An improved Safari browser:** Streamlining Safari gives you faster Internet browsing.

⟶ **Two (one front-facing; one rear-facing) cameras:** Both cameras can be used to capture still photos or HD video. If you use FaceTime, a video calling service, you and your caller can watch each other on live video.

⟶ **Video mirroring capability:** You can use the Apple Digital AV Adapter (see "Consider iPad Accessories," later in this chapter) to connect the iPad to your HDTV or other HDMI-friendly devices and mirror what's on your iPad display on the other device.

⟶ **A built-in, three-axis gyroscope:** Gamers will find this element useful to shift around in a more versatile manner as they move virtually through games that involve motion. With iPad 2 the gyroscope, accelerometer, and compass also help apps like Maps to pinpoint your location and movements as you stroll around town.

 Throughout this book, I highlight features that are relevant only in using the iPad 2, so you can use this book no matter which version of the device you own.

In addition, iPad 2 may have iOS 4 *or* 5 installed, depending on when you bought it. Any iPad device can make use of iOS 5 if you update the operating system (discussed in detail in Chapter 2); this book is based on version 5 of the iOS. This update to the operating system adds many new features, including

⟹ **Integration with iCloud,** including the ability to backup and restore your iPad. *iCloud* is a new service from Apple that allows you to save and retrieve files from an online account, sync content with other Apple devices, and update your iPad operating system without having to sync your device to your computer.

⟹ **Newsstand,** an app that allows you to subscribe to and read online versions of many popular magazines and newspapers that are "pushed" to your iPad so you have the latest editions without having to do a thing once you've bought a subscription.

⟹ **Reminders,** a great place to centralize all your upcoming events, set reminders, and organize your commitments by date or in a list format. You can also have iPad remind you to take actions when you leave or arrive at a location (leaving the grocery store, remember to call your spouse to ask if there's anything else for you to get!).

⟹ Notifications delivered in the **Notification Center,** where you can control how iPad lets you know about FaceTime alerts, new messages or reminders, events in your Calendar, and Game Center items such as badges, sounds, and banners.

⟹ **iMessage,** a new, integrated instant-messaging feature utilized by the Messages app for sending text messages to people using other Apple devices in real time (now you send it, now they see it).

⟱ A **split keyboard** allows those of you who have mas-
tered texting with your thumbs on a mobile phone
to do the same trick on the wider screen of an iPad.
By splitting the keyboard with half of it on the right
of the screen and half of it on the left, you can reach
all keys with your thumbs from the side of the tab-
let. Young people of your acquaintance will be
impressed.

⟱ Additional **touchscreen gestures** provide shortcuts
for getting things done, such as dragging e-mail
addresses to address fields in Mail and multitasking.

⟱ **Accessibility features** such as LED Flash and
Vibration settings that help to alert those with hearing or vision challenges to incoming calls or
messages.

⟱ **Integration with Twitter** from several apps —
including Photos, Maps, and the Safari web browser.

⟱ **E-mail tools** allow you to apply bold, italic, under-
lining, and indentation settings to your e-mail
messages, as well as offer improved searching of
messages.

⟱ **PC Free** is all about liberating your device from your
computer so you can control many actions — such
as registering and updating your iOS wirelessly and
creating calendars and mailboxes — directly from
iPad.

⟱ The **Calendar app** sports a new Year view.

⟱ **Game Center** offers new features such as posting
profile pictures, playing turn-based games, and helping you to compare your scores with your friends'.

Choose the Right iPad for You

iPads don't come in different sizes. In fact, if you pick up an iPad (see **Figure 1-1**), you're not likely to be able to tell one model from another, except that some are black and some are white. Their differences are primarily under the hood.

Figure 1-1

iPad 2 models have three variations:

➡ Black or white

➡ Amount of built-in memory

➡ Method used for connecting to the Internet (Wi-Fi only or Wi-Fi and 3G)

Your options in the first bullet point are pretty black and white, but if you're confused about the other two, read on as I explain these variations in more detail in the following sections.

Decide How Much Memory Is Enough

Memory is a measure of how much information — for example, movies, photos, and software applications, or *apps* — you can store on a computing device. Memory can also affect your iPad's performance when handling tasks such as streaming favorite TV shows from the World Wide Web or downloading music.

Streaming refers to watching video content from the web (or from other devices) rather than playing a file stored on your computing device. You can enjoy a lot of material online without ever downloading its full content to your hard drive — and given that every iPad model has a relatively small amount of memory, that's not a bad idea. See Chapters 11 and 13 for more about getting your music and movies online.

Your memory options with an iPad are 16, 32, or 64 gigabytes (GB). You must choose the right amount of memory because you can't open the unit and add memory, as you usually can with a desktop computer. There is also no way to insert a *flash drive* (also known as a *USB stick*) to add backup capacity, because iPad 2 has no USB port — or CD/DVD drive, for that matter. However, Apple has thoughtfully provided iCloud, a service you can use to back up content to the Internet (you can read more about that in Chapter 2).

With an Apple Digital AV Adapter accessory, you can plug into the Dock connector slot to attach an HDMI–enabled device such as an external hard drive for additional storage capacity. See Chapter 13 for more about using these AV features (most of which have not yet hit the market — but they're coming!). As of this writing ViewSonic is offering three new HDMI projectors; DVDO is offering a HD Travel Kit for smartphones and tablets; and Belkin has introduced a new line of tools for HDTV streaming, for example.

So how much memory is enough for your iPad? Here's a rule of thumb: If you like lots of media, such as movies or TV shows, and you want to store them on your iPad (rather than experiencing or accessing this content online on sites such as Hulu or Netflix), you might need 64 GB. For most people who manage a reasonable number of photos, download some music, and watch heavy-duty media such as movies online, 32 GB is probably sufficient. If you simply want to check e-mail, browse the web, and write short notes to yourself, 16 GB *might* be enough.

 Do you have a clue how big a gigabyte (GB) is? Consider this: Just about any computer you buy today comes with a minimum of 250 GB of storage. Computers have to tackle larger tasks than iPads do, so that number makes sense. The iPad, which uses a technology called *flash* for memory storage, is meant (to a great extent) to help you experience online media and e-mail; it doesn't have to store much and in fact pulls lots of content from online. In the world of memory, 16 GB for any kind of storage is puny if you keep lots of content and graphics on the device.

What's the price for larger memory? For the iPad 2, a 16GB Wi-Fi unit (see the next section for more about Wi-Fi) costs $499; 32 GB jumps the price to $599; and 64 GB adds another $100, setting you back a whopping $699.

Determine Whether You Need Wi-Fi Only or Wi-Fi and 3G

One variation on price and performance for the iPad is whether your model has Wi-Fi or Wi-Fi and 3G. Because iPad is great for browsing online, shopping online, e-mailing, and so on, having an Internet connection for it is important. That's where Wi-Fi and 3G enter the picture. Both technologies are used to connect to the Internet. You use *Wi-Fi* to connect to a wireless network at home or at your local coffee shop or an airport that offers Wi-Fi. This type of network uses short-range radio to connect to the Internet; its range is reasonably limited — so if you leave home or walk out of the coffee shop, you can't use it. (These limitations are changing as some towns are installing community-wide Wi-Fi networks.)

The *3G* cellphone technology allows an iPad to connect to the Internet via a cellular-phone network that's widespread. You use it in much the same way you make calls from just about anywhere using your cellphone.

You can buy an iPad with only Wi-Fi or one with both Wi-Fi *and* 3G capabilities. Getting a 3G iPad costs an additional $130 (see **Table 1-1**), but it also includes GPS so you can get more accurate driving directions. You have to buy an iPad model that fits your data connection provider — either AT&T or Verizon.

Also, to use your 3G network, you have to pay AT&T or Verizon a monthly fee. The good news is that neither carrier requires a long-term contract, as you probably had to commit to with your cellphone and its data connection — you can pay for a connection during the month you visit your grandkids, for example, and then get rid of it when you arrive home. AT&T offers prepaid and postpaid options, but Verizon offers only a prepaid plan. AT&T offers plans that top out at 2 GB of data connection, and Verizon offers several levels, including 3GB, 5GB, and 10GB.

Table 1-1	iPad 2 Models and Pricing	
Memory Size	*Wi-Fi Price*	*Wi-Fi and 3G Price*
16GB	$499	$629
32GB	$599	$729
64GB	$699	$829

Of course, these two carriers could change their pricing and options at any time, so go to these links for more information about iPad data plans: AT&T is at `www.att.com/shop/wireless/devices/ipad.jsp`, and Verizon is at `http://phones.verizonwireless.com/ipad2`.

Sprint now offers the iPhone 4S and, at this time, there's a pretty plausible rumor going around that they will eventually offer iPad to their customers as well. Check their website (http://sprint.com) when you're ready to sign up to see what they have to offer.

So how do you choose? If you want to wander around the woods or town — or take long drives with your iPad continually connected to the Internet — get 3G and pay the price. But if you'll use your iPad mainly at home or using a Wi-Fi *hotspot* (a location where Wi-Fi access to the Internet is available), don't bother with 3G. And frankly, you can now find *lots* of hotspots out there, including restaurants, hotels, airports, and more.

You can use the hotspot feature on a smartphone, which allows iPad to use your phone's 3G connection to go online if you pay for a higher-data-use plan that supports hotspot usage with your phone service carrier. Check out the features of your phone to turn hotspot on.

Because the 3G iPad is a GPS device, it knows where you are and can act as a navigation system to get you from here to there. The Wi-Fi–only model uses a digital compass and triangulation method for locating your current position, which is much less accurate; with no constant Internet connection, it won't help you to get around town. If getting accurate directions is one iPad feature that excites you, get 3G and then see Chapter 15 for more about the Maps feature.

Understand What You Need to Use Your iPad

Before you head off to buy your iPad, you should know what other devices, connections, and accounts you'll need to work with it optimally. At a bare minimum, you need to be able to connect to the Internet to take advantage of most of iPad's features. You can open an iCloud account to store and share content online, or you can use a computer to download photos, music, or applications from non-Apple online sources such as stores or sharing sites like your local library and transfer them to your iPad through a process called *syncing*. You can also use a computer or iCloud to register your iPad the first time you start it, although you can have the folks at the Apple Store handle registration for you if you have one nearby.

Can you use iPad without owning a computer and just using public Wi-Fi hotspots to go online (or a 3G connection if you have a 3G model)? Yes. However, to be able to go online using a Wi-Fi–only iPad and to use many of its built-in features at home, you need to have a home Wi-Fi network available. You also need to use iCloud or sync to your computer to get updates for the iPad operating system.

Apple's *iPad User Guide* recommends that you have

➠ A Mac or PC with a USB 2.0 port and one of the following operating systems:

  • Mac OS X version 10.5.8 or later

  • Windows 7, Windows Vista, or Windows XP Home or Professional with Service Pack 3 or later

➠ iTunes 10.5 or later, available at www.itunes. com/download

➠ An iTunes Store account

➠ Internet access

➠ An iCloud account

Apple has set up its iTunes software and the iCloud service to give you two ways to manage content for your iPad — including movies, music, or photos you've downloaded — and specify how to sync your calendar and contact information. Chapter 3 covers those settings in more detail.

Know Where to Buy Your iPad

Apple didn't offer iPad from every major retail store such as Sears or from all major online retailers, such as Newegg. However, with the launch of iPad 2, Apple expanded its retailer partner network quite a bit. As of this writing, you can buy an iPad at the Apple Store and from several brick-and-mortar stores such as BestBuy, Walmart, Sam's Club, and Target, and at online sites such as MacMall.com. You can also buy 3G models (models that require an account with a phone service provider) from AT&T and Verizon.

If you get your iPad from Apple, either at a retail store or the online store, here's the difference in the buying experience:

➠ The Apple Store advantage is that the sales staff will help you unpack your iPad and make sure it's working properly, register the device (which you have to do before you can use it; see Chapter 2 for more about this process), and help you learn the basics of using it. Occasional workshops are held to help people learn about using the iPad. Apple employees are famous for being helpful to customers.

➠ Apple Stores aren't on every corner, so if visiting one isn't an option (or you just prefer to go it alone), you can go to the Apple Store website (`http://store.apple.com/us/browse/home/shop_ipad/family/ipad`) and order one to be shipped to you. Standard shipping typically is free, and if there's a problem, Apple's online store customer service reps, who are known for being helpful, will help you solve the problem or replace your iPad.

Consider iPad Accessories

At present, Apple offers a few accessories you might want to check out when you purchase your iPad (or purchase down the road), including

➟ **iPad Case/Smart Cover:** Your iPad isn't cheap and, unlike a laptop computer, it has an exposed screen that can be damaged if you drop or scratch it. Investing in the iPad Case or Smart Cover (note that the Smart Cover works only with iPad 2) is a good idea if you intend to take your iPad out of your house — or if you have a cat or grandchildren. The iPad Smart Cover (see **Figure 1-2**) costs about $40 for polyurethane and $70 for leather, and other cases vary in price depending on design and material.

Figure 1-2

➟ **iPad Camera Connection Kit:** Because there's no USB port on an iPad, you can't use a USB connection to upload photos from your digital camera to your iPad. If you want to send digital photos directly to your iPad you can use this handy kit. It will set you back about $30 for the privilege.

➠ **iPad Dock:** The iPad is light and thin, which is great, but holding it all the time can get tedious. The iPad Dock lets you prop up the device so that you can view it hands-free and then charge the battery and sync to your computer. At about $30, it's a good investment for ease and comfort.

➠ **iPad Keyboard Dock:** The iPad provides an onscreen keyboard that's passable, especially if you position it to view material in *landscape* orientation (with the long side across the top). However, if you're a touch typist who wants to write long notes or e-mails, or if you have larger hands and have trouble pressing the virtual keys on the screen, the iPad Keyboard Dock (which works with the first generation iPad) or a wireless keyboard might be the answer. The iPad Keyboard Dock and Apple Wireless Keyboard both cost about $70.

➠ **iPad 10W USB Power Adapter:** This accessory is similar to the 10W USB Power Adapter that ships with the iPad. However, the power adapter makes charging easier if you need to place your iPad a bit farther from a power outlet, because this adapter sports a 6-foot-long cord.

➠ **Apple Digital AV Adapter:** To connect devices to output high definition media, you can buy this adapter. There are more devices coming out that use this technology such as projectors and TVs. See **Figure 1-3.**

➠ **Apple Component AV Cable:** This accessory sells for about $40 and lets you connect your iPad 2 to certain TV or stereo systems.

Figure 1-3

 Printers: Apple has teamed with Hewlett-Packard (HP) to produce several printers that work with iPad's native printing capability to handle wireless printing. These printers range from about $100 to about $250, and you can browse all models at the online Apple Store (`http://store.apple.com`). AirPrint Activator 2 and Printopia are apps that can make any printer shared on a network accessible to AirPrint.

 Several companies are already producing iPad accessories such as cases, and more will undoubtedly pop up, so feel free to search for different items and prices.

Don't bother buying a wireless mouse to connect with your iPad via Bluetooth — the iPad recognizes your finger as its primary input device, and mice need not apply.

Explore What's in the Box

When you fork over your hard-earned money for your iPad, you'll be left holding one box about the size of a package of copy paper. Here's a rundown of what you'll find when you take off the shrink-wrap and open the box:

⟶ **iPad:** Your iPad is covered in a thick, plastic sleeve-thingie that you can take off and toss (unless you think there's a chance you'll return it, in which case you might want to keep all packaging for 14 days — Apple's standard return period).

⟶ **Documentation (and I use the term loosely):** Notice, under the iPad itself, a small, white envelope about the size of a half-dozen index cards. Open it and you'll find:

- *A tiny pamphlet:* This pamphlet, named *Important Product Information Guide,* is essentially small print (that you mostly don't need to read) from folks like the FCC.

- *A label sheet:* This sheet has two white Apple logos on it. (I'm not sure what they're for, but my husband and I use one sticker to differentiate my iPad from his.)

- *A small card:* This card displays a picture of the iPad and callouts to its buttons on one side, and the other side contains brief instructions for setting it up and information about where to find out more.

⟶ **Dock Connector to USB Cable:** Use this cord (see **Figure 1-4**) to connect the iPad to your computer, or use it with the last item in the box, the USB Power Adapter.

⟶ **10W USB Power Adapter:** The power adapter (refer to **Figure 1-4**) attaches to the dock connector cord so that you can plug it into the wall and charge the battery.

That's it. That's all there is in the box. It's kind of a study in Zen-like simplicity.

Dock Connector to USB Cable   10W USB Power Adapter

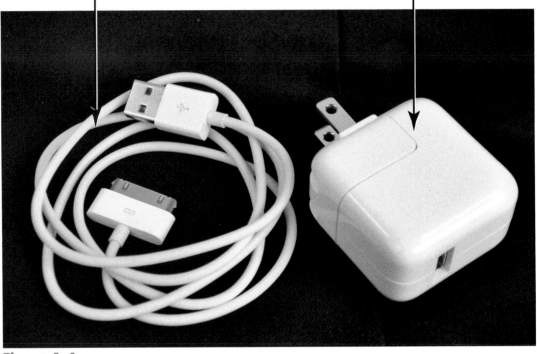

Figure 1-4

Take a First Look at the Gadget

The little card contained in the documentation (see the preceding section) gives you a picture of the iPad with callouts to the buttons you'll find on it. In this section, I give you a bit more information about those buttons and other physical features of the iPad. **Figure 1-5** shows you where each of these items is located.

Here's the rundown on what the various hardware features are and what they do:

➡ **(The all-important) Home button:** On the iPad, you can go back to the Home screen to find just about anything. The Home screen displays all your installed and preinstalled apps and gives you access to your iPad settings. No matter where you are or what you're doing, push Home and you're back at home base. You can also double-tap the Home button to pull up a scrolling list of apps so you can quickly move from one to another.

➠ **Sleep/Wake button:** You can use this button (whose functionality I cover in more detail in Chapter 2) to power up your iPad, put it in Sleep mode, wake it up, or power it down.

➠ **Dock Connector slot:** Plug in the Dock Connector to USB Cable to charge your battery or sync your iPad with your computer (which you find out more about in Chapter 3).

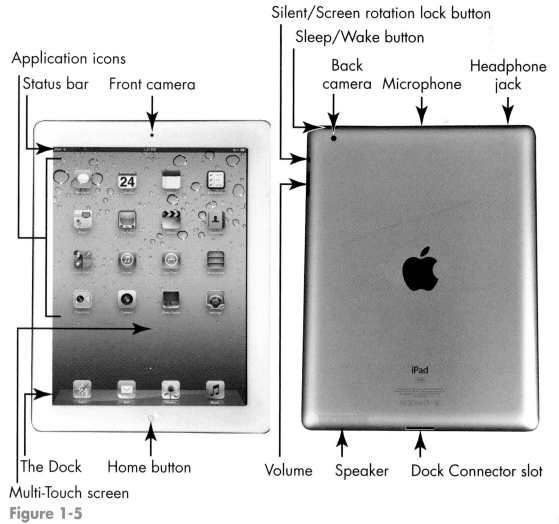

Figure 1-5

➥ **Cameras:** The iPad 2 offers front and rear-facing cameras which you can use to shoot photos or video. The rear one is on the top-right corner, and you need to be careful not to put your thumb over it when taking shots (I have several very nice photos of my thumb already).

➥ **Silent/Screen rotation lock button:** In case you hadn't heard, the iPad screen rotates to match the angle you're holding it. If you want to stick with one orientation even if you spin the iPad in circles, you can use this little switch to lock the screen, which is especially handy when reading an e-book. You can also customize the function of this switch using iPad General Settings to make the switch lock screen rotation rather than mute sound, which it does by default (see Chapter 2 for instructions).

➥ **(A tiny, mighty) Speaker:** One nice surprise when I first got my iPad was hearing what a great little sound system it has and how much sound can come from this tiny speaker. The speaker is located on the bottom edge of the screen, below the Home button.

➥ **Volume:** Tap the volume rocker up for more volume and down for less. With iOS 5 you can use this rocker as a camera shutter button when the camera is activated.

➥ **Headphone jack and microphone:** If you want to listen to your music in private, you can plug in a 3.5mm minijack headphone (including an iPhone headset if you have one, which gives you bidirectional sound). A tiny microphone makes it possible to speak into your iPad to do things such as make phone calls using the Internet, video calling services, or other apps that accept audio input.

Looking Over the Home Screen

I won't kid you: You have a slight learning curve ahead of you because iPad is different from other computers you may have used (although, if you own an iPhone or iPod touch, you've got a head start). That's mainly because of its Multi-Touch screen and onscreen keyboard — no mouse necessary. The iPad doesn't have a Windows or Mac operating system: It does have a modified iPhone operating system, so some of the methods you may have used on computers before (such as right-clicking) don't work on the touchscreen.

The good news is that getting anything done on the iPad is simple, once you know the ropes. In fact, using your fingers instead of a mouse to do things onscreen is a very intuitive way to communicate with your computing device.

In this chapter, you turn on your iPad and register it and then take your first look at the Home screen. You also practice using the onscreen keyboard, see how to interact with the touchscreen in various ways, get pointers on working with cameras, and get an overview of built-in applications.

Chapter 2

Get ready to . . .

Have a soft cloth handy, like the one you might use to clean your eyeglasses. You're about to deposit a ton of fingerprints on your iPad — one downside of a touchscreen device.

See What You Need to Use iPad

You need to be able, at minimum, to connect to the Internet to take advantage of most iPad features, which you can do using a Wi-fi network. You might want to have a computer so that you can download photos, videos, music, or applications and transfer them to your iPad through a process called *syncing*. With iOS 5 a new Apple service called iCloud has arrived, which syncs content from all your Apple iOS devices so anything you buy on your iPhone, for example, will automatically be pushed to your iPad.

You can register your iPad the first time you start it using iCloud or by syncing with your computer via a cable, although you can have the folks at the Apple Store handle registration for you if you have one nearby.

Can you use iPad if you don't own a computer and you use public Wi-Fi hotspots to go online (or a 3G connection if you have a 3G model)? Yes. However, to be able to go online using a Wi-Fi–only iPad and to use many of its built-in features at home, you need to have a Wi-Fi network available.

Apple's *iPad User Guide* recommends that you have

➭ An Apple ID for some features including iCloud

➭ An Internet connection (broadband is recommended)

➭ A Mac or PC with a USB 2.0 port and one of these operating systems:

  • Mac OS X Lion version 10.5.8 or later

- Windows 7, Windows Vista or Windows XP Home
  or Professional with Service Pack 3 or later

➡ iTunes 10.5 or later, available at `www.itunes.com/download`

Apple has set up both iCloud and its iTunes software to help you manage content for your iPad — which includes the movies, music, or photos you've downloaded — and specify where to transfer your calendar and contact information from. Chapter 3 covers these settings in more detail.

Turn On iPad and Register It

1. The first time you turn on your iPad, you have to register it. You can do this using a physical connection to a computer with the latest version of iTunes installed. To register using iTunes on your computer, hold the iPad with one hand on either side, oriented like a pad of paper.

2. Press and hold the Sleep/Wake button on the top of your iPad until the Apple logo appears. In another moment, a screen appears asking if you'd like to register via iCloud or use iTunes. Tap the iTunes option and proceed.

3. Plug the Dock Connector to USB Cable that comes with your device into your iPad.

4. Plug the other end of the cable into a USB port on a computer. Both your computer and the iPad think for a few moments while they exchange data.

5. Sign into your iTunes account in the dialog that appears on your computer screen, and then follow the simple onscreen instructions to register your iPad and choose whether to use iCloud (see Chapter 3 for more about this feature) and whether to allow location services to use your current location. (You can change these settings later; these steps are covered in Chapter 3.) When you're done, your iPad Home screen appears and you're in business.

6. Unplug the Dock Connector to USB Cable.

 If you buy your iPad at an Apple Store, an employee will register it for you and you can skip this whole process.

 You can choose to have certain items transferred to your iPad from your computer when you sync: music, videos, downloaded applications, contacts, audiobooks, calendars, e-books, podcasts, and browser bookmarks. You can also transfer to your computer any content you download directly to your iPad using the iTunes and App Store apps. See Chapters 8 and 9 for more about these features.

 If you have set up iCloud when registering or after registering (see Chapter 3), updates to your operating system will be pushed to your iPad without having to plug it into a computer running iTunes. Apple refers to this feature as PC Free, simply meaning that your device has been liberated from having to use a physical connection to get upgrades.

Meet the Multi-Touch Screen

When the iPad Home screen appears (see **Figure 2-1**), you see a pretty background and two sets of icons. One set appears in the Dock, along the bottom of the screen. The *Dock* contains the Safari, Mail, Photos, and Music app buttons by default, though you can add other apps to it. The Dock appears on every Home screen. You can add new apps to populate as many as 11 additional Home screens. Other icons appear above the Dock and are closer to the top of the screen. (I cover all these icons in the "Take Inventory of Built-in Applications" section, later in this chapter.) Different icons appear in this area on each Home screen.

Application icons

The Dock

Figure 2-1

 Treat the iPad screen carefully. It's made of glass and will smudge when you touch it (and will break if you throw it at the wall).

The iPad uses *touchscreen technology:* When you swipe your finger across the screen or tap it, you're providing input to the device. You hear more about the touchscreen in the next task, but for now, go ahead and play with it for a few minutes — really, you can't hurt anything. Use the pads of your fingertips (not your fingernails) and follow these steps:

1. Tap the Settings icon. The various settings (which you read more about throughout this book) appear, as shown in **Figure** 2-2.

2. To return to the Home screen, press the Home button.

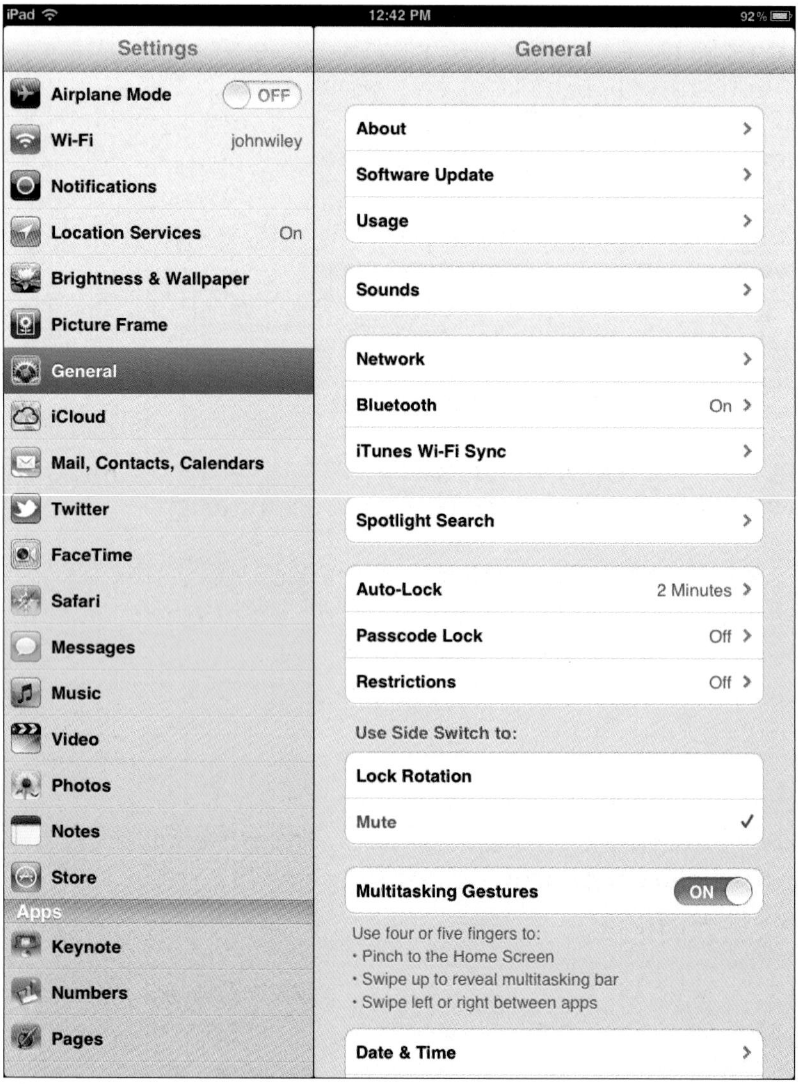

Figure 2-2

3. Swipe a finger or two from right to left on the screen. If downloaded apps fill additional Home screens, then this action moves you to the next Home screen. Note that the little dots at the bottom of the screen, above the Dock icons, indicate which Home screen is displayed. The dot on the far left represents the Spotlight search screen.

4. To experience the screen rotation feature, hold the iPad firmly while turning it sideways. The screen flips to the horizontal orientation. To flip the screen back, just turn the device so it's oriented like a pad of paper again.

 You can customize the Home screen by changing its *wallpaper* (background picture) and brightness. You can read about making these changes in Chapter 4.

Say Goodbye to Click-and-Drag, Hello to Tap-and-Swipe

You can use several methods for getting around and getting things done in iPad using its Multi-Touch screen, including

➡ **Tap once:** To open an application on the Home screen, choose a field such as a search box, select an item in a list, select an arrow to move back or forward one screen, or follow an online link, tap the item once with your finger.

➡ **Tap twice:** Use this method to enlarge or reduce the display of a web page (see Chapter 5 for more about using the *Safari* web browser) or to zoom in or out in the Maps app.

➡ **Pinch:** As an alternative to the tap-twice method, you can pinch your fingers together or move them apart on the screen (see **Figure 2-3**) when you're looking at photos, maps, web pages, or e-mail messages to quickly reduce or enlarge them, respectively.

Figure 2-3

You can use the three-finger tap to zoom your screen to be even larger or use Multitasking gestures to swipe with 4 or 5 fingers (see the "Explore Multitasking Gestures" task later in this chapter). This method is handy if you have vision challenges. Go to Chapter 4 to discover how to turn on this feature using Accessibility settings.

➠ **Drag to scroll (known as *swiping*):** When you press your finger to the screen and drag to the right or left or drag up or down, the screen moves (see **Figure 2-4**). Swiping to the right on the Home screen, for example, moves you to the *Spotlight* screen (the iPad search screen). Swiping down while reading an online newspaper moves you down the page; swiping up moves you back up the page.

➠ **Flick:** To scroll more quickly on a page, quickly flick your finger on the screen in the direction you want to move.

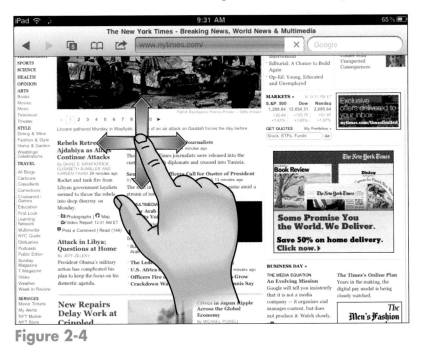

Figure 2-4

⫸ **Tap the Status bar:** To move quickly to the top of a list, web page, or e-mail message, tap the Status bar at the top of the iPad screen.

⫸ **Press and hold:** If you're using Notes or Mail or any other application that lets you select text, or if you're on a web page, pressing and holding text selects a word and displays editing tools you can use to select, cut, or copy the text.

Try these methods now by following these steps:

1. Tap the Safari button to display the web browser. (You may be asked to enter your network password to access the network.)

2. Tap a link to move to another page.

3. Double-tap the page to enlarge it; then pinch your fingers together on the screen to reduce its size.

4. Drag one finger around the page to scroll.

5. Flick your finger quickly on the page to scroll more quickly.

6. Press and hold your finger on a word that isn't a link. The word is selected and the Copy/Define tool is displayed, as shown in **Figure 2-5**. (This step is tricky, so if you don't get it right the first time, don't worry — I cover text editing in more detail in Chapter 18.)

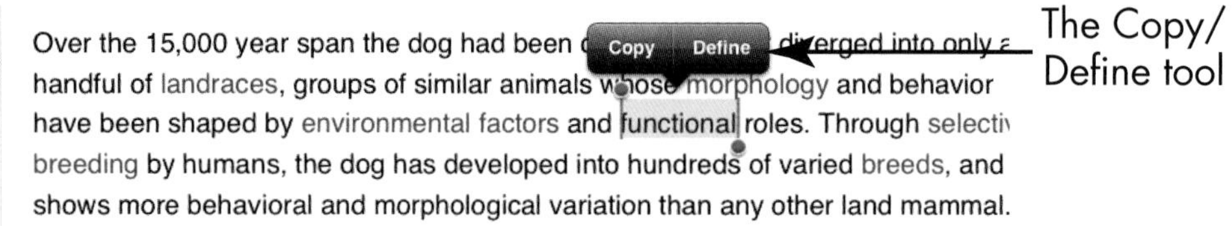

Over the 15,000 year span the dog had been ~~Copy   Define~~ diverged into only a handful of landraces, groups of similar animals whose morphology and behavior have been shaped by environmental factors and functional roles. Through selectiv breeding by humans, the dog has developed into hundreds of varied breeds, and shows more behavioral and morphological variation than any other land mammal.

The Copy/Define tool

Figure 2-5

7. Press and hold your finger on a link or an image. A menu appears with commands you select to open the link or picture, open it in a new page, add it to your Reading List (see Chapter 5), or copy it. The image menu also offers the Save Image command.

8. Position your fingers slightly apart on the screen, and then pinch your fingers together to reduce the page; with your fingers already pinched together, place them on the screen, and then move them apart to enlarge the page.

9. Press the Home button to go back to the Home screen.

Display and Use the Onscreen Keyboard

1. The built-in iPad keyboard appears whenever you're in a text-entry location, such as a search field or an e-mail message. Tap the Notes icon on the Home screen to open this easy-to-use notepad.

2. Tap the note; the onscreen keyboard appears.

3. Type a few words using the keyboard. To make the keyboard display as wide as possible, rotate your iPad to landscape (horizontal) orientation, as shown in **Figure 2-6**.

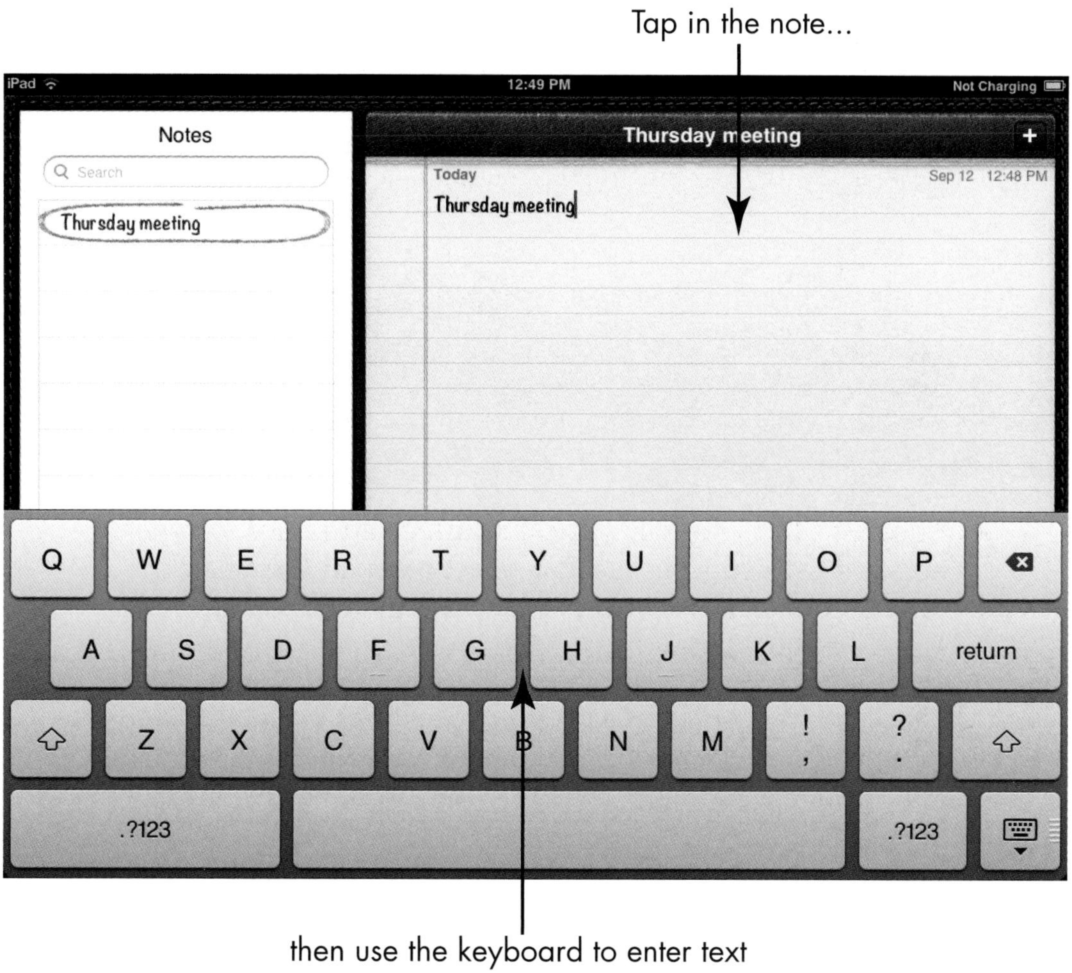

Tap in the note...

then use the keyboard to enter text

Figure 2-6

4. If you make a mistake while using the keyboard — and you will, when you first use it — press the Delete key (it's in the top-right corner, with the little *x* on it) to delete text to the left of the insertion point.

5. To create a new paragraph, press the Return button, just as you would do on a regular computer keyboard.

6. To type numbers and symbols, press the number key
(labeled . ?123) on either side of the spacebar (refer to
Figure 2-6). The characters on the keyboard change. If you
type a number and then tap the spacebar, the keyboard
returns to the letter keyboard automatically. To return to
the letter keyboard at any time, simply tap one of the letter
keys (labeled ABC) on either side of the spacebar.

7. Use the Shift buttons just as you would on a regular keyboard to type uppercase letters or alternate characters.

8. Double-tap the Shift key to turn on the Caps Lock feature; tap the Shift key once to turn off Caps Lock. (You
can control whether this feature is available in iPad
General Settings under Keyboard).

9. To type a variation on a symbol (for example, to see
alternate currency symbols when you press the dollar
sign on the number keyboard), hold down the key; a set
of alternate symbols appears (see **Figure 2-7**). Note that
this trick only works with certain symbols.

A set of alternate symbols

Figure 2-7

10. To hide the keyboard, press the Keyboard key in the bottom right corner.

11. Tap the Home button to return to the Home screen.

 You can undock the keyboard to move it around the
screen. To do this, press and hold the Keyboard button on the keyboard and from the popup menu that

appears, choose Undock. Now by pressing the Keyboard button and swiping up or down you can move the keyboard up and down on the screen. To dock the keyboard again at the bottom of the screen, press and hold the Keyboard button and choose Dock from the popup menu.

 To type a period and space, just double-tap the spacebar.

Use the Split Keyboard

1. With iOS 5 comes the new *split keyboard* feature. This allows you to split the keyboard so that each side appears nearer the edge of the iPad screen. For those who are into texting or one-finger typing, this feature makes it easier to reach all the keys from the sides of the device. Open an application such as Notes where you can use the onscreen keyboard.

2. Tap in an entry field which displays the onscreen keyboard.

3. Place two fingers in the middle of the onscreen keyboard and spread them toward the left and right. The keyboard splits, as shown in **Figure 2-8.**

4. Now hold the iPad with a hand on either side and practice using your thumbs to enter text.

5. To rejoin the keyboard, place two fingers on each side of the keyboard and swipe to join them together again.

 When the keyboard is docked and merged at the bottom of your screen, you can also simply press the Keyboard key and swipe upward. This undocks and splits the keyboard. To revert this you can press and swipe the Keyboard key and swipe downward. The keyboard is docked and merged.

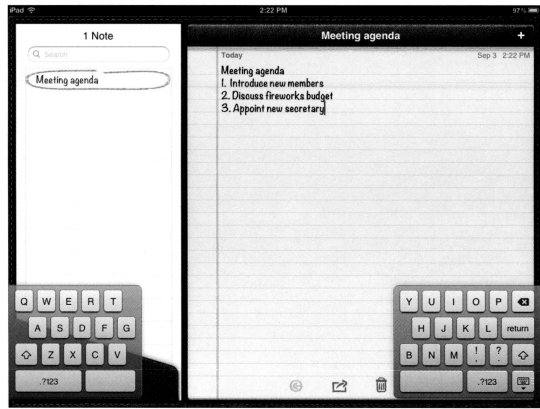

Figure 2-8

Flick to Search

1. The search feature in iPad helps you find photos, music, e-mails, contacts, movies, and more. Press and drag from left to right on the Home screen or tap the small magnifying glass symbol furthest to the left at the bottom of the Home screen to display the Spotlight screen. (You can also, from the primary Home screen, click the left side of the Home button to move one screen to the left.)

2. Tap in the Search iPad field (see **Figure 2-9**); the keyboard appears.

3. Begin entering a search term. In the example in **Figure 2-10**, after I typed the letter *S*, the search results displayed a contact, a couple of built-in apps, and some music I had downloaded, as well as a few e-mail messages. As you continue to type a search term, the results narrow to match it.

4. Tap an item in the search results to open it.

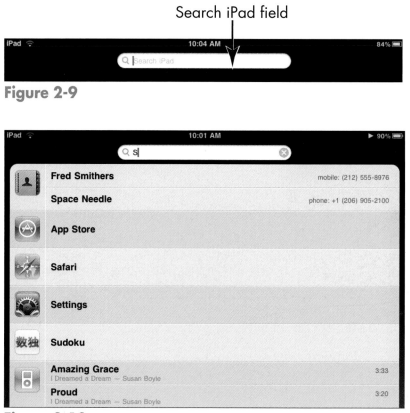

Search iPad field

Figure 2-9

Figure 2-10

Update the Operating System to iOS 5

1. This book was based on the latest version of the iPad operating system at the time: iOS 5. To make sure you have the latest and greatest features in iPad, update to the latest iOS now (and periodically). If you have set up and iCloud account on your iPad updates will happen automatically, or you can use a physical connection to a computer to update the iOS. To use the latter method, plug the 30-pin end of the Dock Connector to USB Cable into your iPad and plug the USB end into your computer.

2. When iTunes opens, click your iPad (in the Devices section of the Source List on the left side of the screen) and then click the Summary tab if it isn't already displayed (see **Figure 2-11**).

Click on your iPad...   then click the Summary tab

Figure 2-11

3. Read the note next to the Check for Update button to see whether your iOS is up to date. If it isn't, click the Check for Update button. iTunes checks to find the latest iOS version and walks you through the updating procedure.

 A new iOS version may introduce new features for your iPad. If a new iOS appears after you buy this book, go to the companion website at `www.iPad MadeClear.com` for updates on new features introduced in major updates.

Follow Multitasking Basics

1. *Multitasking* lets you easily switch from one app to another without closing the first one and returning to the Home screen. First, open an app.

2. Double-tap the Home button.

3. On the horizontal bar that appears beneath the Dock at the bottom of the screen (see **Figure 2-12**), flick to scroll to the left or right to locate another app you want to display.

Figure 2-12

4. Tap the app to open it.

 At the left end of the multitasking bar are controls for volume and playback, as well as a button that locks and unlocks screen rotation or mutes the sound, depending on which feature you've set the side switch to activate (you do that in the General Settings).

Explore Multitasking Gestures

 Multitasking involves jumping from one app to another. New to iOS 5 are some gestures you can tell the system to activate so you can use four or five fingers to multitask. Here are the three gestures you can make:

➥ Swipe up with four or five fingers on any Home screen to reveal the multitasking bar.

➡ Swipe down with four or five fingers to remove the multitasking bar from the Home screen.

➡ With an app open, swipe left or right using four or five fingers and you move to another app.

You can turn on these gestures by tapping Settings on the Home screen, and then in the General settings tap the On/Off button for Multitasking Gestures.

Examine the iPad Cameras

 iPad 2 introduces front and back-facing cameras to the hardware feature list. You can use the cameras to take still photos (covered in more detail in Chapter 12) or shoot videos (covered in Chapter 13).

For now, take a quick look at your camera by tapping the Camera app icon on the Home screen. The app opens, as shown in **Figure 2-13**.

You can use the controls on the screen to

➡ Switch between the front and rear cameras.

➡ Change from still-camera to video-camera operation by using the Camera/Video slider.

➡ Take a picture or start recording a video.

➡ Turn on a grid to help you autofocus on still photo subjects.

➡ Open previously captured images or videos.

When you view a photo or video, you can use an iPad feature to send the image via a tweet or e-mail, print images, use a still photo as wallpaper or assign it to represent a contact, or run a slide show or edit a video. See Chapters 12 and 13 for more detail about using the iPad cameras.

Switch between front and rear cameras

Options button to display Grid

Take photo or start recording video

Previously captured image or video

Figure 2-13

Customize the Screen Rotation Lock/Silent Switch

Starting with iOS 4.3, you can customize the switch on the top-right side of your iPad (in portrait orientation). Use these steps to set up the switch to control screen rotation or mute the sound:

1. From the Home screen, tap the Settings icon.

2. Under General settings, tap either the Lock Rotation or Mute option in the Use Side Switch To section to choose which feature you want the switch to control.

3. Tap the Home button to return to the Home screen.

4. Move the side switch up or down to toggle between the settings you chose: lock or unlock screen rotation or mute or unmute sound.

Explore the Status Bar

Across the top of the iPad screen is the *Status bar* (see **Figure 2-14**). Tiny icons in this area can provide useful information, such as the time, battery level, and wireless-connection status. **Table 2-1** lists some of the most common items you find on the Status bar:

| iPad | 3:30 PM | ⊕ ▶ 79% ▭ |

Figure 2-14

Table 2-1	Common Status Bar Icons	
Icon	**Name**	**What It Indicates**
📶	Wi-Fi	You're connected to a Wi-Fi network.
✳	Activity	A task is in progress — a web page is loading, for example.
3:30 PM	Time	You guessed it: You see the time.
🔒	Screen Rotation Lock	The screen is locked and doesn't rotate when you turn the iPad.
▶	Play	A media element (such as a song or video) is playing.
79% ▭	Battery Life	The charge percentage remaining in the battery. The indicator changes to a lightning bolt when the battery is charging.

If you have GPS, 3G, or Bluetooth service or a connection to a virtual private network (VPN), a corresponding symbol appears on the Status bar whenever
one of these features is active. The GPS and 3G icons
appear only with 3G-enabled iPad models. (If you
can't even conceive of what a virtual private network
is, my advice is not to worry about it.)

Take Inventory of Built-in Applications

The iPad comes with certain functionality and applications — or *apps*,
for short — built in. When you look at the Home screen, you see icons
for each app. This section gives you an overview of what each app
does. (You can find out more about every one of them as you read different chapters in this book.) The icons in the Dock (see the "Meet the
Multi-Touch Screen" task, earlier in this chapter) are, from left to right:

→ **Safari:** You use the Safari web browser (see **Figure
2-15**) to navigate on the Internet, create and save
bookmarks of favorite sites, and add web clips to
your Home screen so that you can quickly visit favorite sites from there. You may have used this web
browser (or another such as Internet Explorer) on
your desktop computer.

→ **Mail:** You use this application to access mail
accounts that you have set up in iPad. Your e-mail is
then displayed without your having to browse to the
site or sign in. Then you can use tools to move
among a few preset mail folders, read and reply to
mail, and download attached photos to your iPad.
Read more about e-mail accounts in Chapter 6.

→ **Photos:** The photo application in iPad (see **Figure
2-16**) helps you organize pictures in folders, e-mail
photos to others, use a photo as your iPad wallpaper, and assign pictures to contact records. You can
also run slide shows of your photos, open albums,
pinch or unpinch to shrink or expand photos, and
scroll photos with a simple swipe.

➠ **Music:** Music is the name of your media player. Though its main function is to play music, you can use it to play podcasts or audiobooks as well.

Figure 2-15

Figure 2-16

Apps with icons above the Dock and closer to the top of the Home screen include:

➟ **Calendar:** Use this handy onscreen daybook to set up appointments and send alerts to remind you about them.

➟ **Contacts:** In the address book feature (see **Figure 2-17**), you can enter contact information (including photos, if you like, from your Photos or Cameras app) and share contact information by e-mail. You can also use the search feature to find your contacts easily.

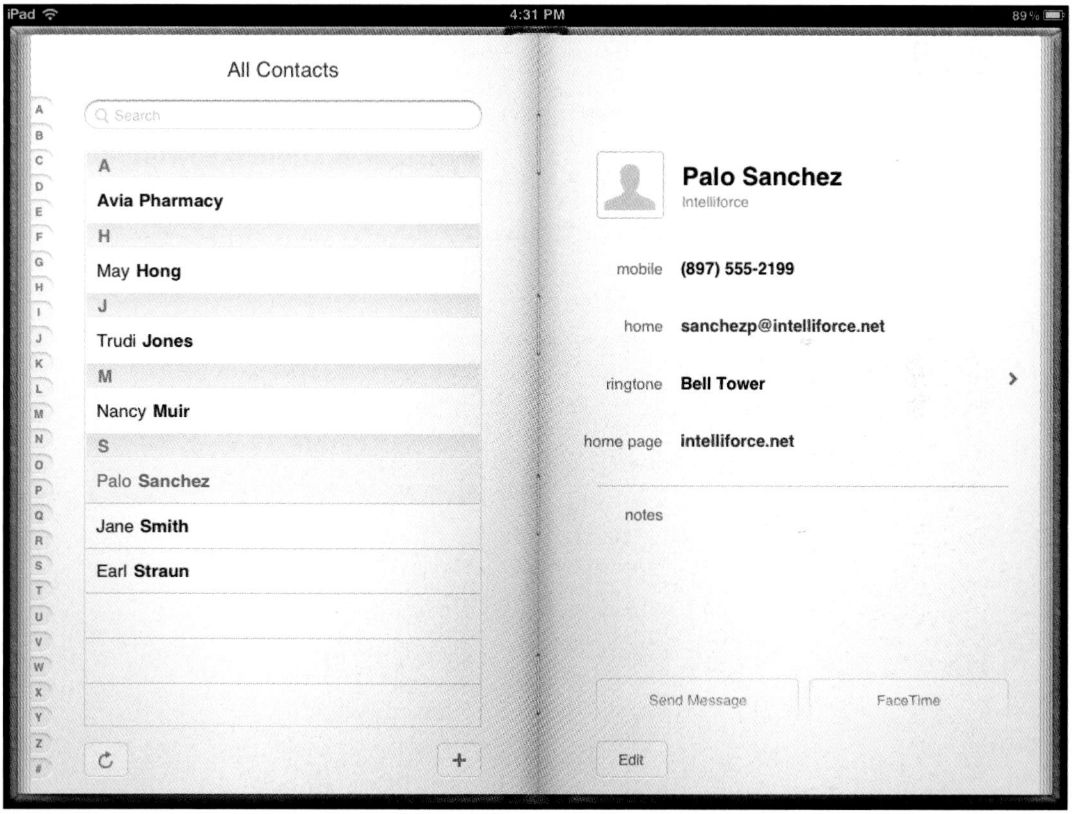

Figure 2-17

➟ **Notes:** Enter text or cut and paste text from a website into this simple notepad app. You can't do much except save notes or e-mail them — the app has no features for formatting text or inserting objects. You'll find Notes handy, though, for simple notes on the fly.

➡ **Maps:** In this cool iPad version of Google Earth, you can view classic maps or aerial views of addresses, find directions from one place to another by car, foot, or public transportation, and even view some addresses as though you're standing in front of the building at street level (though not every street image is totally up to date).

➡ **Videos:** This media player is similar to Music but specializes in playing videos and offers a few features specific to this type of media, such as chapter breakdowns and information about a movie's plot and cast.

➡ **YouTube:** Tap this icon to go to the popular online video-sharing site, where you can watch videos that people have posted and then comment on the videos or share them with others.

➡ **iTunes:** Tapping this icon takes you to the iTunes store, where you can shop 'til you drop (or until your iPad battery runs out of juice) for music, movies, TV shows, audiobooks, and podcasts and then download them directly to your iPad. (See Chapter 8 for more about how iTunes works.)

➡ **App Store:** At the Apple Store online, you can buy and download applications that do everything from enabling you to play games to building business presentations. Some of these are even free!

➡ **Settings:** Settings isn't exactly an app, but it's an icon you should know about, anyway: It's the central location on the iPad where you can specify settings for various functions and do administrative tasks such as set up e-mail accounts or create a password.

➡ **Game Center:** The Game Center app helps you browse games in the App Store and play them with other people online. You can add friends and track your scores. See Chapter 14 for more about Games Center.

➠ **FaceTime:** The FaceTime video calling app lets you use the new iPad 2 video camera to talk face-to-face with someone who has an iPad 2, Mac, fourth-generation iPod touch, or iPhone 4 or 4S. Chapter 7 fills you in on FaceTime features.

➠ **Camera:** As you may have read earlier in this chapter, the Camera app is control central for the still and video cameras built into the iPad 2.

➠ **PhotoBooth:** This fun app, which has been supplied with Mac computers for some time, lets you add effects to photos you take using your iPad camera in weird and wonderful ways.

➠ **Newsstand:** Similar to an e-reader for books, Newsstand is a handy reader app for subscribing to and reading magazines, newspapers, and other periodicals.

➠ **Reminders:** This is a useful app that centralizes all your calendar entries and alerts to keep you on schedule, as well as allowing you to create to-do lists.

➠ **iMessage:** For those who have been waiting for instant messaging on iPad, the iMessage feature comes to the rescue. Using the Messages app, you can engage in live text- and image-based conversations with others via their phones or other devices that use e-mail.

The iBooks application isn't built in to the iPad out of the box. Though iBooks is free, you have to download it from the App Store. Because the iPad has been touted as an outstanding *e-reader* — a device that enables you to read books on an electronic device, similar to the Amazon Kindle — you should definitely consider downloading the app as soon as possible. (For more about downloading applications for your iPad, see Chapter 9. To work with the iBooks e-reader application itself, go to Chapter 10.)

Lock iPad, Turn It Off, or Unlock It

Earlier in this chapter, I mention how simple it is to turn on the power to your iPad. Now it's time to put it to *sleep* (a state in which the screen goes black, though you can quickly wake up the iPad) or to turn off the power to give your new toy a rest. Here are the procedures you can use:

➡ **Press the Sleep/Wake button.** The iPad goes to sleep: The screen goes black and is locked.

 If you bought a Smart Cover with your iPad, just fold the cover over the front of the screen and iPad goes to sleep; open the cover to wake up the iPad. See Chapter 1 for more about iPad accessories.

➡ **Press the Home button or slide the Sleep/Wake slider.** The iPad wakes up. Swipe the onscreen arrow on the Slide to Unlock bar (see **Figure 2-18**) on the bottom of the screen to unlock the iPad.

Figure 2-18

➡ **Press and hold the Sleep/Wake button until the Slide to Power Off bar appears at the top of the screen, and then swipe the bar.** You've just turned off your iPad.

 The iPad automatically enters sleep mode after a few minutes of inactivity. You can change the time interval at which it sleeps by adjusting the Auto-Lock feature in Settings. See this book's companion Cheat Sheet at www.dummies.com/cheatsheet/ipad forseniors to review tables of various settings.

Getting Going

$\mathcal{Y}$our first step in getting to work with the iPad is to make sure that its battery is charged. Next, if you want to find free or paid content for your iPad from Apple, from movies to music to e-books to audiobooks, look into opening an iTunes account.

After that, connect your iPad to your computer and sync them so that you can exchange content between them (for example, to transfer your saved photos or music to the iPad).

If you prefer, you can take advantage of the new iCloud service from Apple to store and push all kinds of content and data to all your Apple devices — wirelessly.

This chapter also introduces you to the *iPad User Guide*, which you access using the Safari browser on your iPad. The guide essentially serves as your iPad Help system, to provide advice and information about your magical new device.

Charge the Battery

1. My iPad showed up in the box fully charged, and let's hope yours did, too. Because all batteries run down eventually, one of your first priorities is to know how to recharge your iPad battery. Gather your iPad and its connector cord and power adapter.

Chapter

3

Get ready to . . .

2. Gently plug the USB end (the smaller of the two connectors) of the Dock Connector to USB Cable into the USB Power Adapter.

3. Plug the other end of the cord into the cord connector slot on the iPad (see **Figure 3-1**).

Attach the USB connector...

to the power adapter.

Then plug this end into the iPad.

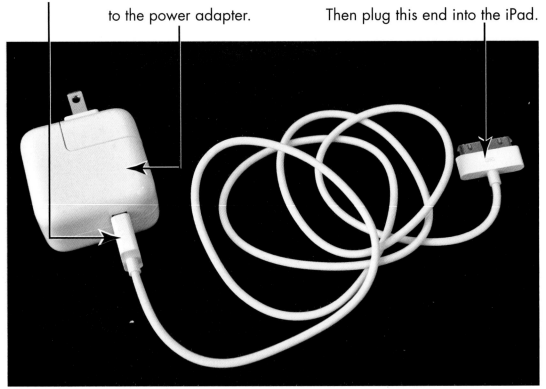

Figure 3-1

4. Unfold the two metal prongs on the power adapter (refer to **Figure 3-1**) so they extend from it at a 90-degree angle, and then plug the adapter into an electrical outlet.

 If you buy the iPad Dock accessory, you can charge your iPad while it's resting in the Dock. Just plug the larger connector into the back of the Dock instead of at the bottom of the iPad.

Download iTunes to Your Computer

1. If you are using a Mac, you already have iTunes installed. For Windows users, you should download the iTunes application to your computer so that you have the option of using it to *sync* (transfer) downloaded content to your iPad. Go to www.apple.com/itunes using your computer's browser.

2. Click the iTunes Free Download link. On the screen that opens, click the Download Now button (see **Figure 3-2**).

Figure 3-2

3. In the dialog that appears (see **Figure 3-3**), or using the Internet Explorer 9 download bar if you have that version, click Run. The iTunes application downloads.

Click Run

Figure 3-3

4. When the download is complete, another dialog appears, asking whether you want to run the software. Click Run and the iTunes Installer appears (see **Figure** 3-4).

Figure 3-4

5. Click Next.

6. Click the I Accept the Terms of the License Agreement check box in the following dialog and click Next.

7. Review the installation options, click to deselect the ones you don't want to use, and then click the Install button, as shown in **Figure** 3-5. A dialog appears, showing the installation progress.

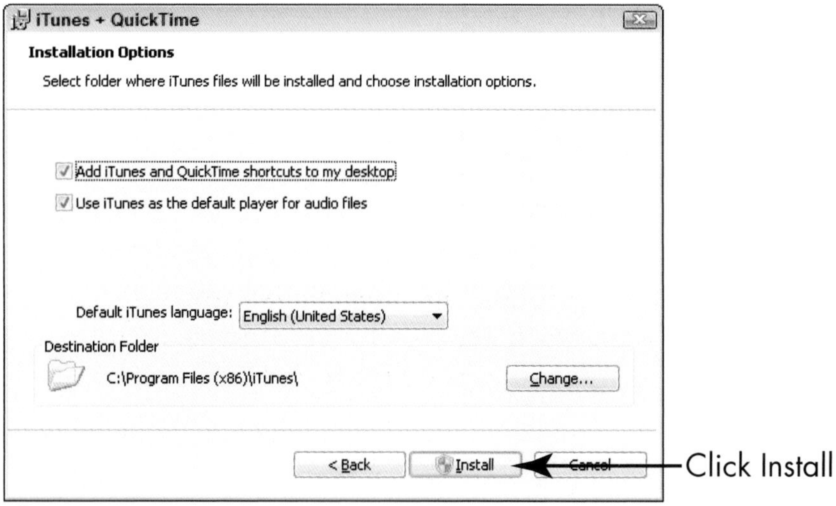

Figure 3-5

8. When a dialog appears and tells you that the installation is complete, click Finish. You have to restart your computer for the configuration settings that were made during the installation to take effect.

> As of this writing, iTunes 10.5 is the latest version of this software. iTunes 10 requires that you have Windows XP SP3 (a freely downloaded service pack update) or later on your PC, or Mac OS X version 10.5 or later on your Apple computer.

Open an iTunes Account for Music, Movies, and More

1. To be able to buy or download free items from the Apple Store on your computer or iPad, you must open an iTunes account. First, open the iTunes app (you download it to your computer in the preceding task). You can open iTunes by clicking its option on your computer's Start menu in Windows or by clicking the iTunes item in the Mac Dock or Launchpad).

2. Click the Store tab to open the Store menu and choose Create Account from the menu that appears (see **Figure 3-6**).

Select this option

Figure 3-6

3. On the Welcome to the iTunes Store screen that appears, click Continue.

4. On the following screen (see **Figure 3-7**), click to select the I Have Read and Agree to the iTunes Terms and Conditions check box, and then click the Continue button.

5. In the Create iTunes Store Account (Apple ID) screen that follows (see **Figure 3-8**), fill in the information fields, click the last two check boxes to deselect them if you don't want to receive e-mail from the Apple Store, and then click the Continue button.

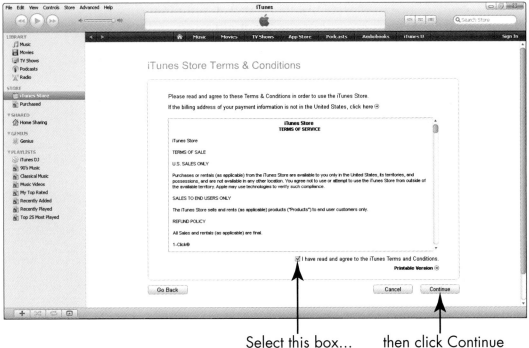

Select this box...   then click Continue

Figure 3-7

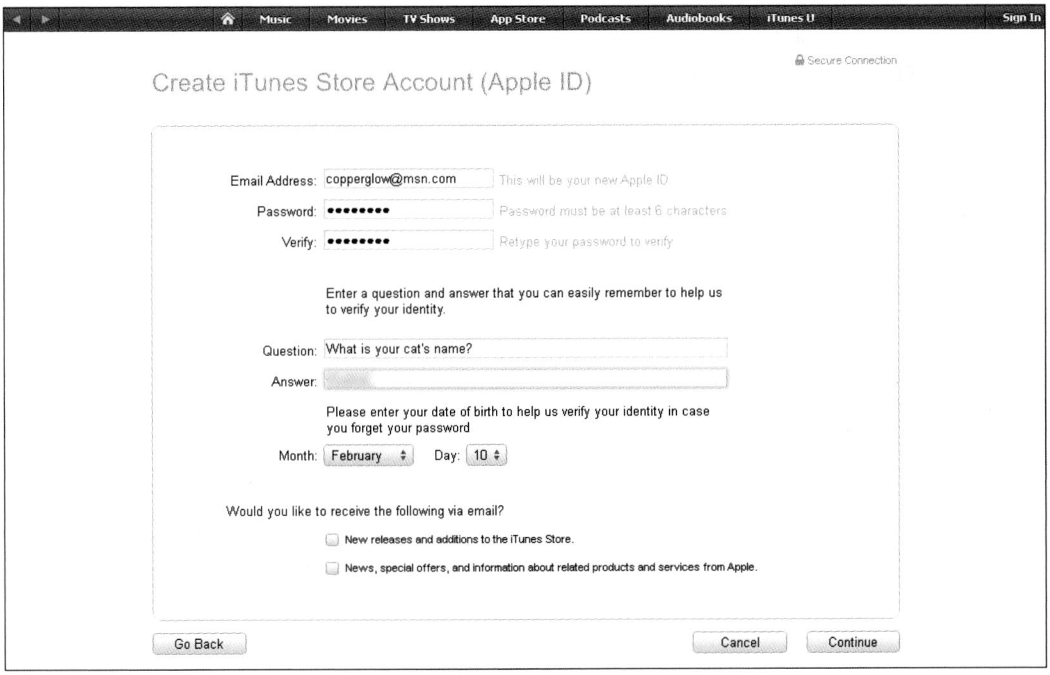

Figure 3-8

6. On the Provide a Payment Method screen that appears (see **Figure 3-9**), enter your payment information and click the Continue button.

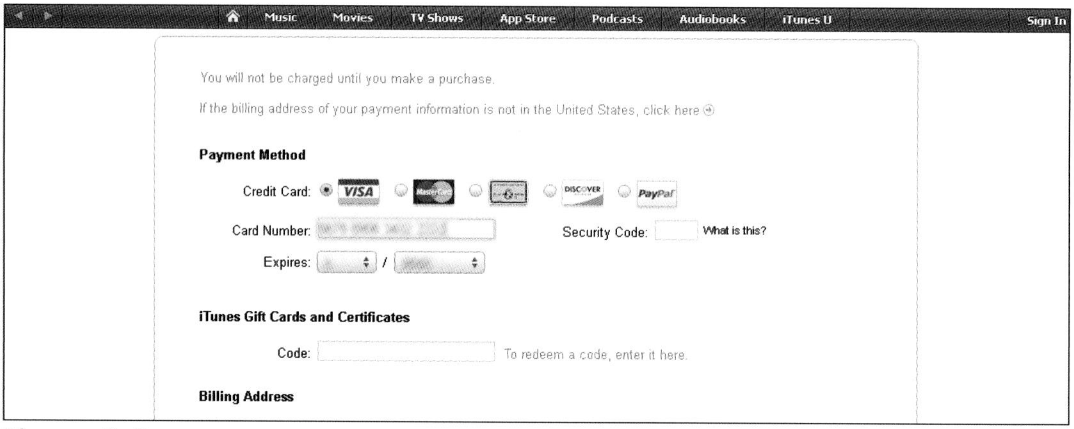

Figure 3-9

7. A screen appears confirming that your account has been opened. Click the Done button to return to the iTunes Store.

Make iPad Settings Using iTunes

1. Open your iTunes software. (On a Windows computer, choose Start⇨All Programs⇨iTunes; on a Mac, click the iTunes icon in the Dock or Launchpad.)

2. iTunes opens and if you've connected it to your computer using the Dock Connector to USB Cable, your iPad is listed in the Devices section of the Source List on the left, as shown in **Figure 3-10.** Click on your iPad and a series of tabs displays. The tabs offer information about your iPad and settings to determine how to download music, movies, or podcasts, for example. (You can see the simple choices on the Music tab in **Figure 3-11.**) The settings relate to the kind of content you want to download and whether you want to download it automatically (when you sync) or manually. See **Table 3-1** for an overview of the settings that are available on each tab.

Click on your iPad...   to display this series of tabs

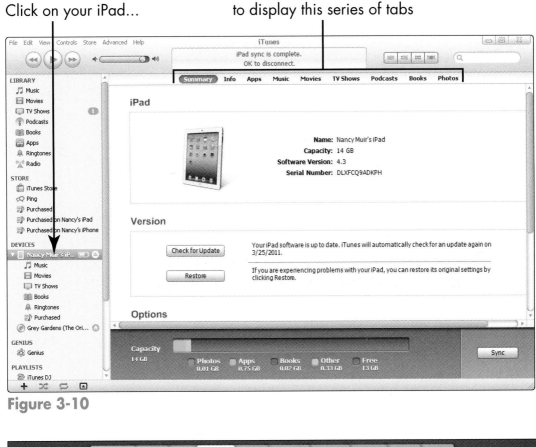

Figure 3-10

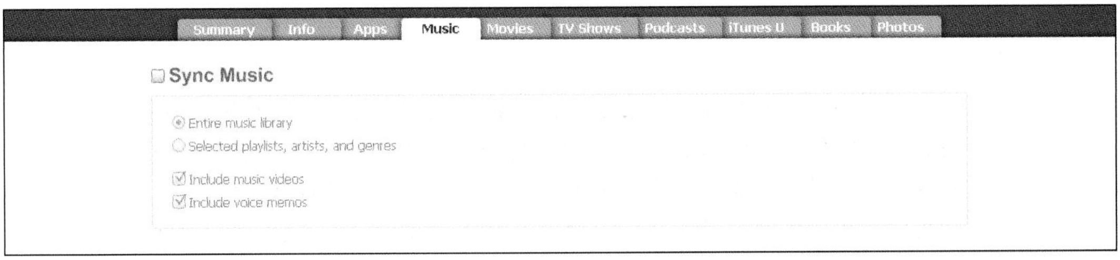

Figure 3-11

3. Make all settings for the types of content you plan to obtain on your computer. **Table 3-1** provides information about settings on the different tabs.

Table 3-1	iPad Settings in iTunes
Tab Name	**What You Can Do with the Settings on the Tab**
Summary	Perform updates to the iPad software and set general syncing options
Info	Specify which information to sync: Contacts, Calendars, E-mail, Bookmarks, or Notes
Apps	Sync with iPad the apps you've downloaded to your computer and manage the location of those apps and folders
Music	Choose which music to download to your iPad when you sync
Movies	Specify whether to automatically download movies
TV Shows	Choose shows and episodes to sync automatically
Podcasts	Choose podcasts and episodes to sync automatically
Books	Choose to sync all, or only selected, books, and audiobooks to your iPad
Photos	Choose the folders from which you want to download photos or albums

Sync the iPad to Your Computer Using iTunes

1. After you specify which content to download in iTunes (see the preceding task), you can use the Dock Connector to USB Cable to connect your iPad and computer at any time and sync files, contacts, calendar settings and more. You can also use the iTunes Wi-Fi Sync setting to allow cordless syncing (Tap Settings, General, iTunes Wi-Fi Sync, and then tap Sync Now to sync with a computer connected to the same Wi-Fi network). After iTunes is downloaded to your computer and your iTunes account is set up, plug the data connection cord into your iPad (using the wider connector).

2. Plug the other end of the cord into a USB port on your computer.

3. iTunes opens and shows an item for your iPad in the Source List on the left (refer to **Figure 3-10**). Your iPad screen shows the phrase *Sync in Progress*.

4. When the syncing is complete, the Lock screen returns on the iPad; iTunes shows a message above the series of tabs (refer to **Figure 3-10**), indicating that the iPad sync is complete and that you can disconnect the cable. Any media you chose to transfer in your iTunes settings, and any new photos in the photos folder on your computer, have been transferred to your iPad.

Understand iCloud

There's an alternative to syncing content using iTunes. When iOS 5 launched it also introduced iCloud, a service that allows you to back up all your content and certain settings such as bookmarks to online storage. That content and those settings are then pushed automatically to all your Apple devices through a wireless connection.

All you need to do is get an iCloud account, which is free, and then make settings on each device for which types of content you want pushed to each device. After you've done that, any content you create or purchase on one device — such as music, apps, books, and TV shows, as well as documents created in Apple's iWork apps, photos, and so on — can be synced among your devices automatically.

When you get an iCloud account, you get 5GB of free storage; content you purchase (such as apps, books, music, and TV shows) won't be counted against your storage. If you want additional storage, you can buy an upgrade from one of your devices. 10GB costs $20 per year; 20GB is $40; and 50GB is $100 a year. Most people will do just fine with the free 5GB of storage.

To upgrade your storage, go to iCloud in Settings, tap Storage & Backup, and then tap Manage Storage. In the dialog that appears, tap Buy More Storage. Tap the amount you need and then tap Buy.

 You can make settings for backing up your content to iCloud in the iCloud section of Settings. You can have content backed up automatically, or do it manually.

Get an iCloud Account

Before you can use iCloud, you need an iCloud account, which is tied into the Apple ID you probably already have. You can turn on iCloud when first setting up your iPad or use Settings to sign up using your Apple ID.

1. When first setting up your phone after upgrading to iOS 5, in the sequence of screens that appear you'll see the one in **Figure 3-12**. Tap Use iCloud.

2. In the next dialog tap Backup to iCloud.

Your account is now set up based on the Apple ID you entered earlier in the set up sequence.

Here are the steps to set up iCloud on your iPad if you didn't do so when first setting up iPad:

1. Tap Settings and then tap iCloud.

2. Tap the On/Off button to turn on iCloud.

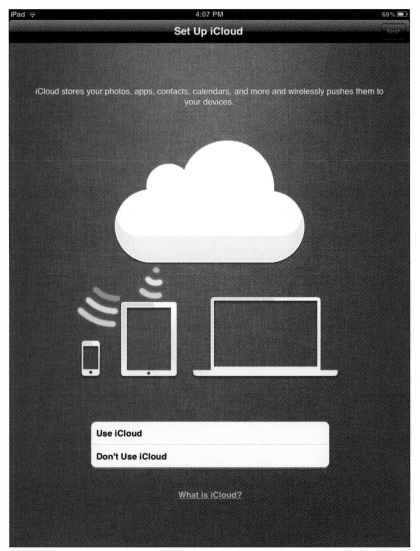

Figure 3-12

3. Enter your Apple ID and password and tap the Sign In button. (See **Figure 3-13.**) (If you don't have an Apple ID, tap the Get a Free Apple ID button and follow the instructions to get your ID.) A dialog appears, asking whether you'd like to merge your iPad calendars, reminders, and bookmarks with iCloud.

Figure 3-13

4. A dialog may appear asking if you want to allow iCloud to use the location of your iPad. Tap OK. Your account is now set up.

Make iCloud Sync Settings

When you have an iCloud account up and running (see the preceding section), you have to specify which type of content should be synced with your iPad via iCloud. Note that content that you purchase and download will be synced among your devices automatically via iCloud.

1. Tap Settings and then tap iCloud.

2. In the iCloud settings shown in **Figure 3-14,** tap the On/ Off button for any item that's turned off that you want to turn on (or vice versa). You can sync Mail, Contacts, Calendars, Reminders, Bookmarks, and Notes.

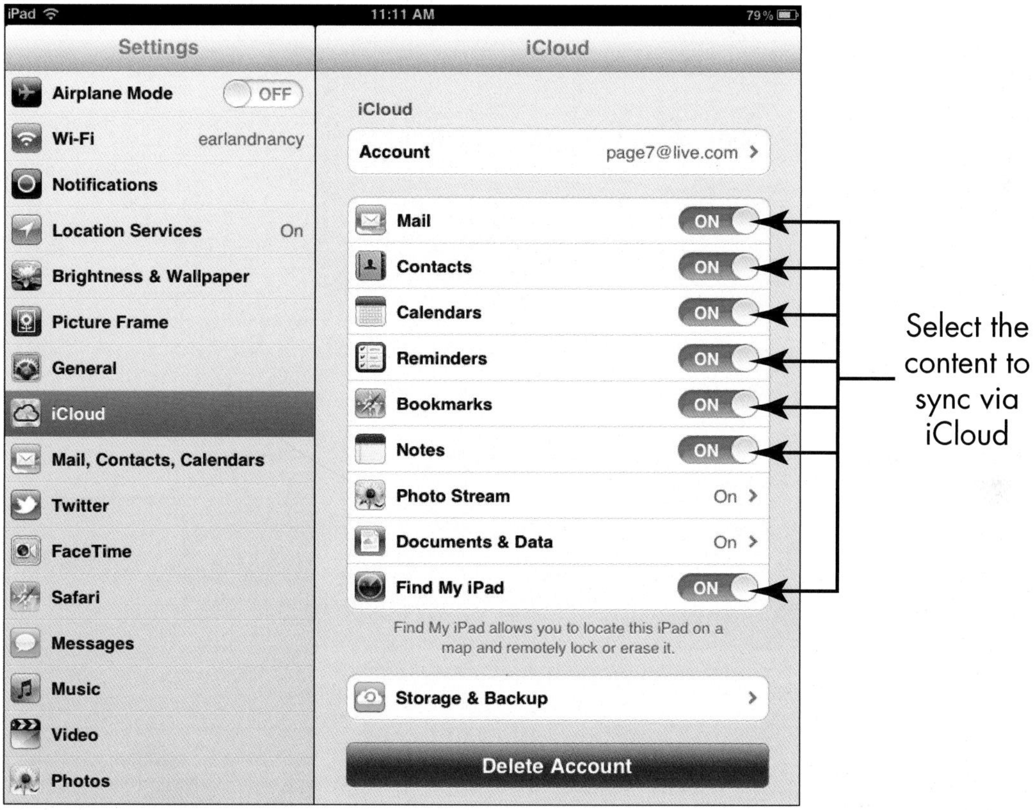

Figure 3-14

3. To turn Photo Stream, Documents & Data, or Storage & Backup on or off (so you can sync photos, documents created in iWork, or settings data, respectively), tap those options on the list (refer to **Figure 3-14**) and then tap the On/Off button for each particular setting in the subse-quent screen.

_4._ To enable automatic downloads of music, apps, and book, tap Store in the Settings pane.

_5._ Tap the On/Off button for Music, Apps, or Books to set up automatic downloads of any of this content to your iPad via iCloud.

 If you want to allow iCloud to provide a service for locating a lost or stolen iPad, tap the On/Off button in the Find My iPad field to activate it. This service helps you locate, send a message to, or delete content from your iPad if it falls into other hands.

View the User Guide Online

_1._ The *iPad User Guide* is equivalent to the Help system you may have used on a Windows or Mac computer. You access the guide online as a bookmarked site in the Safari browser. From the iPad Home screen, tap the Safari icon.

_2._ Tap the Bookmark icon. On the Bookmarks menu that appears (see **Figure 3-15**), tap iPad User Guide.

Tap this option

Figure 3-15

3. Tap a topic on the left to display subtopics, as shown in **Figure 3-16**.

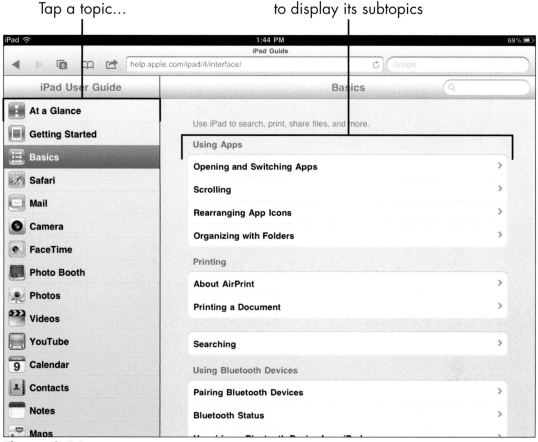

Figure 3-16

4. Tap a subtopic to display information about it, as shown in **Figure 3-17**.

5. Tap any link in the subtopic information to access additional topics.

6. Tap the Home screen button to close the browser.

 To find the PDF version of the *iPad User Guide* on your browser, see http://manuals.info. apple.com/en_US/iPad_User_Guide.pdf.

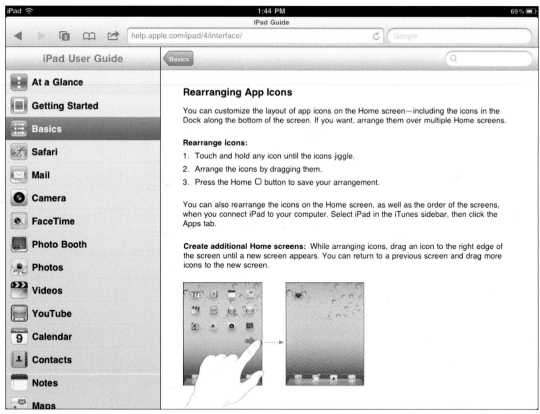

Figure 3-17

Taking Advantage of Accessibility Features

*i*Pad users are all different; some face visual, dexterity, or hearing challenges. If you're one of these folks, you'll be glad to hear that iPad offers some handy accessibility features.

To make your screen easier to read, you can adjust the brightness or wallpaper. The Zoom feature lets you enlarge the screen even more than the standard unpinch gesture does. The black-and-white screen option even offers a black background with white lettering that some people find easier when reading text. You can also set up the VoiceOver feature to read onscreen elements out loud.

If hearing is your challenge, you can do the obvious and adjust the system volume. The iPad also has a setting for mono audio that's useful when you're wearing headphones. Rather than breaking up sounds in a stereo effect, this setting puts all the sound in each ear. If you have more trouble hearing in one ear than in the other, this option can help make sounds clearer. iPad uses the Speak Auto-text feature to tell you whenever text you enter in any iPad application is auto-corrected or capitalized.

Finally, you can set a larger text size for your iPad to bring text into better focus and turn on the AssistiveTouch Control Panel to help you with making gestures and choices if you struggle with the touchscreen interface.

Set Brightness

1. Especially when using iPad as an e-reader, you may find that a slightly less-bright screen reduces strain on your eyes. To begin, tap the Settings icon on the Home screen.

2. In the Settings dialog shown in **Figure 4-1,** tap Brightness & Wallpaper.

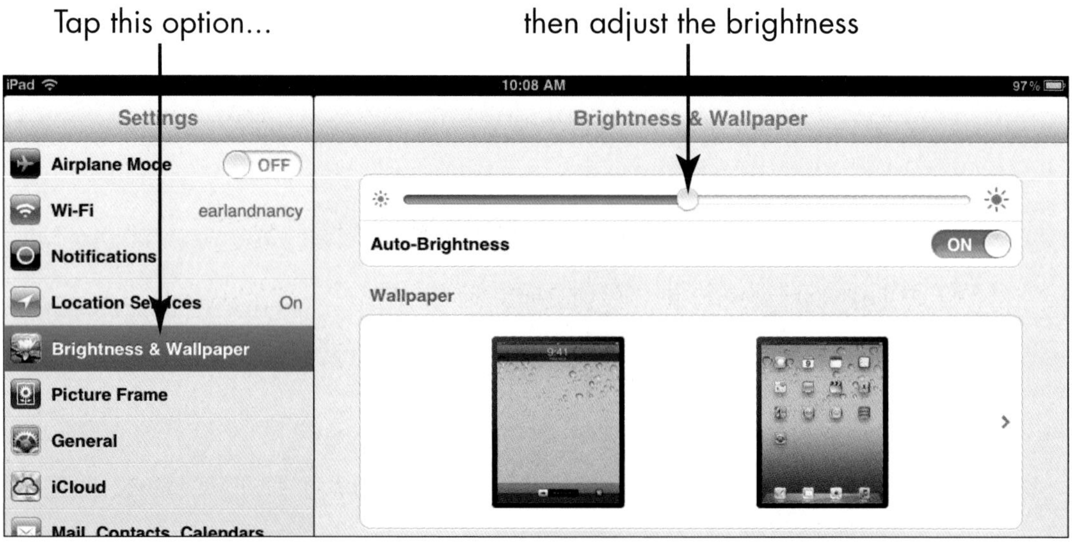

Tap this option...   then adjust the brightness

Figure 4-1

3. To control brightness manually, tap the Auto-Brightness On/Off button (refer to **Figure 4-1**) to turn off this feature.

4. Tap and drag the Brightness slider to the right to make the screen brighter, or to the left to make it dimmer.

5. Tap the Home button to close the Settings dialog.

 If glare from the screen is a problem for you, consider getting a *screen protector*. This thin film not only protects your screen from damage but can also reduce glare.

 In the iBooks e-reader app, you can set a sepia tone for the page, which might be easier on your eyes. See Chapter 10 for more about using iBooks.

Change the Wallpaper

1. The picture of water drops — the default iPad background image — may be pretty, but it may not be the one that works best for you. Choosing different wallpaper may help you to see all the icons on your Home screen. Start by tapping the Settings icon on the Home screen.

2. In the Settings dialog, tap Brightness & Wallpaper.

3. In the Brightness & Wallpaper settings that appear, tap the arrow to the right of the iPad images displayed in the Wallpaper section (refer to **Figure 4-1**) and then tap Wallpaper.

4. The wallpaper options shown in **Figure 4-2** appear. Tap one to select it.

5. In the preview that appears (see **Figure 4-3**), tap either Set Lock Screen (the screen that appears when you lock the iPad by tapping the power button), Set Home Screen, or Set Both.

6. Tap the Home button to return to your Home screen with the new wallpaper set as the background.

Tap a wallpaper sample

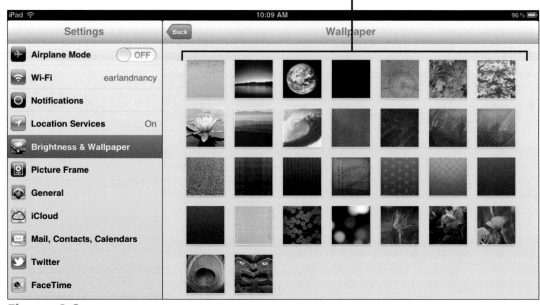

Figure 4-2

Tap to set one or both screens

Figure 4-3

Turn On Zoom

1. The Zoom feature enlarges the contents displayed on the iPad screen when you double-tap the screen with three fingers. Tap the Settings icon on the Home screen and then tap General. In the General settings, tap Accessibility. The Accessibility pane, shown in **Figure 4-4,** appears.

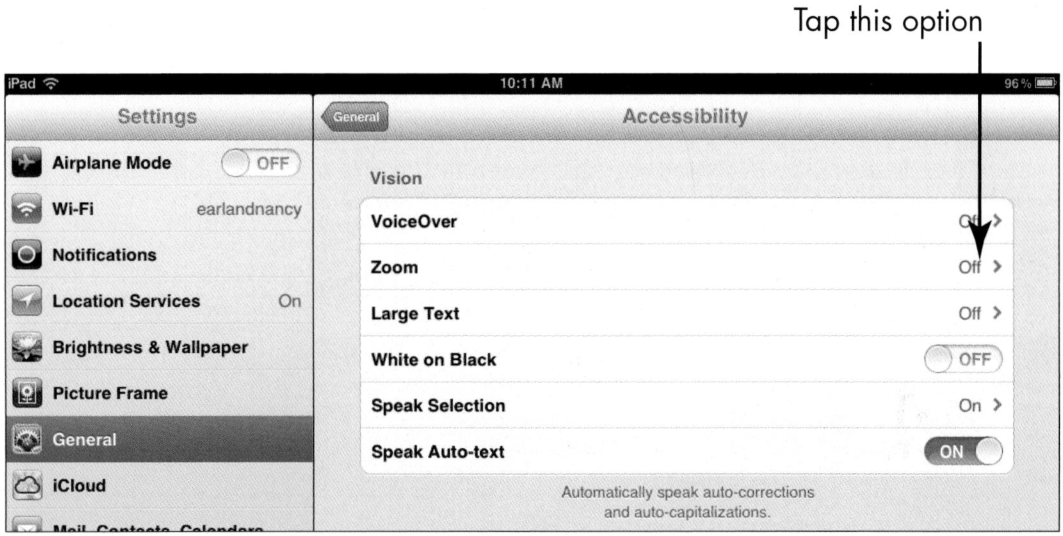

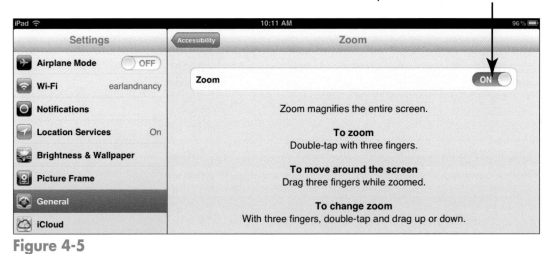

Tap this option

Figure 4-4

2. Tap Zoom (refer to **Figure** 4-4).

3. In the Zoom pane shown in **Figure** 4-5, tap the Zoom On/Off button to turn on the feature.

Tap to turn on Zoom

Figure 4-5

4. Go to a website (`www.ipadmadeclear.com`, for example) and double-tap the screen using three fingers; it enlarges.

5. Press three fingers on the screen and drag to move around it.

6. Double-tap with three fingers again to go back to regular magnification.

7. Tap the Home button to close Settings.

 The Zoom feature works almost everywhere in iPad: in Photos, on web pages, in your Mail, in Music and Video — give it a try!

Turn on White on Black

1. The White on Black accessibility setting reverses colors on your screen so that backgrounds are black and text is white. To turn on this feature, tap the Settings icon on the Home screen.

2. Tap General and then tap Accessibility.

3. In the Accessibility dialog, tap the White on Black On/Off button to turn on this feature (see **Figure 4-6**).

Settings		Accessibility	
		1:34 PM	88%
Airplane Mode	OFF	Vision	
Wi-Fi	johnwiley	VoiceOver	Off >
Notifications		Zoom	Off >
Location Services	On	Large Text	Off >
Brightness & Wallpaper		White on Black	ON
Picture Frame		Speak Selection	Off >
General		Speak Auto-text	OFF

Figure 4-6

4. The colors on the screen reverse. Tap the Home button to leave Settings.

The White on Black feature works well in some places and not so well in others. For example, in the Photos application, pictures appear almost as photo negatives. Your Home screen image will likewise look a bit strange. And, don't even think of playing a video with this feature turned on! However, if you need help reading text, White on Black can be useful in several applications.

Set Up VoiceOver

1. *VoiceOver* reads the names of screen elements and settings to you, but it also changes the way you provide input to the iPad. In Notes, for example, you can have VoiceOver read the name of the Notes buttons to you and, when you enter notes, it will read words or characters you've entered. It can also tell you whether features such as AutoCorrect are on. To turn on this feature, tap the Settings icon on the Home screen. Tap General and then Accessibility.

2. In the Accessibility pane shown in **Figure 4-7,** tap the VoiceOver button.

3. In the VoiceOver pane shown in **Figure 4-8,** tap the VoiceOver On/Off button at the top to turn on this feature. You see a dialog noting that turning on VoiceOver changes gestures that you use to interact with the iPad. Tap OK once to select the button, and then tap OK twice to proceed. With VoiceOver on you must first single-tap to select an item such as a button, which causes VoiceOver to read the name of the button to you. Then you double-tap the button to activate its function. (VoiceOver reminds you about this if you turn on Speak Hints, which is helpful when you first use VoiceOver but soon becomes annoying.)

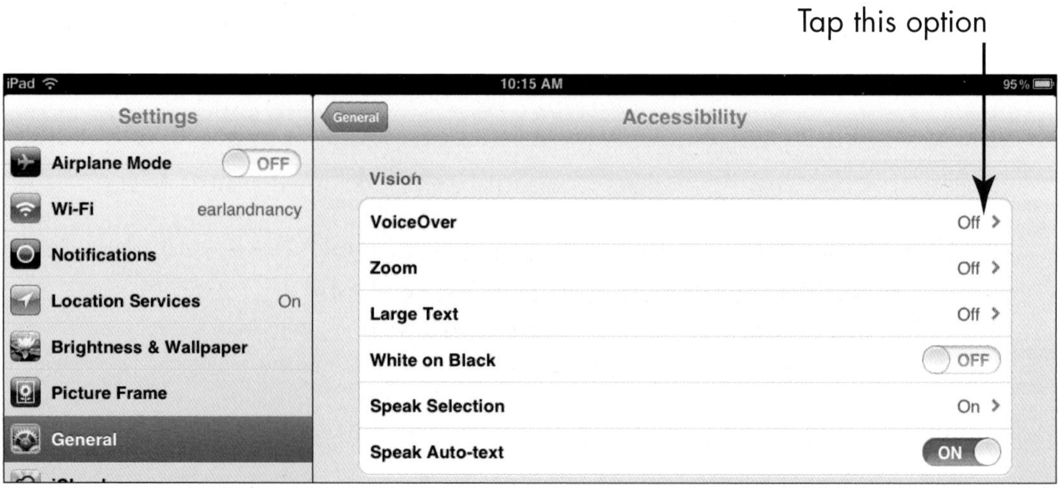

Tap this option

Figure 4-7

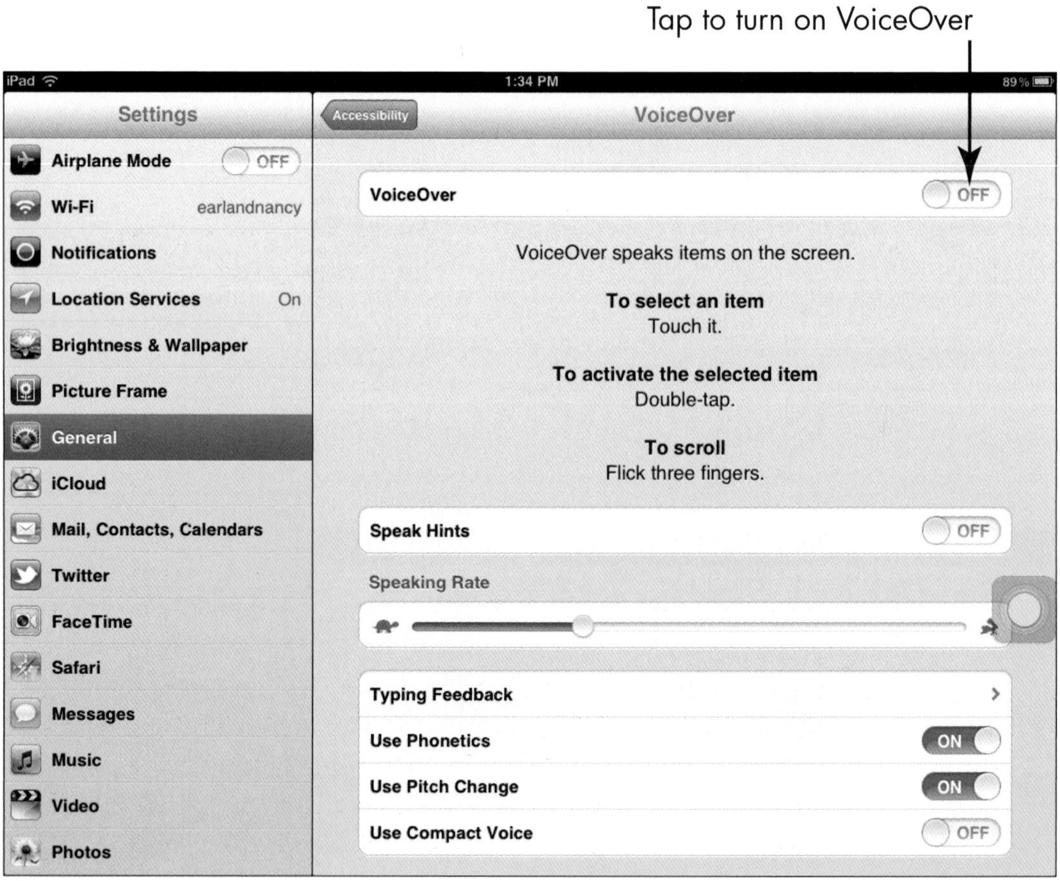

Tap to turn on VoiceOver

Figure 4-8

4. Tap the VoiceOver Practice button to select it, and then double-tap the button to open VoiceOver Practice. (This is the new method of tapping that VoiceOver activates). Practice using gestures such as pinching or flicking left and VoiceOver tells you what action each gesture initiates.

5. Tap the Done button and then double-tap it to return to the VoiceOver dialog. Tap the Speak Hints field and VoiceOver speaks the name of the item. Double-tap the slider to turn off Speak Hints.

6. If you want VoiceOver to read words or characters to you (for example, in the Notes app), double-tap Typing Feedback.

7. In the Typing Feedback dialog, tap to select the option you prefer. The Words option causes VoiceOver to read words to you, but not characters, such as "dollar sign" ($). The Characters and Words option causes VoiceOver to read both.

8. Tap the Home button to return to the Home screen. Read the next task to find out how to navigate your iPad after you have turned on VoiceOver.

 You can change the language that VoiceOver speaks. In General settings, choose International and then Language and select another language. This action, however, also changes the language used for labels on Home icons and various settings and fields in iPad.

 You can use the Set Triple-Click Home setting to help you more quickly turn the VoiceOver and White on Black features on and off. In the Accessibility dialog, tap Triple-Click Home. In the dialog that appears, choose what you want a triple-click of the Home button to do: toggle VoiceOver on or off; toggle White on Black on or off; toggle the Zoom feature on or off; toggle on the AssistiveTouch Control Panel; or display a menu of options using the Ask choice. Now a triple-click with a single finger on the Home button provides you with the option you selected wherever you go in iPad.

Use VoiceOver

After VoiceOver is turned on, you need to figure out how to use it. I won't kid you; using it is hard at first, but you'll get the hang of it! Here are the main onscreen gestures you should know how to use:

➡ **Tap an item to select it.** VoiceOver then speaks its name.

➡ **Double-tap the selected item.** This action activates the item.

➡ **Flick three fingers.** It takes three fingers to scroll around a page with VoiceOver turned on.

Table 4-1 provides additional gestures to help you use VoiceOver. I suggest that, if you want to use this feature often, you read the VoiceOver section of the iPad online User Guide, which goes into a great deal of detail about the ins and outs of using VoiceOver.

Table 4-1	VoiceOver Gestures
Gesture	**Effect**
Flick right or left	Select the next or preceding item
Tap with two fingers	Stop speaking the current item
Flick two fingers up	Read everything from the top of the screen
Flick two fingers down	Read everything from the current position
Flick three fingers up or down	Scroll one page at a time
Flick three fingers right or left	Go to the next or preceding page
Tap three fingers	Speak the scroll status (for example, line 20 of 100)
Flick four fingers up or down	Go to the first or last element on a page
Flick four fingers right or left	Go to the next or preceding section (as on a web page)

If tapping with two or three fingers seems difficult for you, try tapping with one finger from one hand and one or two from the other. When double- or triple-tapping, you have to perform these gestures as quickly as you can for them to work.

 Check out some new settings in iOS 5 for VoiceOver, including a choice for Braille, language choices, the ability to navigate images, and a setting to have iPad speak notifications.

Adjust the Volume

1. Though individual applications such as Music and Video have their own volume settings, you can set your iPad system volume as well to help you better hear what's going on. Tap the Settings icon on the Home screen.

2. In the General settings, tap Sounds.

3. In the Sounds pane that appears (see **Figure** 4-9), tap and drag the slider to the right to increase the volume, or to the left to lower it.

4. Tap the Home button to close Settings.

 In the Sounds pane you can turn on or off the sounds that iPad makes when certain events occur (such as receiving new mail or Calendar alerts). These sounds are turned on by default. Conversely, if you need the audio clue and this feature has been turned off, just tap the On/Off button for the item to turn it back on.

Adjust iPad volume here

Figure 4-9

Use Mono Audio

1. Using the stereo effect in headphones or a headset breaks up sounds so that you hear a portion in one ear and a portion in the other ear, to simulate the way your ears process sounds. However, if you're hard of hearing or deaf in one ear, you're hearing only a portion of the sound in your hearing ear, which can be frustrating. If you have such hearing challenges and want to use iPad with a headset connected, you should turn on Mono Audio. When it's turned on, you can set up iPad to play all sounds in each ear. Tap the Settings icon on the Home screen.

2. In the General settings, tap Accessibility.

3. In the Accessibility pane shown in **Figure 4-10,** tap the Mono Audio On/Off button to turn on the feature.

Tap to turn on Mono Audio

iPad 🔋	10:27 AM	94% 🔋
Settings	‹ General **Accessibility**	

Airplane Mode	OFF
Wi-Fi	earlandnancy
Notifications	
Location Services	On
Brightness & Wallpaper	
Picture Frame	
General	
iCloud	
Mail, Contacts, Calendars	
Twitter	
FaceTime	

Vision

VoiceOver	Off ›
Zoom	Off ›
Large Text	Off ›
White on Black	OFF
Speak Selection	On ›
Speak Auto-text	ON

Automatically speak auto-corrections and auto-capitalizations.

Hearing

Mono Audio	ON
L ———————●——— R	

Figure 4-10

4. Tap and drag the slider to L for sending sound to only your left ear or R for right ear.

5. Tap the Home button to close Settings.

 If you have hearing challenges, another good feature that iPad provides is support for closed-captioning. In the video player, you can use the closed-captioning feature to provide onscreen text representing dialogue and actions in a movie (if it supports closed-captioning) as it plays. For more about playing videos, see Chapter 13.

Have iPad Speak Auto-Text

1. The *Speak Auto-text* feature speaks auto-corrections and auto-capitalizations (two features that you can turn on using Keyboard settings). When you enter text in an application such as Pages or Mail the app then makes either type of change, while Speak Auto-text lets you know what change was made. To turn on Speak Auto-text, tap the Settings icon on the Home screen.

2. Under the General settings, tap Accessibility.

3. In the Accessibility pane shown in **Figure 4-11,** tap the Speak Auto-text On/Off button to turn on the feature.

Tap to turn on Speak Auto-text

iPad 🛜		10:33 AM	93% 🔋
Settings	General	**Accessibility**	
✈️ **Airplane Mode** ⚪ OFF		**Vision**	
🛜 **Wi-Fi** earlandnancy		**VoiceOver**	Off ›
⭕ **Notifications**		**Zoom**	Off ›
📍 **Location Services** On		**Large Text**	Off ›
🖼️ **Brightness & Wallpaper**		**White on Black**	⚪ OFF
🖼️ **Picture Frame**		**Speak Selection**	Off ›
⚙️ **General**		**Speak Auto-text**	ON ⚪
☁️ **iCloud**		*Automatically speak auto-corrections and auto-capitalizations.*	

Figure 4-11

4. Tap the Home button to leave Settings.

 Why would you want iPad to tell you whenever an auto-correction has been made? If you have vision challenges and you know that you typed *ain't* when writing dialogue for a character in your novel, but iPad corrected it to *isn't,* you would want to know. Similarly, if you type the poet's name *e.e. Cummings* and auto-capitalization corrects it (incorrectly), you need to know immediately so that you can change it back again!

Turn On Large Text

1. If having larger text in the Contacts, Mail, and Notes apps would be helpful to you, you can turn on the Large Text feature and choose the text size that works best for you. To turn on Large Text, tap the Settings icon on the Home screen.

2. Under the General settings, tap Accessibility.

3. In the Accessibility pane, tap the Large Text button to turn on the feature.

4. In the list of text sizes shown in **Figure 4-12**, tap the one you prefer.

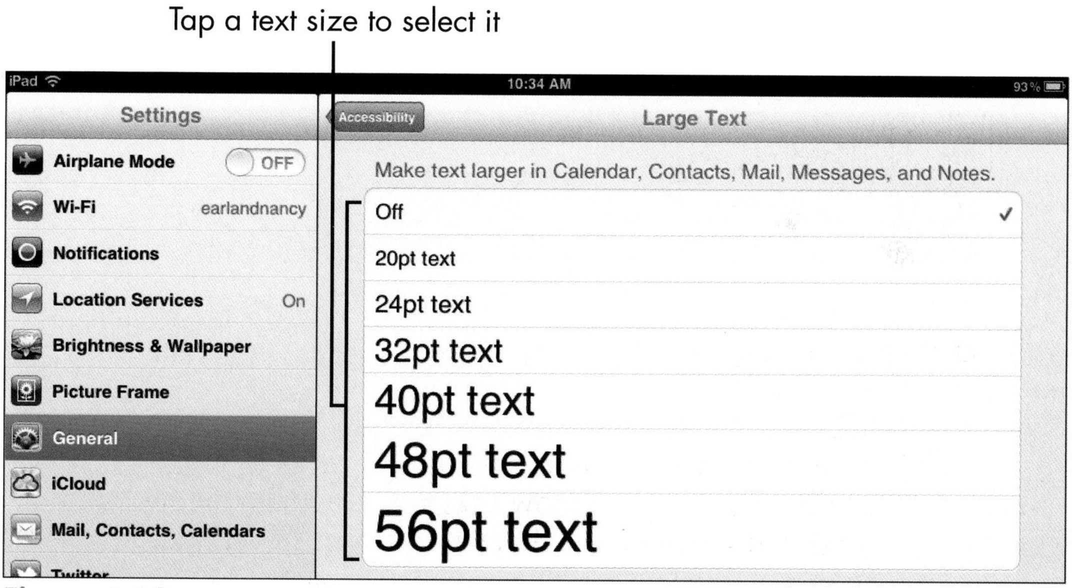

Tap a text size to select it

iPad	10:34 AM	93%

Settings / **Accessibility** **Large Text**

Make text larger in Calendar, Contacts, Mail, Messages, and Notes.

Airplane Mode — OFF

Wi-Fi — earlandnancy

Notifications

Location Services — On

Brightness & Wallpaper

Picture Frame

General

iCloud

Mail, Contacts, Calendars

Twitter

Off ✓

20pt text

24pt text

32pt text

40pt text

48pt text

56pt text

Figure 4-12

5. Tap the Home button to close the Settings dialog.

Turn On and Work with AssistiveTouch

1. The AssistiveTouch Control Panel helps those who have challenges working with buttons to provide input to iPad using the touchscreen. To turn on AssistiveTouch, tap Settings on the Home screen and then tap General and Accessibility.

2. In the Accessibility pane tap AssistiveTouch. In the pane that appears, tap the On/Off button for AssistiveTouch to turn it on (see **Figure 4-13**). Note the gray square that appears on the right side of the pane. This square now appears on the screen in whatever apps you display on your iPad.

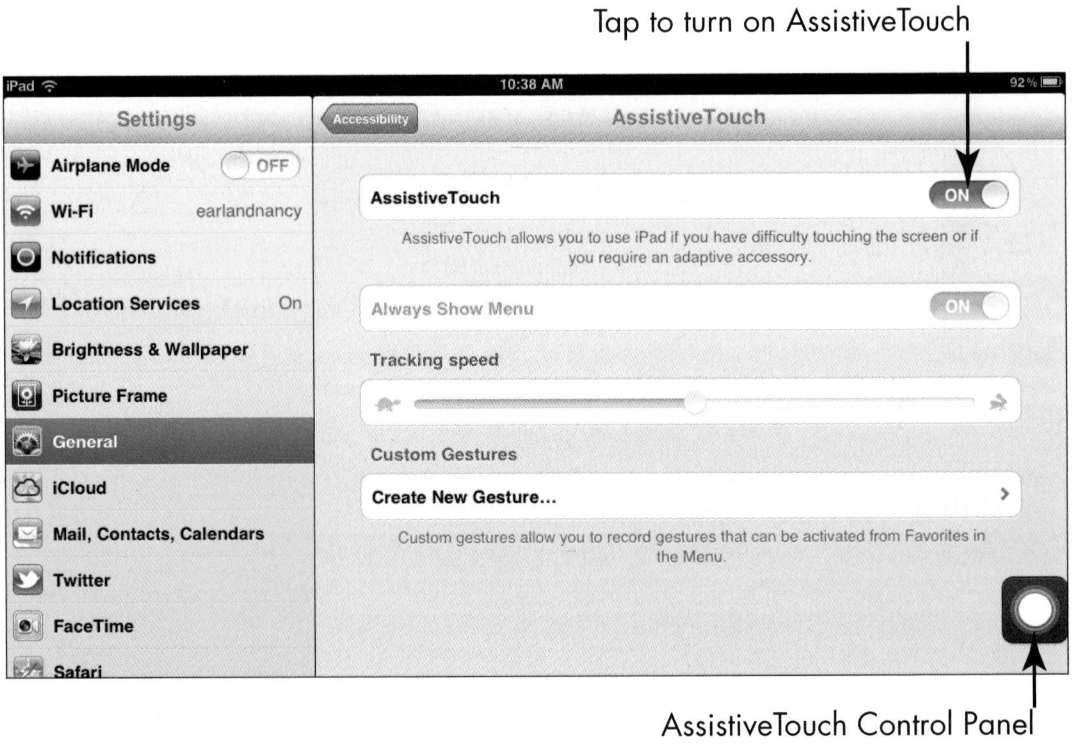

Tap to turn on AssistiveTouch

AssistiveTouch Control Panel

Figure 4-13

3. Tap the AssistiveTouch Control Panel to display options, as shown in **Figure 4-14**.

4. You can tap Gestures, Favorites, or Device on the panel
to see additional choices, or tap Home to go directly to
the Home screen. Once you've chosen an option, tapping
the Back arrow takes you back to the main panel.

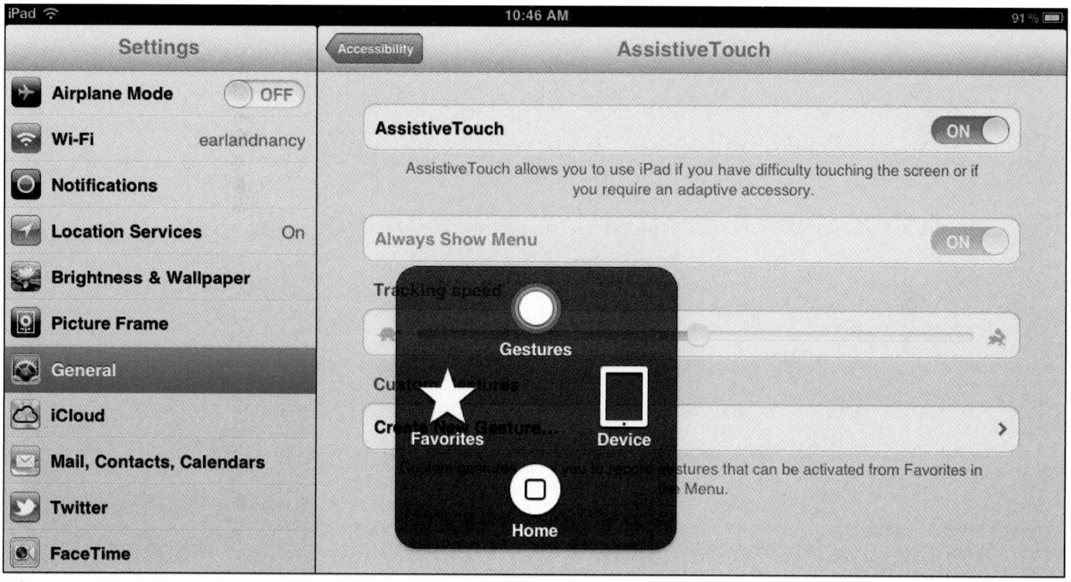

Figure 4-14

Table 4-2 shows the major options available in the AssistiveTouch
Control Panel:

Table 4-2	AssistiveTouch Controls
Control	**Purpose**
Gestures	Choose the number of fingers to use for gestures on the touchscreen.
Favorites	Displays a set of gestures with only the Pinch gesture preset; you can tap any of the other blank squares to add your own favorite gestures.
Device	You can rotate the screen, lock the screen, turn volume up or down, mute or unmute sound, or shake iPad to undo an action using the presets in this option.
Home	Sends you to the Home Screen.

Part II
Taking the Leap Online

The 5th Wave   By Rich Tennant

"Hold on Barbara. I'm pretty sure there's an app for this."

Browsing the Internet with Safari

Getting on the Internet with your iPad is easy, using its Wi-Fi or 3G capabilities. After you're online, the built-in browser, *Safari*, is your ticket to a wide world of information, entertainment, education, and more. Safari will look familiar to you if you've used it on a PC or Mac device before, though the way you move around by using the iPad touchscreen might be new to you. If you've never used Safari, this chapter takes you by the hand and shows you all its ins and outs.

In this chapter, you discover how to connect your iPad to the Internet and navigate among web pages. Along the way, you see how to place a bookmark for a favorite site or place a web clip on your Home screen. You can also view your browsing history, save online images to your Photo Library, or e-mail or tweet a hotlink to a friend. You explore the Safari Reader and Safari Reading List features and learn how to keep yourself safer while online using private browsing. Finally, you review the simple steps involved in printing what you find online.

Connect to the Internet

How you connect to the Internet depends on which iPad model you own:

⟹ The Wi-Fi–only iPad connects to the Internet only via a Wi-Fi network. You can set up this type of network in your own home using your computer and some equipment from your Internet provider. You can also connect over public Wi-Fi networks, referred to as *hotspots*. You'll probably be surprised to discover how many hotspots your town or city has: Look for Internet cafés, coffee shops, hotels, libraries, and transportation centers such as airports or bus stations, for example. Many of these businesses display signs alerting you to their free Wi-Fi.

⟹ If you own a Wi-Fi- and 3G-enabled iPad, you can still use a Wi-Fi connection, but you can also use the paid data network provided by AT&T or Verizon to connect from just about anywhere you can get cellphone coverage via a cellular network.

If you have a 3G model, you don't have to do anything; with a contract for 3G coverage the connection is made automatically wherever cellular service is available, just as it is on your cellphone. To connect to a Wi-Fi network you have to complete a few steps.

1. When you're in range of a hotspot, if access to several nearby networks is available, you may see a message asking you to tap a network name to select it. After you select one (or if only one network is available), you see a message similar to the one shown in **Figure 5-1**.

2. If you're required to enter a network password, do so.

3. Tap the Join button and you're connected.

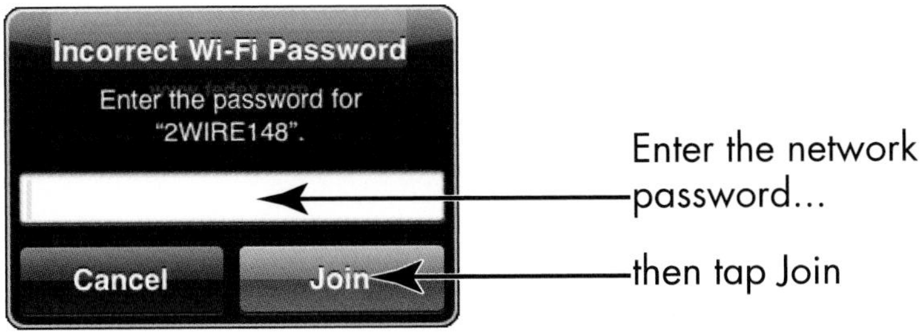

Incorrect Wi-Fi Password

Enter the password for "2WIRE148".

Cancel   Join

Enter the network password...

then tap Join

Figure 5-1

 See Chapter 1 for more about the capabilities of different iPad models and the costs associated with 3G.

 Free public Wi-Fi networks typically don't require passwords. However, it's then possible for someone else to track your online activities over these *unsecured* networks. Avoid accessing financial accounts or sending sensitive e-mail when connected to a public hotspot.

Explore Safari

1. After you're connected to a network, tap the Safari icon on the Home screen. Safari opens, probably displaying the Apple iPad home page the first time you go online (see **Figure 5-2**).

2. Put two fingers together on the screen and swipe them outward to enlarge the view, as shown in **Figure 5-3**. Double-tap the screen with a single finger to restore the default screen size.

3. Put your finger on the screen and flick upward to scroll down on the page.

4. To return to the top of the web page, put your finger on the screen and drag downward or tap the Status bar at the top of the screen.

Using the pinch method to enlarge or reduce the size of a web page on your screen allows you to view what's displayed at various sizes, giving you more flexibility than the double-tap method.

 When you enlarge the display, you gain more control using two fingers to drag from left to right or from top to bottom on the screen. On a reduced display, one finger works fine for making these gestures.

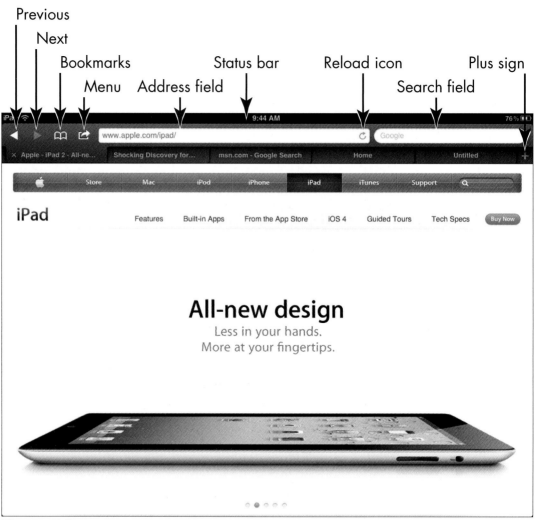

Figure 5-2

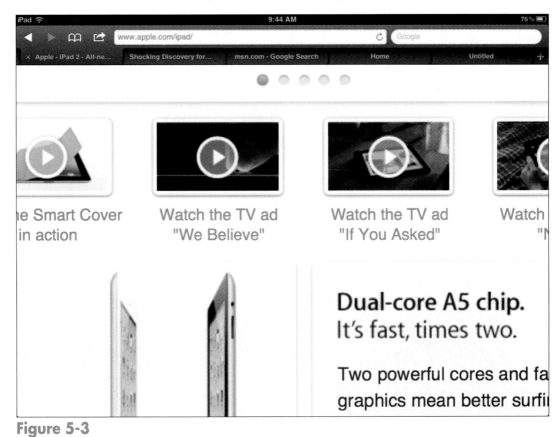

Figure 5-3

Navigate among Web Pages

1. Tap in the Address field. The onscreen keyboard appears (see **Figure 5-4**).

2. To clear the field, press the Delete key on the keyboard. Enter a web address; for example, you can go to this book's companion website: www.iPadMadeClear.com.

3. Tap the Go key on the keyboard (refer to **Figure 5-4**). The website appears.

- If, for some reason, a page doesn't display, tap the Reload icon on the right end of the Address field.

- If Safari is loading a web page and you change your mind about viewing the page, you can tap the Stop icon (the X), which appears on the right end of the Address field during this process, to stop loading the page.

4. Tap the Previous arrow to go backward to the last page you displayed.

5. Tap the Next arrow to go forward to the page you just came from.

6. To follow a link to another web page, tap the link with your finger. To view the destination web address of the link before you tap it, just touch and hold the link; a menu appears that displays the address at the top, as shown in **Figure 5-5**.

By default, AutoFill is turned on in iPad, causing entries you make in fields such as the Address field to automatically display possible matching entries. You can turn off AutoFill by using iPad Settings.

Figure 5-4

The link's web address

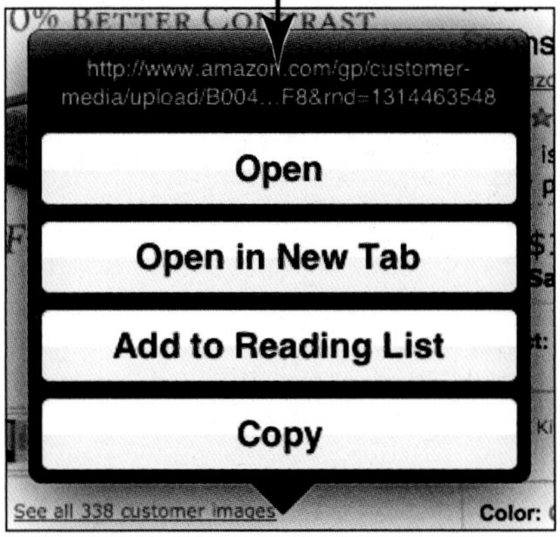

Figure 5-5

Use Tabbed Browsing

1. With iOS 5 comes *tabbed browsing*, a feature that allows you to have several websites open at once on separate tabs so you can move easily among those sites. To add a tab, tap the plus sign near the upper-right corner of the screen (refer to **Figure 5-2**).

2. The search field becomes active and a drop-down list and the onscreen keyboard appear (see **Figure 5-6**). You can tap an item from a recent search, or tap in the search field and enter the name of a site to open. The site opens on a new tab.

3. You can now switch among open sites by tapping another tab.

Using tabbed browsing you can not only place a site on a tab but also a search results screen. If you recently searched for something, those search results will be on your Recent Searches list. Also, if you are displaying a search results page when you tap the plus sign to add a tab, the first ten suggested sites in the results will be listed there for you to choose from.

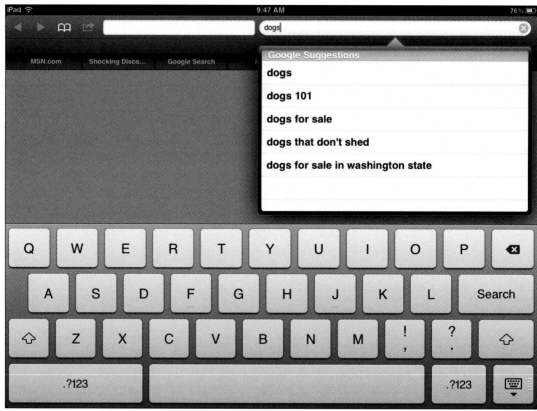

Figure 5-6

View Browsing History

1. As you move around the web, your browser keeps a record of your browsing history. This record can be handy when you want to visit a site that you viewed previously but have forgotten its address. With Safari open, tap the Bookmark icon.

2. On the menu shown in **Figure 5-7**, tap History.

3. In the History list that appears (see **Figure 5-8**), tap a date if available, and then tap a site to navigate to it.

Tap this option

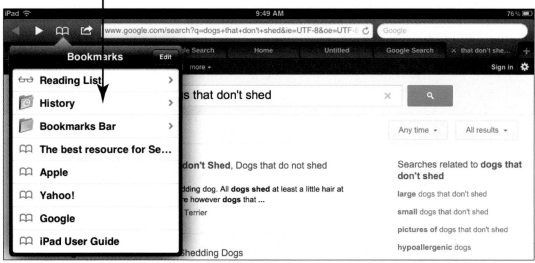

Figure 5-7

History list

Clear History button

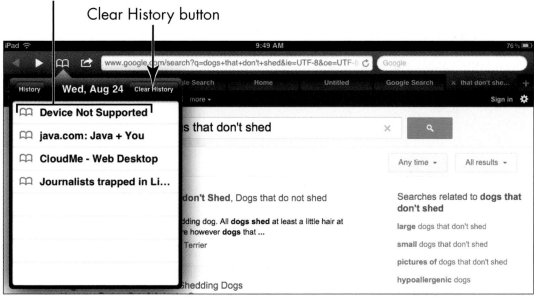

Figure 5-8

To clear the history, tap the Clear History button (refer to **Figure 5-8**). This button is useful when you don't want your spouse or grandchildren to see where you've been browsing for birthday or holiday presents!

You can tap and hold the Previous button to quickly display a list of your browsing history.

Search the Web

1. If you don't know the address of the site you want to visit (or you want to research a topic or find other information online), get acquainted with Safari's Search feature on iPad. By default, Safari uses the Google search engine. With Safari open, tap in the Search field. The onscreen keyboard appears.

2. You can tap on one of the suggested sites, or enter a search word or phrase, and tap the Search key (see **Figure 5-9**) on your keyboard.

3. In the search results that are displayed, tap a link to visit that site.

To change your default search engine from Google to Yahoo! or Bing, in iPad Settings, tap Safari and then tap Search Engine. Tap Yahoo! or Bing and your default search engine changes.

You can browse for specific items such as images, videos, or maps by tapping the corresponding link at the top of the Google results screen. Also, tap the More button in this list to see even more options to narrow your results such as searching for books or YouTube videos on the subject.

Suggested sites

Search field

Figure 5-9

Add and Use Bookmarks

 **1.** Bookmarks are a way to save favorite sites so you can easily visit them again. With a site you want to bookmark displayed, tap the Menu icon.

2. On the menu that appears (see **Figure 5-10**), tap Add Bookmark.

3. In the Add Bookmark dialog, shown in **Figure 5-11,** edit the name of the bookmark if you want. To do so, tap the name of the site and use the onscreen keyboard to edit its name.

Tap this option

Figure 5-10

Edit the name here

Figure 5-11

4. Tap the Save button.

 5. To go to the bookmark, tap the Bookmarks icon.

6. On the Bookmarks menu that appears (see **Figure 5-12),** tap the bookmarked site you want to visit.

Tap a bookmarked site to visit it

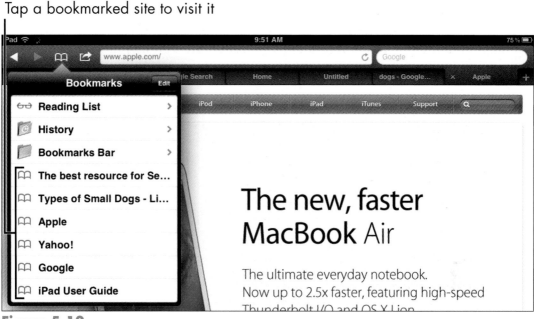

Figure 5-12

 If you want to sync your bookmarks on your iPad browser to your computer, connect your iPad to your computer and make sure that the Sync Safari Bookmarks setting on the Info tab of iTunes is activated.

 When you tap the Bookmarks icon, you can use the Bookmarks Bar option to create folders to organize your bookmarks. When you next add a bookmark, you can then choose, from the dialog that appears, any folder to which you want to add the new bookmark.

Use Safari Reading List

1. The Safari Reading List provides a way to save sites that contain content you want to read at a later time so you can easily visit them again. With a site you want to add to your Reading List displayed, tap the Menu icon.

2. On the menu that appears (refer to **Figure 5-10**), tap Add to Reading List. The site is added to your list.

3. To view your Reading List, tap the Bookmarks icon and tap Reading List.

4. On the Reading List that appears (see **Figure 5-13**), tap the content you want to revisit and resume reading.

Tap an item to resume reading

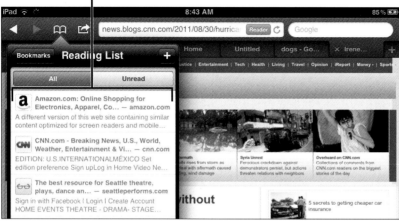

Figure 5-13

If you want to see both Reading List material you've read and that material you haven't read, tap the All tab in the Reading List pane (refer to **Figure 5-13**). To see just the material you haven't read, use the Unread tab.

To save an image to your Reading List, tap and hold the image until a menu appears, and then tap Add to Reading list. To delete an item, with the Reading List displayed swipe left or right on an item and a Delete button appears. Tap it to delete the item from Reading List.

Utilize Safari Reader

1. The Safari Reader feature gives you an e-reader type of experience right within your browser, removing other stories and links as well as those distracting advertisements. When you are on a site where you're reading content such as an article, Safari displays a Reader button on the right side of the address field (see **Figure 5-14**). Tap the Reader button. The content appears in a reader format (see **Figure 5-15**).

The Reader button

Figure 5-14

Tap here to increase/decrease the text size

Figure 5-15

2. Scroll down the page. The entire content is contained in this one long page.

3. When you finish reading the material, just tap the Previous button to go back to its source.

 To enlarge the text in the Reader tap the large *A* in the top-left corner (refer to **Figure 5-15**).

Add Web Clips to the Home Screen

1. The *Web Clips* feature allows you to save a website as an icon on your Home screen so that you can go to the site at any time with one tap. With Safari open and displaying the site you want to add, tap the Menu icon.

2. On the menu that appears (refer to **Figure 5-10**), tap Add to Home Screen.

3. In the Add to Home dialog that appears (see **Figure 5-16**), you can edit the name of the site to be more descriptive, if you like. To do so, tap the name of the site and use the onscreen keyboard to edit its name.

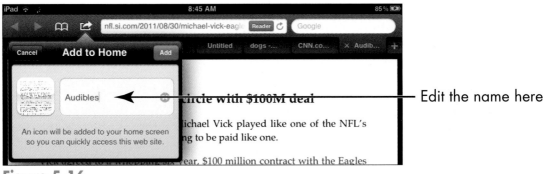

Edit the name here

Figure 5-16

4. Tap the Add button. The site is added to your Home screen.

Remember that you can have as many as 11 Home screens on your iPad to accommodate all the web clips and apps you download (though there is a limit to how many will fit). If you want to delete an item from your Home screen for any reason, press and hold the icon on the Home screen until all items on the screen start to jiggle and Delete icons appear on all items except the preinstalled apps. Tap the Delete icon on each item you want to delete, and it's gone. (To get rid of the jiggle, tap the Home button again.)

Save an Image to Your Photo Library

1. Display a web page that contains an image you want to copy.

2. Press and hold the image. The menu shown in **Figure 5-17** appears.

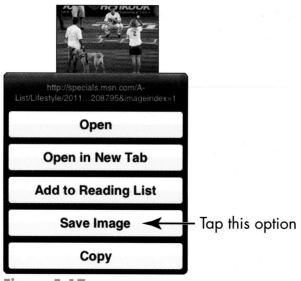

Tap this option

Figure 5-17

3. Tap the Save Image option (refer to **Figure 5-17**). The image is saved to your library.

Be careful about copying images from the Internet and using them for business or promotional activities. Most images are copyrighted, and you may violate the copyright even if you simply use an image in (say) a brochure for your association or a flyer for your community group. Note that some search engines' advanced search settings offer the option of browsing only for images that aren't copyrighted.

Send a Link

1. If you find a great site that you want to share, you can do so easily by sending a link in an e-mail. With Safari open and the site you want to share displayed, tap the Menu icon.

2. On the menu that appears (refer to **Figure 5-10**), tap Mail Link to this Page.

3. On the message form that appears (see **Figure** 5-18), enter a recipient's e-mail address, a subject, and your message.

iPad	2:23 PM	53%
Cancel	Software	Send

To: copperglow@msn.com

Cc/Bcc:

Subject: Software

Check out this site. You might want to link to it:

http://techsmartsenior.com/page7.html

Helen

Sent from my iPad

Figure 5-18

4. Tap Send and the e-mail goes on its way.

 The e-mail is sent from the default e-mail account you have set up on iPad. For more about setting up an e-mail account, see Chapter 6.

 To tweet the link using your Twitter account, in Step 2 of this task choose Tweet, enter your tweet message in the form that appears, and then tap Send. For more about using Twitter with iPad, see Chapter 7.

Make Private Browsing and Cookie Settings

Apple has provided some privacy settings for Safari that you should consider using. *Private Browsing* automatically removes items from the download list, stops Safari from letting AutoFill save information used to complete your entries in the search or address fields as you type, and doesn't save some browsing history information. These features can keep your online activities more private. The *Accept Cookies* setting allows you to stop the downloading of cookies (small files that document your browsing history so you can be recognized the next time you go to or move within a site) to your iPad.

You can control both settings by choosing Safari in the Settings window. Tap to turn Private Browsing on or off (see **Figure 5-19**). Tap the arrow on Accept Cookies and choose to never save cookies, always save cookies, or only save cookies from visited sites.

 You can also use those two settings to clear your browsing history, saved cookies, and other data manually (refer to **Figure 5-19**).

Turn on Private Browsing here

Figure 5-19

Print a Web Page

 1. If you have a wireless printer that supports Apple's AirPrint technology (Hewlett-Packard is the only manufacturer that makes these at present), you can print web content using a wireless connection. With Safari open and the site you want to print displayed, tap the Menu icon.

2. On the menu that appears (refer to **Figure 5-10**), tap Print.

3. In the Printer Options dialog that appears (see **Figure 5-20**), tap Select Printer. In the list of printers that appears, tap the name of your wireless printer.

Tap Select Printer

Figure 5-20

4. Tap either the plus or minus button in the Copy field to adjust the number of copies to print.

5. Tap Print to print the displayed page.

The apps Printopia and AirPrint Activator 2 make any shared or network printer on your home network visible to your iPad. Printopia has more features, but is more expensive, while AirPrint Activator is free.

If you don't have an AirPrint-compatible wireless printer or don't wish to use an app to help you print wirelessly, just e-mail a link to the web page to yourself, open the link on your computer, and print from there.

Working with E-Mail in Mail

Staying in touch with others by using e-mail is a great way to use your iPad. You can access an existing account using the handy Mail app supplied with your iPad or sign in to your e-mail account using the Safari browser. Using Mail involves adding an existing e-mail account by way of iPad Settings. Then you can use Mail to write, format, retrieve, and forward messages from that account.

Mail offers the capability to mark the messages you've read, delete messages, and organize your messages in a small set of folders, as well as a handy search feature. In this chapter, you read all about Mail and its various features.

Add a Gmail, Yahoo!, or AOL Account

1. You can add one or more e-mail accounts, including the e-mail account associated with your iCloud account, using iPad Settings. If you have a Gmail, Yahoo!, or AOL account, iPad pretty much automates the setup. To set up iPad to retrieve messages from your e-mail account at one of these popular providers (Gmail, Yahoo!, iCloud, AOL, or Windows Live Hotmail), first tap the Settings icon on the Home screen.

2. In the Settings dialog, tap Mail, Contacts, Calendars. The settings shown in **Figure 6-1** appear.

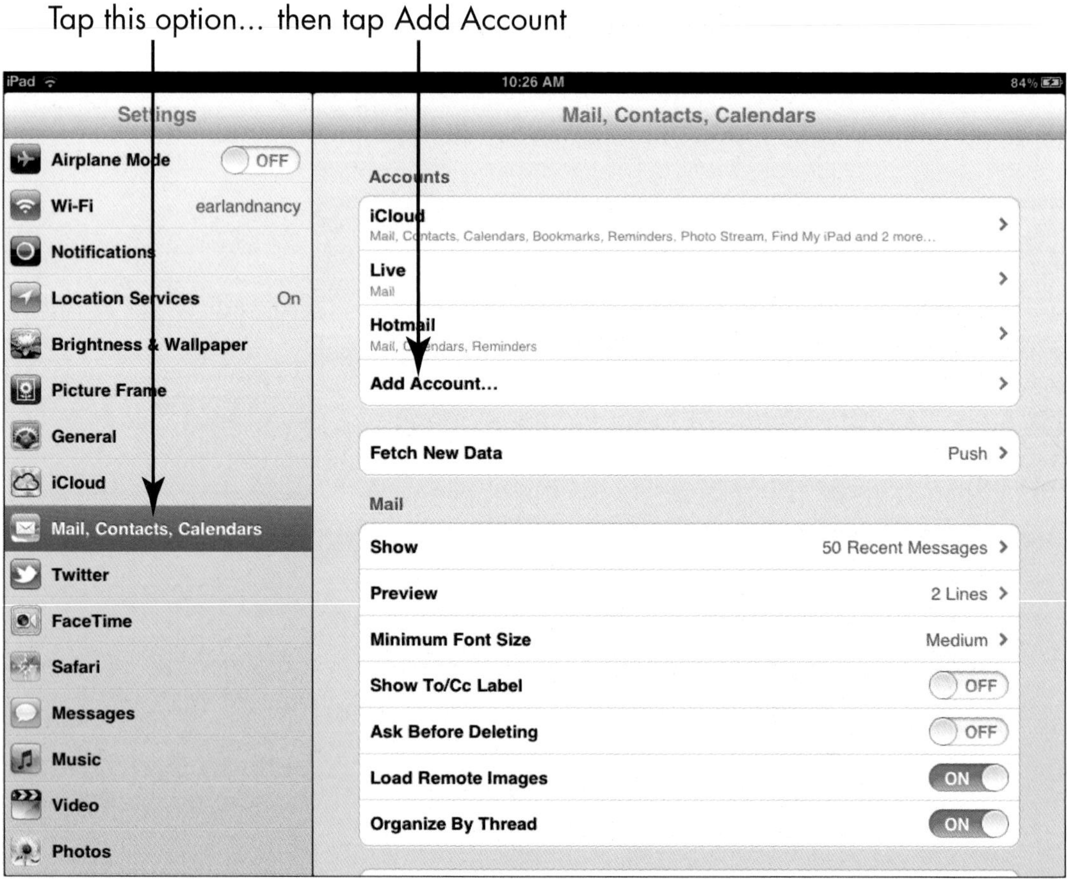

Tap this option... then tap Add Account

Figure 6-1

3. Tap Add Account. The options shown in **Figure 6-2** appear.

4. Tap iCloud, Gmail, Yahoo!, AOL, or Windows Live Hotmail. Enter your account information in the form that appears (see **Figure 6-3**).

5. After iPad takes a moment to verify your account information, you can tap on any on/off button to have Mail, Contacts, Calendars, or Reminders from that account synced with iPad.

6. When you're done, tap Save. The account is saved and you can now open it using Mail.

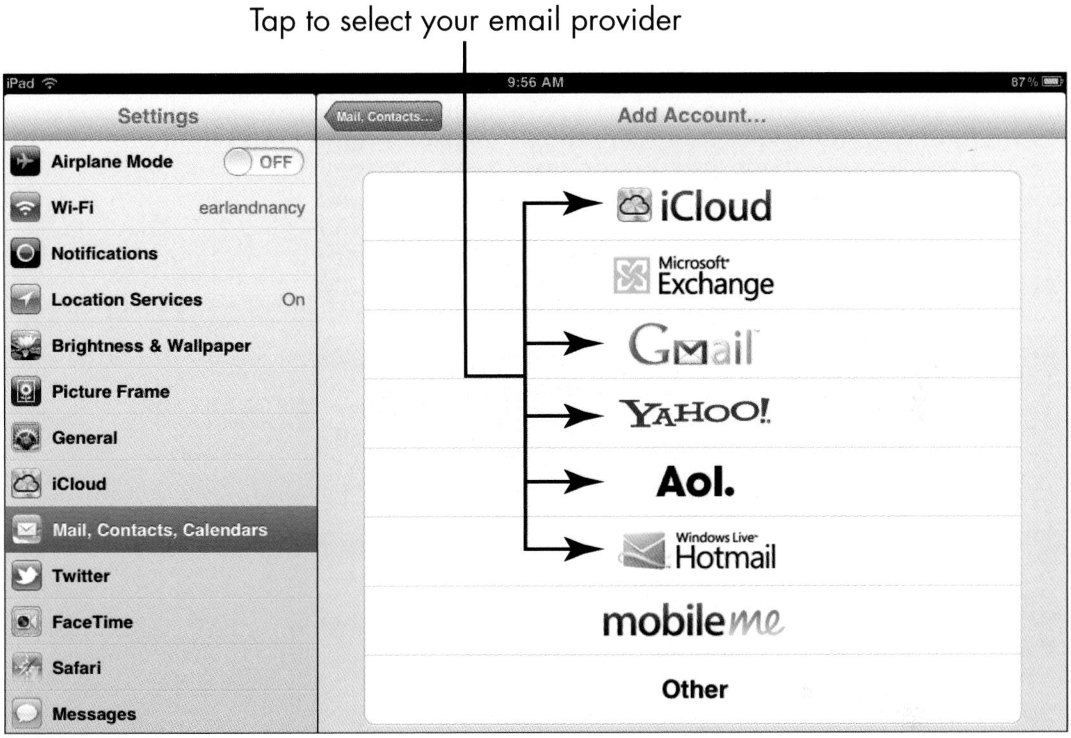

Tap to select your email provider

Figure 6-2

Enter your account info

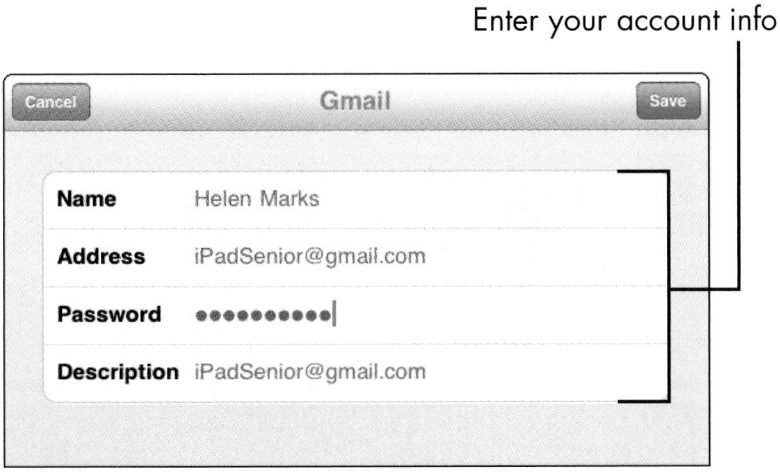

Figure 6-3

Set Up a POP3 E-Mail Account

1. You can also set up most popular e-mail accounts, such as those available through Earthlink or a cable provider's service, by obtaining the host name from the provider. To set up an existing account with a provider other than iCloud, Gmail, Windows Live Hotmail, Yahoo!, or AOL, you enter the account settings yourself. First, tap the Settings icon on the Home screen.

2. In Settings, tap Mail, Contacts, Calendars, and then tap the Add Account button at the top right.

3. On the screen that appears (refer to **Figure 6-2**), tap Other.

4. On the screen shown in **Figure 6-4**, tap Add Mail Account.

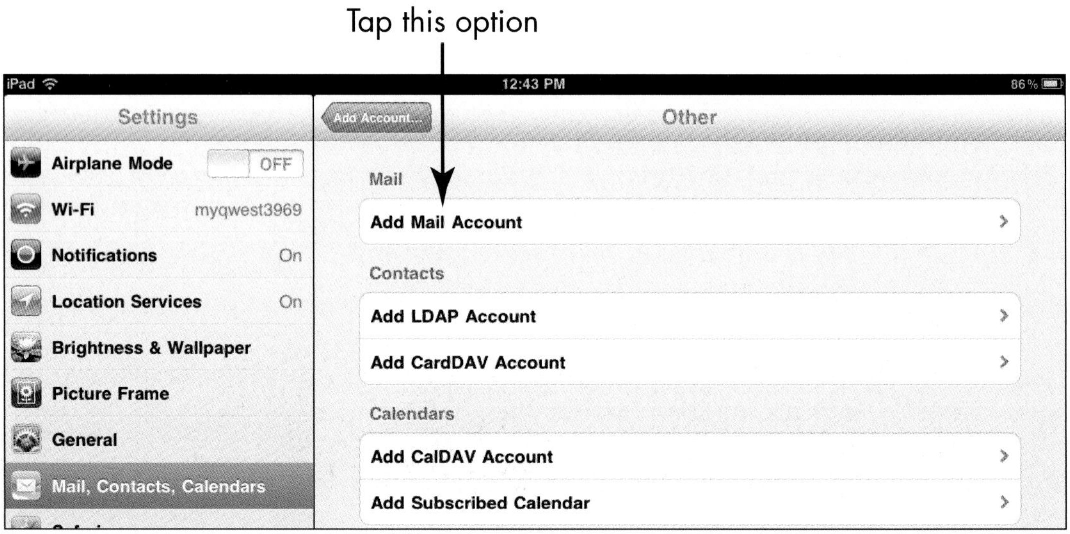

Tap this option

iPad	12:43 PM	86%

Settings	Add Account...	Other

Mail

Add Mail Account >

Contacts

Add LDAP Account >

Add CardDAV Account >

Calendars

Add CalDAV Account >

Add Subscribed Calendar >

Settings:
- Airplane Mode — OFF
- Wi-Fi — myqwest3969
- Notifications — On
- Location Services — On
- Brightness & Wallpaper
- Picture Frame
- General
- Mail, Contacts, Calendars

Figure 6-4

5. In the form that appears (refer to **Figure 6-3**), enter your name and an account address, password, and description, and then tap Next. iPad takes a moment to verify your account and then returns you to the Mail, Contacts, and Calendars page, with your new account displayed.

If you have a less mainstream e-mail service, you may have to enter the mail server protocol (POP3 or IMAP — ask your provider for this information) and your password. iPad will probably add the outgoing mail server (SMTP) information for you, but if it doesn't, you may have to enter it yourself. Your Internet service provider (ISP) can provide it to you.

6. To make sure that the Account field is set to On for receiving e-mail, tap the account name. In the dialog that appears, tap the On/Off button for the Mail field and then tap Done to save the setting. You can now access the account through Mail.

If you turn on Calendars in the Mail account settings, any information you've put into your calendar in that e-mail account will be brought over into the Calendar app on your iPad and reflected in the Notifications Center (discussed in more detail in Chapter 17).

Open Mail and Read Messages

1. Tap the Mail app icon, located in the Dock on the Home screen (see **Figure 6-5**). A red circle on the icon indicates the number of unread e-mails in your Inbox.

Tap this icon

Figure 6-5

2. In the Mail app, if you're holding the iPad in portrait orientation, if the Inbox you want isn't displayed, tap the button to the left of the word Inbox (see **Figure 6-6**) to display your list of inboxes. Tap the inbox whose contents you want to display Note that in landscape orientation, the Mailboxes/Inbox panel is always displayed; in portrait orientation, you display it by clicking the button to the left of the word Inbox.

Tap this button

Figure 6-6

3. Tap a message to read it. It opens (see **Figure** 6-7).

4. If you need to scroll to see the entire message, just place your finger on the screen and flick upward to scroll down. You can also swipe right while reading a message to open the Inbox list of messages, and then swipe left to hide the list.

 You can tap the Hide button (top-right corner of the message) to hide the address details (the To field) so that more of the message appears on your screen. To reveal the field again, tap the Details button (which becomes the Hide button when details are displayed).

 E-mail messages you haven't read are marked with a blue circle in your Inbox. After you read a message, the blue circle disappears. You can mark a read message as unread, to help remind you to read it again later. With a message open and details about it displayed, tap the Mark link on the right side and then tap Mark as Unread. To flag a message, which places a little flag next to it in your inbox, helping you to spot items of more importance or to read again, tap Mark and then tap Flag.

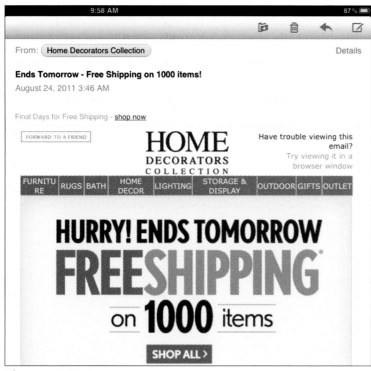

Figure 6-7

To escape your e-mail now and then (or to avoid having messages retrieved while you're at a public Wi-Fi hotspot), you can stop retrieval of e-mail by using the Fetch New Data control of Mail in iPad Settings.

Reply To or Forward E-Mail

1. With an e-mail message open (see the previous task), tap the Reply/Forward button, shown in **Figure 6-8**.

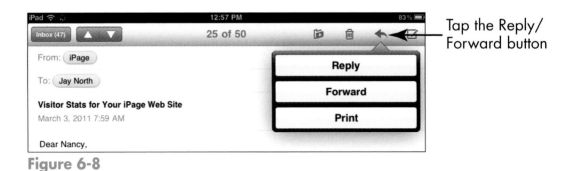

Tap the Reply/
Forward button

Figure 6-8

2. Take one of the following actions:

- Tap Reply to respond to the sender of the message or Reply All to respond to the sender and any other recipients. The Reply Message form, shown in **Figure 6-9**, appears. Tap in the message body and enter a message.

- Tap Forward to send the message to somebody else. The form shown in **Figure 6-10** appears. Enter a recipient in the To field, and then tap in the message body and enter a message.

3. Tap Send. The message goes on its way.

 If you want to copy an address from the To field to the Cc or Bcc field, tap and hold the address and drag it to the other field.

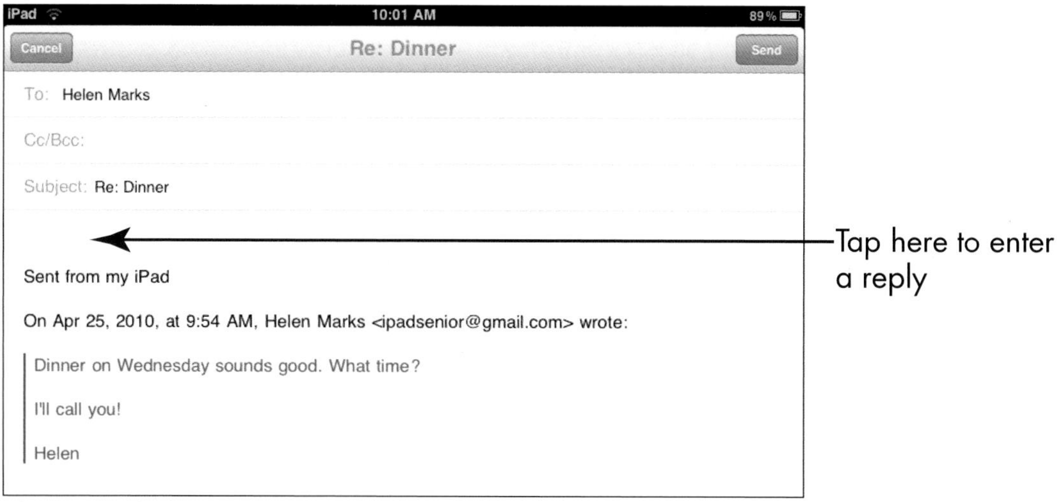

Tap here to enter a reply

Figure 6-9

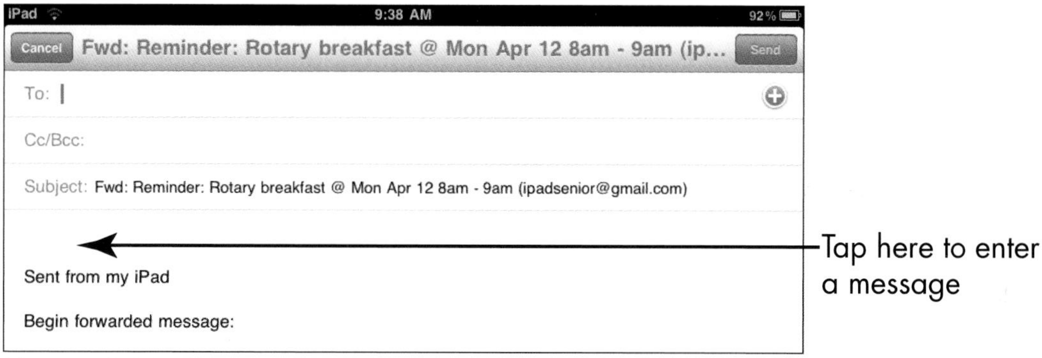

Tap here to enter a message

Figure 6-10

Create and Send a New Message

 1. With Mail open, tap the New Message icon. A blank message form appears (see **Figure 6-11**).

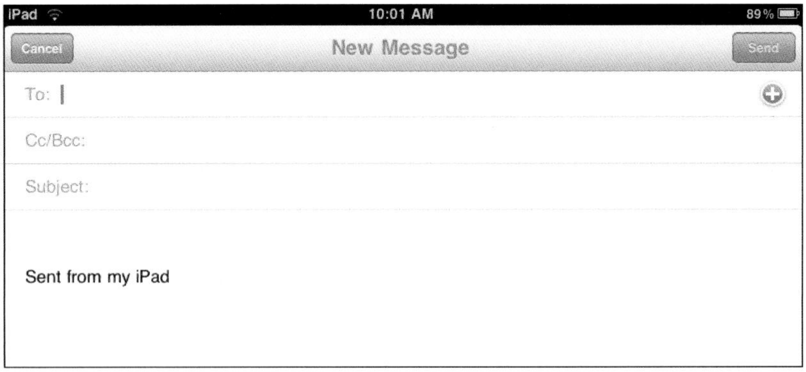

iPad	10:01 AM	89%
Cancel	New Message	Send

To: |

Cc/Bcc:

Subject:

Sent from my iPad

Figure 6-11

2. Enter a recipient's address in the To field. If you have saved addresses in Contacts, tap the plus-sign symbol (+) in the Address field to choose an addressee from the Contacts list.

3. If you want to send a copy of the message to other people, enter their addresses in the Cc/Bcc field. If you want to send both carbon copies and *blind* carbon copies (copies you don't want other recipients to be aware of), note that when you tap the Cc/Bcc field, two fields are displayed; use the Bcc field to specify recipients for blind carbon copies.

4. Enter the subject of the message in the Subject field.

5. Tap in the message body and type your message.

6. Tap Send.

Mail keeps a copy of all deleted messages for a time in the Trash folder. To view deleted messages, tap the Inbox button and then, in the dialog that appears, tap the Mailboxes button to show all mailboxes. If you have more than one mail account (therefore more than one mailbox), tap the account name in the Accounts list and a list of folders opens. Tap the Trash folder and all deleted messages are displayed.

Format E-mail

1. A new feature that comes with iOS 5 is the capability to apply formatting to e-mail text. You can use bold, underline, and italic formats, and indent text using the Quote Level feature.

2. Tap on the text and choose Select or Select All to select a single word or all the words in the e-mail. Note that if you select a single word, handles appear that you can drag to add adjacent words to your selection.

3. Tap the arrow at the far end of the toolbar that appears.

4. To apply Bold, Italic, or Underline formatting, tap the BIU button (see **Figure 6-12**).

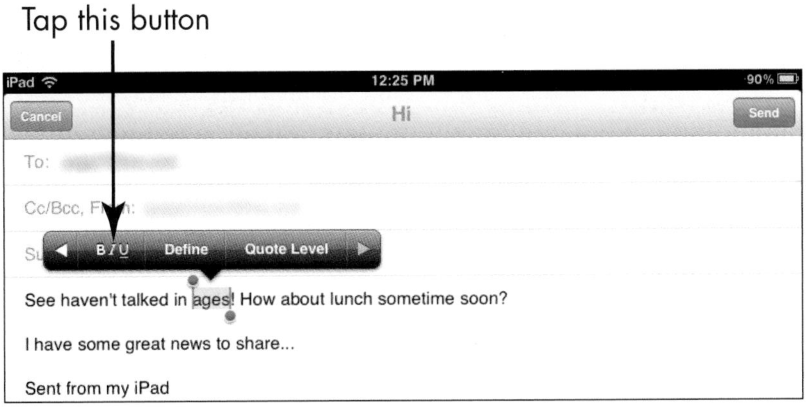

Tap this button

iPad	12:25 PM	90%
Cancel	Hi	Send

To:

Cc/Bcc, From:

Su ◄ **B**/U   Define   Quote Level ►

See haven't talked in ages! How about lunch sometime soon?

I have some great news to share...

Sent from my iPad

Figure 6-12

5. In the toolbar that appears (see **Figure 6-13**) tap Bold, Italics, or Underline to apply formatting.

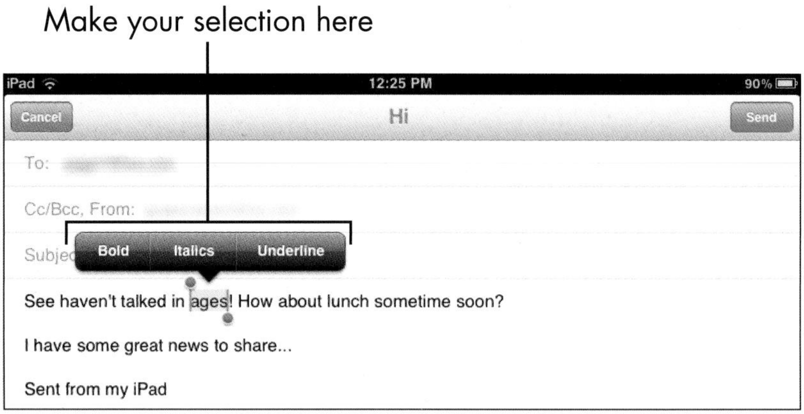

Make your selection here

iPad 🔋		12:25 PM		90% 🔋
Cancel		Hi		Send

To:

Cc/Bcc, From:

Subje   **Bold**   **Italics**   **Underline**

See haven't talked in ages! How about lunch sometime soon?

I have some great news to share...

Sent from my iPad

Figure 6-13

6. To change the indent level, tap at the beginning of a line and then tap the arrow in at the far end of the toolbar. In the toolbar that appears tap Quote Level.

7. Tap Increase to indent the text or Decrease to move indented text further toward the left margin.

   To change the minimum size of text in e-mails use the iPad Settings. Tap Mail, Contacts, Calendars, and then tap the Minimum Font Size setting. Choose from Small, Medium, Large, Extra Large, and Giant in the list that appears.

Search E-Mail

1. Say you want to find all messages from a certain person or containing a certain word in the Subject field. You can use Mail's handy Search feature to find these e-mails. With Mail open, tap the Inbox button.

2. In the Inbox, tap in the Search field. The onscreen keyboard appears.

3. Enter a search term or name as shown in **Figure 6-14.**

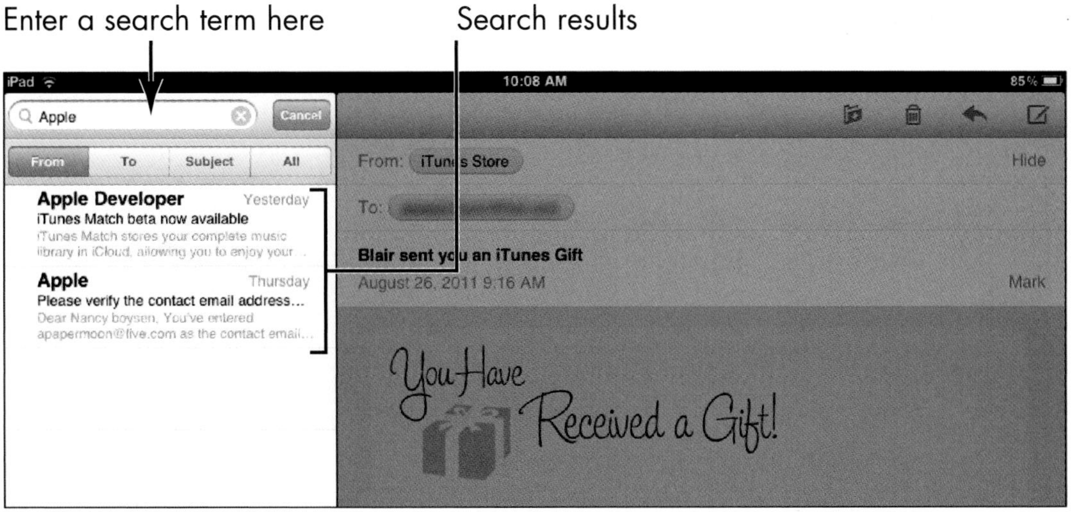

Enter a search term here   Search results

Figure 6-14

4. Tap the From, To, or Subject tab to view messages that contain the search term in one of those fields, or tap the All tab to see messages in which any of these three fields contains the term. Matching e-mails are listed in the results (refer to **Figure 6-14**).

 You can also use the Spotlight Search feature covered in Chapter 2 to search for terms in the To, From, or Subject lines of mail messages.

 To start a new search or go back to the full Inbox, tap the Delete key in the top-right corner of the onscreen keyboard to delete the term or just tap the Cancel button.

Delete E-Mail

1. When you no longer want an e-mail cluttering your Inbox, you can delete it. With the Inbox displayed, tap the Edit button. Circular check boxes are displayed to the left of each message (see **Figure 6-15**).

Tap to select a message   Check marks indicate selected messages

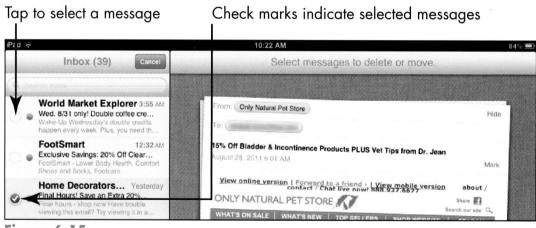

Figure 6-15

2. Tap the circle next to the message you want to delete. (You can tap multiple items if you have several e-mails to delete.) A message marked for deletion shows a check mark in the circular check box (refer to **Figure 6-15**).

3. Tap the Delete button at the bottom of the Inbox dialog. The message is moved to the Trash folder.

 You can also delete an open e-mail by tapping the trashcan icon on the toolbar that runs across the top of Mail or swiping left or right on a message displayed in an inbox and tapping the Delete button that appears.

Organize E-Mail

1. You can move messages into any of several predefined folders in Mail (these will vary depending on your e-mail provider and the folders you've created on their server). After displaying the folder containing the message you want to move (for example, Trash or Inbox), tap the Edit button. Circular check boxes are displayed to the left of each message (refer to **Figure 6-15**).

2. Tap the circle next to the message you want to move.

3. Tap the Move button.

4. In the Mailboxes list that appears on the left (see **Figure 6-16**), tap the folder where you want to store the message. The message is moved.

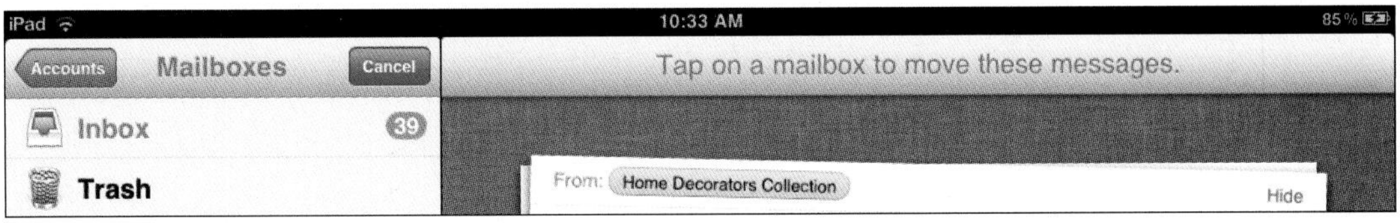

iPad	10:33 AM	85%
Accounts Mailboxes Cancel	Tap on a mailbox to move these messages.	
Inbox 39		
Trash	From: Home Decorators Collection Hide	

Figure 6-16

 If you receive a junk e-mail, you might want to move it to the Spam or Junk folder if your e-mail account provides one. Then any future mail from the same sender is automatically placed in the Spam or Junk folder.

 If you have an e-mail open, you can move it to a folder by tapping the Folder icon on the toolbar along the top. The Mailboxes list displays; tap a folder to move the message.

Getting Social with FaceTime, Twitter, and iMessage

FaceTime is an excellent video-calling app that's been available on the iPhone 4 since its release in mid-2010; it came later to iPad 2. The app lets you call people who have FaceTime on their devices — whether iPhone 4 or 4S, iPad 2, fourth-generation iPod touch, or Mac (running Mac OS X 10.6.6 or later) — using either a phone number (iPhone 4 and 4S) or an e-mail address (Mac, iPod touch, or iPad 2). You and your friend or family member can see each other as you talk, which makes for a much more personal calling experience.

Twitter is a social networking service referred to as a *microblog*, because it involves only short posted messages. Twitter has been incorporated into iOS 5 so you can "tweet" people from within the Safari, Photos, Camera, YouTube, and Maps apps. You can also download the free Twitter app and use it to post tweets whenever you like.

Finally, iMessage is a new feature in iOS 5 (available through the pre-installed Messages app) for instant messaging (IM). IM involves sending a text message to somebody's iPhone (using their phone number) or iPod or iPad (using their e-mail address) to carry on an instant conversation.

In this chapter, I introduce you to FaceTime, Twitter, and iMessage and review their simple controls. In no time, you'll be socializing with all and sundry.

Get an Overview of FaceTime

The *FaceTime* app, built into iOS 4.3 and later for use with the cameras built into the iPad 2, lets you call other folks who have a FaceTime device (iPhone 4 or 4S, iPad 2, a fourth-generation iPod touch, or a compatible Mac computer) and chat while sharing video images of each other. This pre-installed app is useful for seniors who want to keep up with distant family members and friends and see (as well as hear) the latest-and-greatest news.

At this point, you can make and receive calls with FaceTime using a phone number (iPhone 4 or 4S) or an e-mail account (iPad 2, iPod touch, or Mac) and show the person on the other end what's going on around you. Just remember that you can't adjust audio volume from within the app or record a video call. Nevertheless, on the positive side, even though its features are limited, this app is straightforward to use.

You can use your Apple ID and e-mail address to access FaceTime, so it works pretty much right away after you install it. See Chapter 3 for more about getting an Apple ID.

 If you're having trouble using FaceTime, make sure the FaceTime feature is turned on. That's quick to do: Tap Settings on the Home screen, tap FaceTime, and then tap the On/Off button to turn it on, if necessary. You can also select the e-mail account that can be used to make phone calls to you on this Settings page.

Make a FaceTime Call

1. If you know that the person you're calling has FaceTime on an iPhone 4 or 4S, an iPad 2, or a Mac, add that person to your iPad Contacts (see Chapter 18 for how to do this) if he or she isn't already in there.

2. Tap the FaceTime app icon on the Home screen; on the screen that appears, tap the Contacts button in the bottom-right corner of the screen.

3. Scroll to locate a contact and tap the contact's name to display his or her information (see **Figure 7-1**).

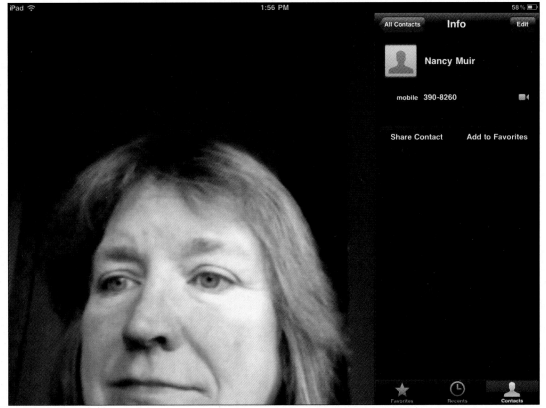

 Figure 7-1

4. Tap on the contact's stored phone number or e-mail address. You've just placed a FaceTime call!

 You have to use the appropriate method for placing a FaceTime call, depending on the kind of device the person you're calling has. If you're calling an iPhone 4 or 4S user, you should use a phone number the first time you call and thereafter you can use the phone number or email address; if you're calling an iPad 2, an iPod touch, or a FaceTime for Mac user, you have to make the call using that person's e-mail address.

 When you call somebody using an e-mail address, the person must be signed in to his or her Apple ID account and have verified that the address can be used for FaceTime calls. iPad 2 and iPod touch (fourth-generation) users can make this setting by tapping Settings and then FaceTime; FaceTime for Mac users make this setting by clicking FaceTime⇨Preferences.

5. When the person accepts the call, you see a large screen that displays the recipient's image alongside a small screen containing your image (see **Figure 7-2**).

 You can also simply go to the Contacts app, find a contact, and tap the FaceTime icon next to that person's phone number or e-mail address in the contact record to make a FaceTime call.

 To view recent calls, tap the Recents button in Step 2. Tap a recent call and iPad displays that person's information. You can tap the contact to call the person back.

 At the time of this writing, you can use FaceTime only over a Wi-Fi network, not over 3G, which limits the places from which you can make or receive video calls to your home wireless network or a public hotspot. On the other hand, you avoid costly data usage over a 3G network with this setup.

Figure 7-2

Accept or End a FaceTime Call

1. If you're on the receiving end of a FaceTime call, accepting the call is about as easy as it gets. When the call comes in, tap the Accept button to take the call or tap the Decline button to reject it (see **Figure 7-3**).

2. Chat away with your friend, swapping video images. To end the call, tap the End button (see **Figure 7-4**).

Figure 7-3

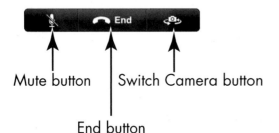

Mute button | Switch Camera button

End button

Figure 7-4

 To mute sound during a call, tap the Mute button (refer to **Figure** 7-4). Tap the button again to unmute your iPad or iPhone.

 To add a caller to your Favorites list, with FaceTime open (refer to **Figure** 7-1), tap the Favorites button and then tap the plus sign (+) and select a name from the contact list to add the person to Favorites. You can then locate the person to make a call to him or her by tapping Favorites rather than Contacts.

Switch Views

1. When you're on a FaceTime call, you might want to use iPad's built-in camera to show the person you're talking to what's going on around you. Tap the Switch Camera button (refer to **Figure 7-4**) to switch from the front-facing camera that's displaying your image to the back-facing camera that captures whatever you're looking at (see **Figure 7-5**).

Figure 7-5

2. Tap the Switch Camera button again to switch back to the front camera displaying your image.

Experience Twitter on iPad

Twitter is a social networking service for *microblogging,* which involves posting very short messages (limited to 140 characters) online so your friends can see what you're up to. You can go to www.twitter.com to sign up with the service; there is also a free Twitter app for iPad you can download and use to manage your Twitter account. Once you have an account you can post "tweets," have people follow your tweets, and follow the tweets that other people post.

With iOS 5 for iPad the ability to tweet has become integrated into several apps. You can post tweets using the Menu button within Safari, Photos, Camera, YouTube, and Maps. First, sign up for an account, then download the free Twitter app to your iPad (see Chapter 9 for more about downloading apps). Go to iPad Settings and tap on Twitter. Then add your account information.

Now when you're using Safari, Photos, Camera, YouTube, or Maps you can choose Tweet from a menu. You'll see a Tweet form like that shown in **Figure 7-6.** Just write your message in the form and then tap Send.

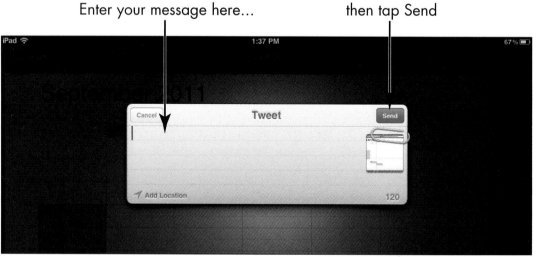

Enter your message here...   then tap Send

Figure 7-6

 See Chapters 5, 12, or 13 for more about tweeting in the Safari, Photos, or YouTube apps.

Set Up an iMessage Account

1. iMessage is a new feature in iOS 5 (available through the pre-installed Messages app) that allows you to send and receive instant messages (IM) to others using an Applie iOS device. Instant messaging differs from e-mail or tweeting in an important way. Where you might e-mail somebody and wait days or weeks before that person responds, or you might post a tweet that could sit there awhile before anybody views it, with instant messaging communication happens immediately. You send an IM and it appears on somebody's iPhone, iPod touch, or iPad right away, and assuming the person wants to participate in a live conversation, it begins immediately, allowing a back and forth dialog in real time. To set up iMessage, tap Settings on the Home screen.

2. Tap Messages and the settings shown in **Figure** 7-7 are displayed.

3. If iMessage is not set to On (refer to **Figure** 7-7), tap the On/Off button to turn it on.

4. Check to be sure the e-mail account associated with your iPad is correct (this should be set up automatically based on your Apple ID).

5. To allow a notice to be sent when you've read somebody's messages, tap the On/Off button for Send Read Receipts.

6. Tap the Home button to leave the settings.

 To change the e-mail account used by iMessage tap the Email button and then tap Remove This Email, then follow the steps above to add another e-mail account.

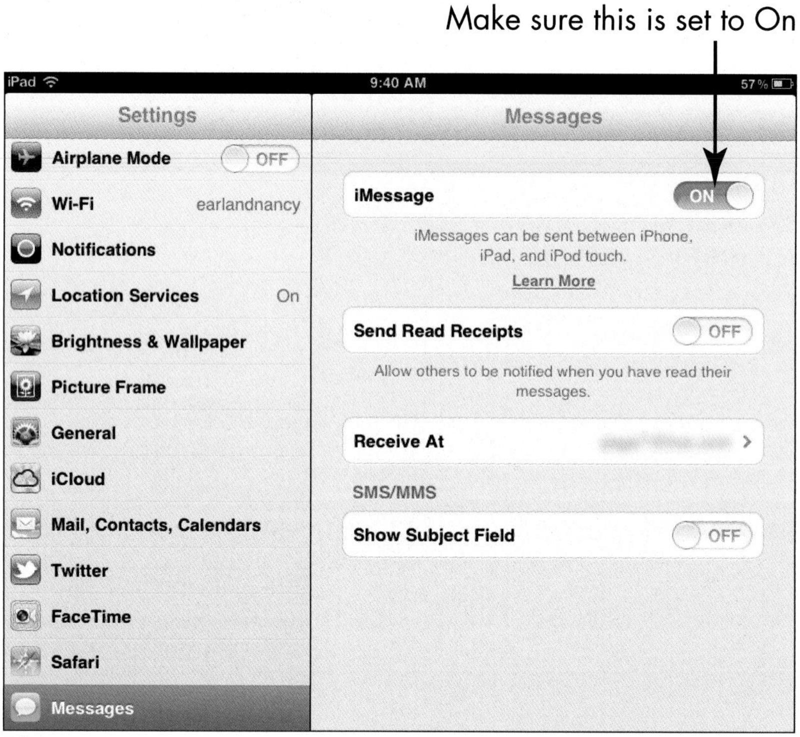

Make sure this is set to On

Figure 7-7

Use iMessage to Address, Create, and Send Messages

1. Now you're ready to use iMessage. From the Home screen, tap the Messages icon. If this is the first time you're using iMessage, on the screen that appears (see **Figure 7-8**), you tap the New Message button to begin a conversation.

2. You can address a message in a couple of ways:

- Begin to type an address in the To: field and a list of matching contacts appears.

- Tap the plus icon on the right of the address field and the All Contacts list is displayed, as shown in **Figure 7-9**.

New Message button · Address field

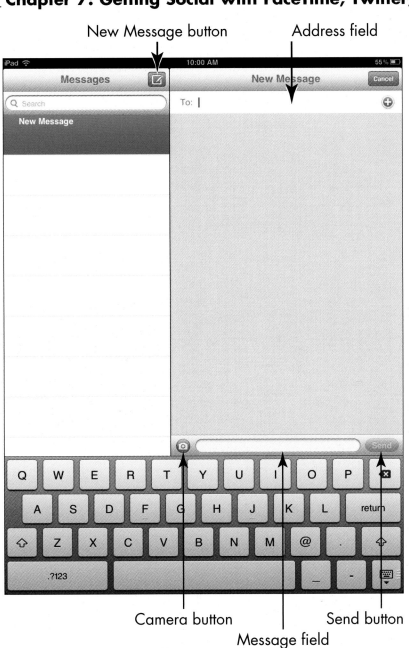

Camera button · Message field · Send button

Figure 7-8

3. Tap a contact on the list you chose to display in Step 2. If the contact has both an e-mail address and phone number stored, the Info dialog appears, allowing you to tap on one or the other, which addresses the message.

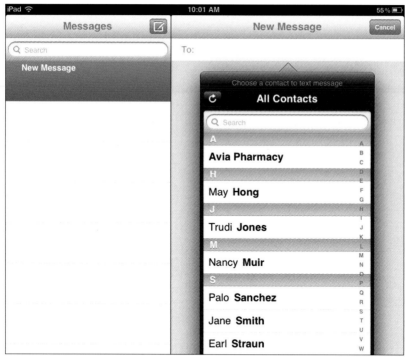

Figure 7-9

4. To create a message, simply tap in the message field near the bottom of the screen and type your message.

5. To send the message, tap the Send button (refer to **Figure 7-8**). When your recipient(s) respond, you'll see the conversation displayed on the right side of the screen, as shown in **Figure 7-10**.

 You can address a message to more than one person by simply choosing more recipients in Step 2.

 If you want to include a photo or video with your message, tap the Camera icon to the left of the message field (refer to **Figure 7-8**). Tap Take Photo or Video or Choose Existing and then Use, depending on whether you want to create a new photo/video or send one you've already taken. When you send your message the photo or video will go along with your text.

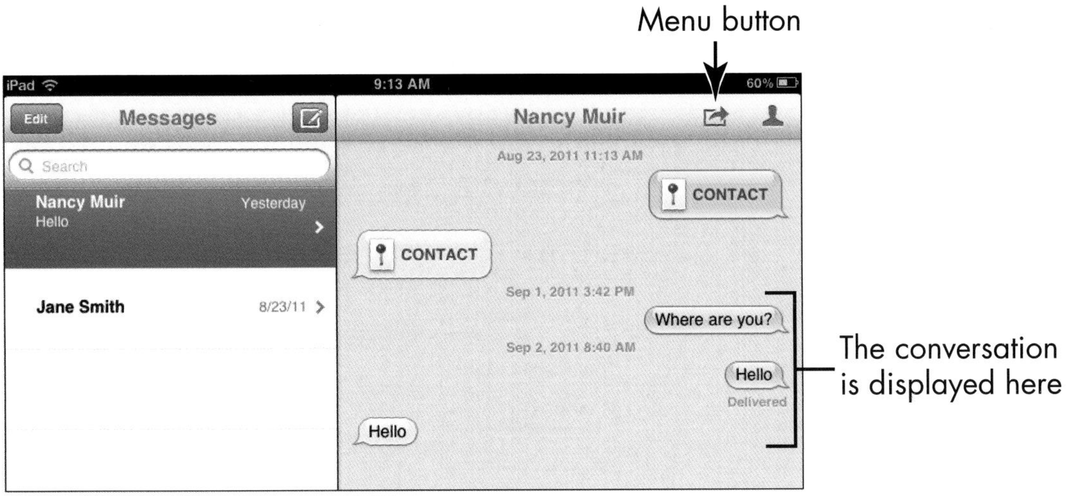

Menu button

Figure 7-10

Clear a Conversation

1. When you're done chatting, you might want to clear a conversation to remove the clutter before you start a new one. With Messages open, tap the menu button (refer to **Figure 7-10**).

2. Tap the Clear All button (see **Figure 7-11**).

3. Tap Clear Conversation.

You can also tap the menu button, tap the text of a particular conversation, and then tap the Delete or Forward button on the bottom of the screen (refer to **Figure 7-11**) to delete that one conversation or forward its contents to somebody.

Clear All button

Delete button   Forward button

Figure 7-11

Shopping the iTunes Store

*T*he iTunes app that comes pre-installed in iPad lets you easily shop for music, movies, TV shows, audiobooks, podcasts, and even online classes at Apple's iTunes Store.

In this chapter, you discover how to find content on the iTunes website. The content can be downloaded directly to your iPad or downloaded to another device and then synced to your iPad. In addition, I cover a few options for buying content from other online stores.

Note that I cover opening an iTunes account and downloading iTunes software to your computer in Chapter 3. If you need to, read Chapter 3 to see how to handle these two tasks before digging into this chapter.

Explore the iTunes Store

1. Visiting the iTunes Store from your iPad is easy with the built-in iTunes app. Tap the iTunes icon on the Home screen.

2. If you're not already signed in to iTunes, the dialog shown in **Figure 8-1** appears, asking for your iTunes password. Enter your password and tap OK.

Tap here and enter your password

Figure 8-1

3. Tap the Music button in the row of buttons at the bottom of the screen, if it's not already selected.

4. Tap the Next or Previous arrow to scroll the featured New and Noteworthy selections, as shown in **Figure 8-2**.

Tap these arrows to scroll through the selections

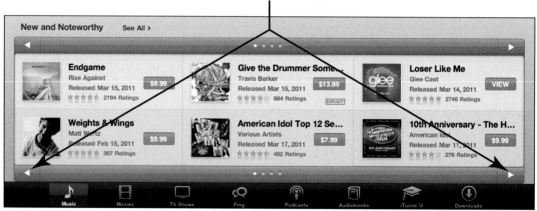

Figure 8-2

5. Tap the Top Charts tab at the top of the screen. This step displays best-selling songs and albums in the iTunes Store.

6. Tap any other listed item to see more detail about it, as shown in **Figure 8-3**.

 The navigation techniques in these steps work essentially the same in any of the content categories (the buttons at the bottom of the screen), which include Music, Movies, TV Shows, Podcasts, Audiobooks, and iTunes U. Just tap on one to explore it.

	Jeff Healey			Artist Page >
	Last Call			Tell a Friend >
	Genre: Jazz			
	Released: Apr 06, 2010			
	14 Songs			
	$9.99			

Tap to Preview

	Name	Time	Popularity	Price
1	Holding My Honey's Hand	2:59	IIIIIIIIIII	$0.99
2	Time On My Hands	5:02	IIIIIIIIIII	$0.99
3	The Wildcat	2:37	IIIIIIIIIII	$0.99

Figure 8-3

 If you want to use the Genius playlist feature, which recommends additional purchases based on the contents of your library, turn on this feature in iTunes on your computer. Then on your iPad, tap the Genius tab at the top of the screen. Song and album recommendations appear.

Find a Selection

There are several ways to look for a selection in the iTunes Store. You can use the Search feature, search by genre or category, or view artists' pages. Here's how these work:

➡ Tap in the Search field shown in **Figure 8-4** and enter a search term using the onscreen keyboard. Tap the Search button on the keyboard or, if a suggestion appeals to you, just tap on it.

➡ Tap the Genres button (in some content types, such as Audiobooks, it's the Categories button). A list of genres or categories like the one shown in **Figure 8-5** appears.

Enter a search term here

Figure 8-4

Tap here to view the list

Figure 8-5

➠ On a description page that appears when you tap a selection, you can find more offerings by people involved. For example, for a music selection, tap the Artist Page link to see all of that artist's selections. For a movie, tap the name of someone in the movie credits to see more of that person's work, as shown for Kate Winslet in **Figure 8-6**.

 If you find a selection you like, tap the Tell a Friend link on its description page to share your discovery with a friend via e-mail. A message appears with a link to the selection. Enter an address in the To field and tap Send. Your friend is now in the know.

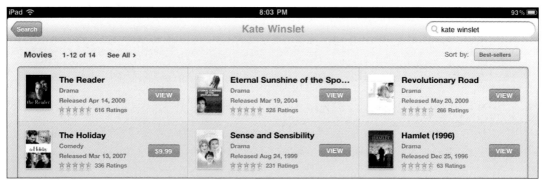

Figure 8-6

 When displaying items on the Featured tab for any type of content, tap the See All link to see all featured selections rather than only the top New and Noteworthy selections.

Sort Your Media Selections

1. You can sort selections by criteria such as bestsellers, name, or release date when you have an Artist Page displayed for movies or music. With an Artist Page open, tap the Sort By field.

2. In the menu shown in **Figure 8-7**, tap the criteria you want to sort by.

Tap here to select a sort criteria

Figure 8-7

3. Selections are sorted by the criteria you chose (for example, alphabetically if you chose Name or with the latest release listed first if you chose Release Date).

Preview Music, a Movie, or an Audiobook

1. Because you have already set up an iTunes account (if you haven't done so yet, refer to Chapter 3), when you choose to buy an item it's automatically charged to the credit card you have on record or against any allowance you have outstanding from an iTunes gift card. You might want to preview an item before you buy it. If you like it, buying and downloading are then easy and quick. Open iTunes and use any method outlined in earlier tasks to locate a selection you might want to buy.

2. Tap the item to see detailed information about it, as shown in **Figure 8-8**.

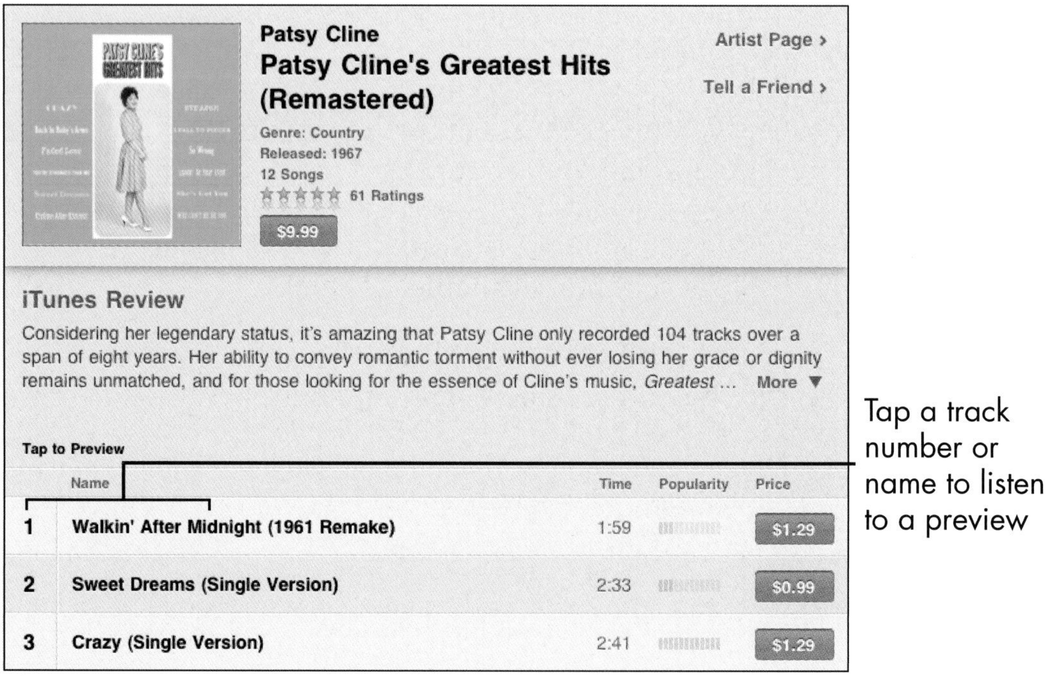

Tap a track number or name to listen to a preview

Figure 8-8

3. If you're looking at a music selection, tap the track number or name of a selection (refer to **Figure 8-8**) to play a preview. For a movie or audiobook selection, tap the Preview button, shown in **Figure 8-9**.

Tap here to preview the selection

Figure 8-9

 The iTunes Store offers several free selections, especially in the Podcast and iTunes U content categories. If you see one you want to try out, download it by tapping the button labeled Free and then tapping the Get Episode (or similarly named) button that appears.

Buy a Selection

1. When you find an item you want to buy, tap the button that shows either the price (if it's a selection available for purchase; see **Figure 8-10**) or the button with the word *Free* on it (if it's a selection available for free).

2. The button label changes to Buy X, where X is the type of content you're buying such as a song or album (refer to **Figure 8-10**).

3. Tap the Buy X button. The iTunes Password dialog appears (refer to **Figure 8-1**).

Tap the price button

Sunny Sweeney
Concrete
Genre: Country
Released: Aug 23, 2011
11 Items
★★★★☆ 59 Ratings

Artist Page >

Tell a Friend >

BUY ALBUM

Tap to Preview

	Name	Time	Popularity	Price
1	**Drink Myself Single**	2:59	▮▮▮▮▮▮▮	$1.29
2	**From a Table Away**	3:35	▮▮▮▮▮▮	$1.29
3	**Staying's Worse Than Leaving**	3:24	▮▮▮▮▮▮▮▮	$1.29

Figure 8-10

4. Enter your password and tap OK. The item begins down-loading (see **Figure 8-11**) and the cost is automatically charged against your account. When the download finishes, you can view the content using the Music or Video app, depending on the type of content.

iPad 🛜	9:43 AM	94% 🔋
	Downloads	Purchased

DOWNLOADS

Robert Schwentke
The Time Traveler's Wife ⬇
Download error. Tap to retry.

Patsy Cline
Crazy (Single Version)
Processing...

The selection being downloaded

iTunes Store Terms and Conditions...

Figure 8-11

 If you want to buy music, you can open the description page for an album and buy individual songs rather than the entire album. Tap on the price for a song, and then proceed to purchase it.

 Note the Redeem button on many iTunes screens. Tap this button to redeem any iTunes gift certificates you might get from your generous friends, or from yourself.

 If you don't want to allow purchases from within apps (for example Music or Videos) but rather want to allow purchases only through the iTunes store, you can go to Settings, General, tap Restrictions, then tap Enable Restrictions, and enter a passcode. Once you've set a passcode you can tap on individual apps to turn on restrictions for them.

 If you have a 3G model iPad you can allow content to be downloaded over your 3G cellular network. Be aware, however, that this could incur hefty data charges with your provider. However, if you aren't near a Wi-Fi hotspot it might be your only option. Go to Settings, Store and tap the On/Off button for the Cellular setting.

Rent Movies

1. In the case of movies, you can either rent or buy content. If you rent, which is less expensive, you have 30 days from the time you rent the item to begin to watch it. After you have begun to watch it, you have 24 hours from that time left to watch it as many times as you like. With iTunes open, tap the Movies button.

2. Locate the movie you want to rent and tap the View button, shown in **Figure 8-12.**

3. In the detailed description of the movie that appears, tap the Rent button, shown in **Figure 8-13.**

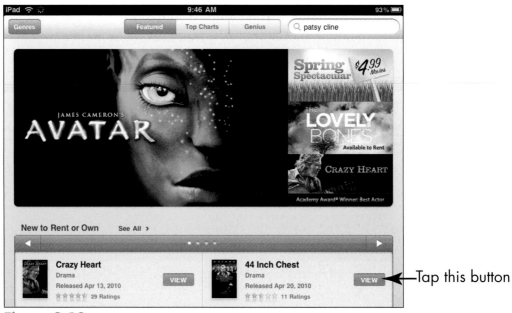

Tap this button

Figure 8-12

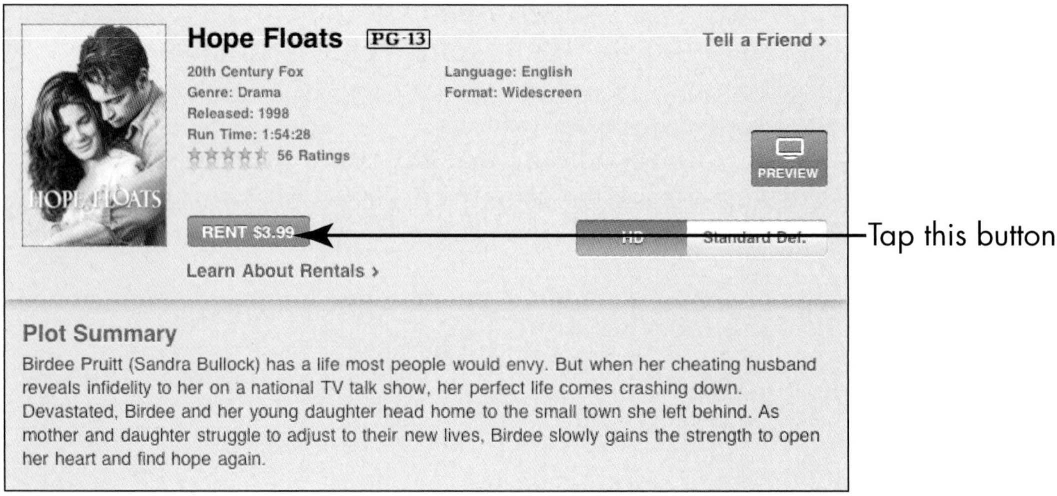

Tap this button

Figure 8-13

4. The gray Rent button changes to a green Rent Movie button; tap it to confirm the rental. The movie begins to download to your iPad immediately, and your account is charged the rental fee.

5. To check the status of your download, tap the Downloads button. The progress of your download is displayed. After the download is complete, you can use either the Music or Videos app to watch it. (See Chapters 11 and 13 to read about how these apps work).

Some movies are offered in high-definition versions. These *HD* movies will look great on that crisp, colorful iPad screen.

You can also download content to your computer and sync it to your iPad. Refer to Chapter 3 for more about this process.

Listen to Podcasts

1. *Podcasts* are audio broadcasts you can listen to on your iPad. Most of them are free and iTunes features a wide variety of broadcast topics. With iTunes open, tap the Podcast button in the row of buttons at the bottom of the screen.

2. Tap on a podcast selection; a detailed listing of podcasts, like the one shown in **Figure 8-14,** appears.

3. Tap on the name or number of a podcast for additional information, or simply tap the Free button, and then tap the Get Episode button (refer to **Figure 8-14**) to download the podcast. After it downloads, you can play it using the Music app.

To save your work you might consider using the subscription feature in iTunes. First, locate a podcast and click the Subscribe button. A URL for the podcast is displayed. Copy the URL, and then, with iTunes open, click the Advanced menu and choose Subscribe to Podcast. In the dialog that opens enter the URL of a podcast you like. Now you'll get all episodes of that podcast delivered to iTunes as they become available and they'll be available to all your devices through iCloud (see more about setting up iCloud for automatically pushing purchases from one device to your other Apple devices in the final task of this chapter).

Figure 8-14

Go to School at iTunes U

1. One very cool feature of iTunes is *iTunes U*, a compilation of free and often excellent online courses from universities and other providers. Tap the iTunes U button in the row of buttons at the bottom of the screen to display selections.

2. Tap one of the three tabs shown in **Figure 8-15**: Universities & Colleges, Beyond Campus, or K-12.

3. On the list that appears, tap an item to select the source for a course. That provider's page appears.

Tap one of these buttons

Figure 8-15

4. Tap either the Next or Previous button to scroll through offerings. When you find a topic of interest, tap a selection and it opens, displaying a list of segments of the course, as shown in **Figure 8-16**.

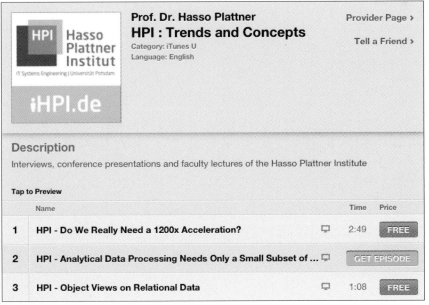

Figure 8-16

5. Tap the Free button next to a course, and then tap the green Download/Get Episode button that appears (if there's only one session this button says Download but if there is more than one session it says Get Episode). The course begins downloading.

 After you're on a provider's page, to return to iTunes U, just tap the button labeled iTunes U (located in the top left corner of the screen) and you return to the page with the three provider tabs (refer to **Figure 8-15**).

 You can also make selections of courses from the Featured or Top Charts tabs of iTunes U. Narrow these down by tapping the Categories button and choosing a category of courses to browse.

Shop Anywhere Else

One feature that's missing from the iPad is support for Flash, a format of video playback that many online video-on-demand services use. However, many online stores that sell content such as movies and music are hurriedly adding iPad-friendly videos to their collections, so you do have alternatives to iTunes for your choice of movies and TV shows. You can also shop for music from sources other than iTunes such as Amazon.com.

You can open accounts at one of these stores by using your computer or your iPad's Safari browser and then following the store's instructions for purchasing and downloading content.

These stores offer iPad-compatible video content, and more are opening all the time:

⟹ **ABC:** http://abc.go.com

⟹ **CBS news:** www.cbsnews.com

⟹ **Clicker:** www.clicker.com

⟱ **Netflix:** www.netflix.com

⟱ **UStream:** www.ustream.tv

 For non-iPad friendly formats, you can download the content on your computer and stream them to your iPad using AirVideo ($2.99) on the iPad and AirVideo Server (which is also free) using your Mac or Windows computer. For more information go to www.inmethod.com/air-video/index.html.

Enable Auto Downloads of Purchases from Other Devices

1. With iCloud you can make a purchase or download free content on any of your Apple devices and have those purchases automatically copied onto all your Apple devices. To enable this auto download feature on iPad, start by tapping Settings on the Home screen.

 To use iCloud, first set up an iCloud account. See Chapter 3 for detailed coverage of iCloud including setting up your account.

2. Tap Store.

3. In the options that appear, tap the On/Off button for any category of purchases you want to auto download to your iPad from other Apple devices: Music, Apps, or Books, as well as Newsstand subscriptions (see **Figure 8-17**).

 At this point, Apple doesn't offer an option of auto-downloading video content using these settings. You can always download video directly to your iPad through the iTunes app or sync to your computer using iTunes to get the content.

Figure 8-17

Expanding Your iPad Horizons with Apps

Chapter 9

Some *apps* (short for *applications*) come pre-installed on your iPad, such as Contacts and Videos. But there's a world of other apps out there that you can get for your iPad, some for free (such as iBooks) and some for a price (typically, from 99 cents to about $10 though some can top out at $90 or more).

Apps range from games to financial tools and productivity applications, such as the iPad version of Pages, the Apple software for word processing and page layout.

In this chapter, I suggest some apps you might want to check out and explain how to use the App Store feature of iPad to find, purchase, and download apps.

Explore Senior-Recommended Apps

As I write this book, apps are being furiously created for iPad, so there will be many more apps available that could fit your needs by the time you have this book in your hands. Still, to get you exploring what's available, I want to provide a quick list of apps that might whet your appetite.

Access the App Store by tapping the App Store icon on the Home screen. Then check out an app by typing its name in the Search box and tapping the Search key on the onscreen keyboard. Here are some interesting apps to explore:

➡ **Sudoku Daily** (Free; see **Figure 9-1**): If you like this mental math puzzle in print, try it out on your iPad. It has three lessons and several levels ranging from easiest to nightmare, making it a great way to make time fly by in the doctor's or dentist's waiting room.

Figure 9-1

➡ **Stocks Portfolio for iPad** ($9.99): Keep track of your investments with this app on your iPad. You can use the app to create a watch list and record your stock performance.

➠ **Price Grabber iPad Edition (Free):** Use this app to find low prices on just about everything. Read product reviews and compare list prices.

➠ **Flickr (Free):** If you use the Flickr photo-sharing service on your computer, why not bring the same features to your iPad? This app is useful for sharing images with family and friends.

➠ **Paint Studio ($1.99):** Get creative! You can use this powerful app to draw, add color, and even create special effects. If you don't need all these features, try Paint Studio Jr.

➠ **GarageBand ($4.99):** If you love to make music, you'll love this app, which has been part of the Mac stable for several years. Play piano, guitar, or a variety of other virtual musical instruments.

➠ **Mediquations Medical Calculator ($4.99):** Use this handy utility to help calculate medications with built-in formulas and read scores for various medications. Check with your physician before using!

 iBooks is the outstanding, free e-reader app that opens up a world of reading on your iPad. See Chapter 10 for details about using iBooks.

 Most iPhone apps will work on your iPad, so if you own the mobile phone and have favorite apps on it, sync them to your iPad!

Search the App Store

1. Tap the App Store icon on the Home screen. The site shown in **Figure 9-2** appears.

New, What's Hot, and Release Date tabs

Previous and Next arrows

Search field

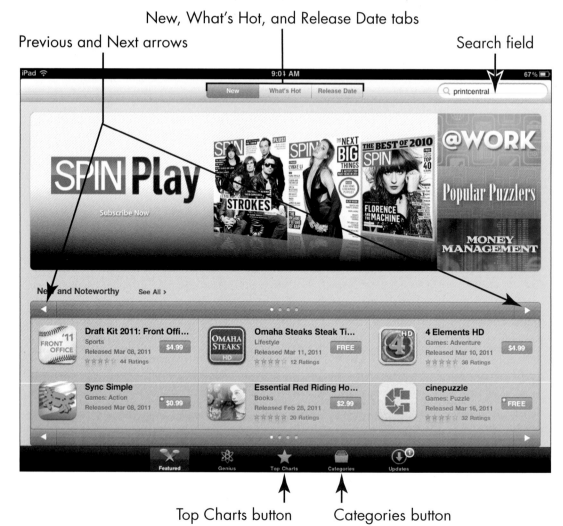

Top Charts button   Categories button

Figure 9-2

2. At this point, you have several options for finding apps:

- Tap in the Search field, enter a search term, and tap the Search button on the onscreen keyboard to see results.

- Tap either the Previous or Next arrow to see more selections, or tap the See All link to display all selections.

- Tap the New, What's Hot, or Release Date tab at the top of the screen to see that category of apps.

- Tap the Top Charts button at the bottom of the screen to see which free and paid apps other people are downloading most.

- Tap the Categories button to search by type of app, as shown in **Figure** 9-3.

Figure 9-3

Get Applications from the App Store

1. Buying apps requires that you have an iTunes account, which I cover in Chapter 3. After you have an account, you can use the saved payment information there to buy apps in a few simple steps or download free apps. I strongly recommend that you install the free iBooks app, so in this task I walk you through the steps for getting it. With the App Store open, tap in the Search field, enter iBooks and then tap the Search button on the onscreen keyboard.

2. Tap on the Free button for iBooks in the results that appear, as shown in **Figure** 9-4. (To get a *paid* app, you tap the same button, which would be labeled with a price.)

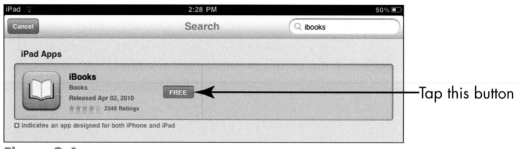

Tap this button

Figure 9-4

3. The Free button changes to read *Install App* (or, in the case of a paid app, the button changes to read *Buy App*). Tap the button; you may be asked to enter your iTunes password and tap the OK button to proceed.

4. The app downloads; if you purchase an app that isn't free, at this point your credit card or gift card allowance is charged for the purchase price.

 Out of the box, only preinstalled apps are located on the first iPad Home screen. Apps you download are placed on additional Home screens and you have to scroll to view and use them, which is covered later in this chapter. See the next task for help in finding your newly downloaded apps using multiple Home screens.

 If you have opened an iCloud account then anything you purchase on your iPad can be set up to automatically be pushed to other Apple iOS devices. See Chapter 3 for more about iCloud.

Organize Your Applications on Home Screens

1. iPad can display up to 11 Home screens. By default, the first contains preinstalled apps; other screens are created to contain any apps you download or sync to your iPad. At the bottom of any iPad Home screen (just above the

Dock), a magnifying-glass icon represents the Search screen to the left of the primary Home screen; dots that appear to the right of the magnifying-glass icon indicate the number of Home screens; and a solid dot specifies which Home screen you're on now, as shown in **Figure 9-5**. Tap the Home button to open the last displayed Home screen.

The screen you're currently on

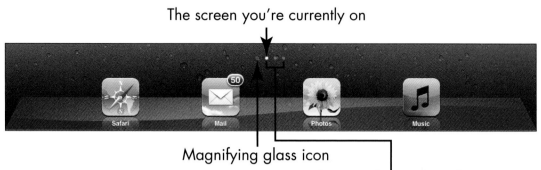

Magnifying glass icon

Dots indicating the number of screens

Figure 9-5

2. Flick your finger from right to left to move to the next Home screen. To move back, flick from left to right.

3. To reorganize apps on a Home screen, press and hold any app on that page. The app icons begin to jiggle (see **Figure 9-6**) and any apps you installed will sport a Delete button (a black circle with a white X on it).

Figure 9-6

4. Press, hold, and drag an app icon to another location on the screen to move it.

5. Tap the Home button to stop all those icons from jiggling!

 To move an app from one page to another, while the apps are jiggling, you can press, hold, and drag an app to the left or right to move it to the next Home screen. You can also manage what app resides on what Home screen from iTunes when you've connected iPad to iTunes via a cable or wireless sync.

Organize Apps in Folders

As with iPhone, iPad lets you organize apps in folders. The process is simple (and specific to each device):

1. Tap and hold an app until all apps do their jiggle dance.

2. Drag an app on top of another app. A bar appears across the screen, showing the two apps and a file with a placeholder name (see **Figure 9-7**).

Placeholder name

Figure 9-7

3. To change the name, tap in the field at the end of the placeholder name and the keyboard appears.

4. Press the Delete key to delete the placeholder name and type one of your own.

5. Tap anywhere outside the bar to save the name.

6. Tap the Home key to stop the icons from dancing around and you'll see your folder appear on the Home screen where you began this process.

Delete Applications You No Longer Need

1. When you no longer need an app you have installed, it's time to get rid of it. (You can't delete apps that are prein-stalled on the iPad.) If you use iCloud to push content across all Apple iOS devices, note that deleting an app on your iPad won't affect that app on other devices. Display the Home screen that contains the app you want to delete.

2. Press and hold the app until all apps begin to jiggle.

3. Tap the Delete button for the app you want to delete (see **Figure 9-8**).

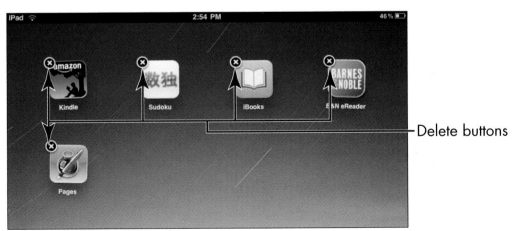

Figure 9-8

4. A confirmation like the one shown in **Figure** 9-9 appears. Tap OK to proceed with the deletion.

Delete "B&N eReader"

Deleting "B&N eReader" will also delete all of its data.

Delete   Cancel

Figure 9-9

5. A dialog asking you to rate an app before deleting it appears after Step 4; you can tap the Rate button to rate it or tap No Thanks to opt out of the survey.

 Don't worry about wiping out several apps at once by deleting a folder. When you delete a folder, the apps that were contained within the folder are placed back on the Home screen.

Update Apps

1. App developers update their apps all the time so you might want to check for those updates. Assuming Notification is set up to alert you to updates, the App Store icon on the Home screen will display the number of available updates. If you have turned this setting off, tap the App Store icon on the Home Screen. At the bottom right of the App Store screen is an Updates icon which will indicate the number of updates available in a red circle.

2. Tap the Updates icon to access the Updates screen (see **Figure 9-10**) and then tap any item you want to update. To update all tap the Update All button.

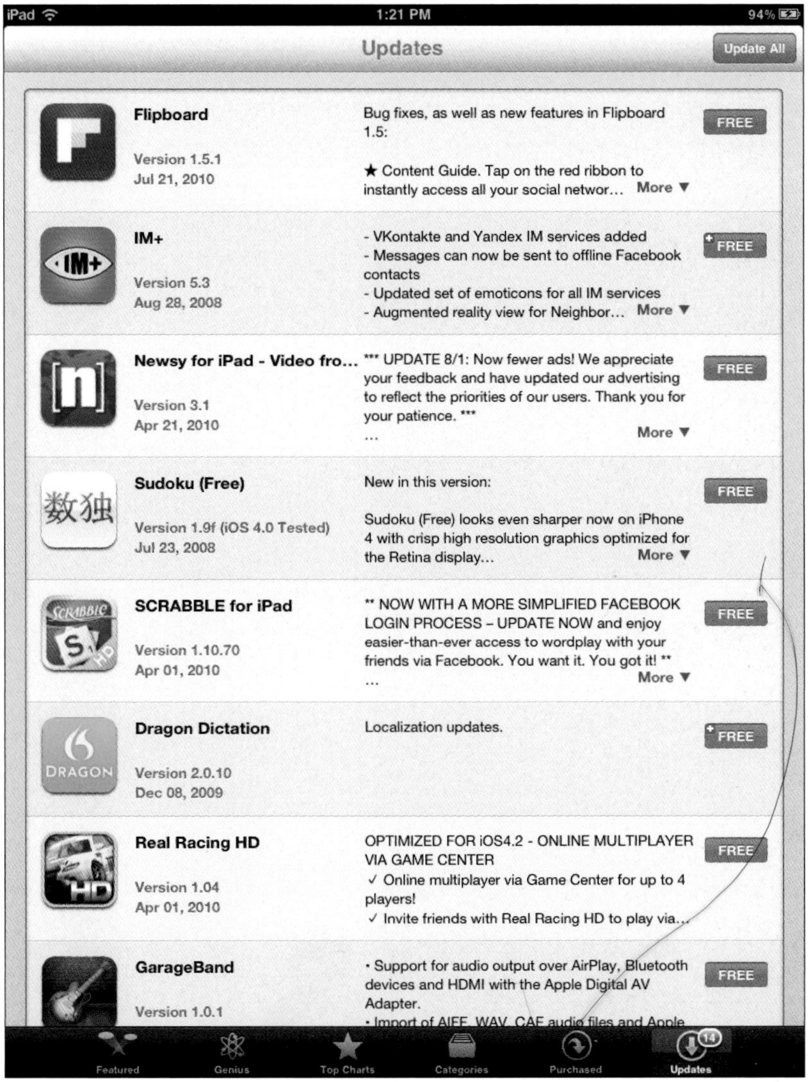

Figure 9-10

3. On the app screen that appears, tap Update. You may be asked to confirm that you want to update, or to enter your Apple ID Password and then tap OK to proceed. You may also be asked to confirm that you are over a certain age or agree to terms and conditions; if so, scroll down the terms dialog and at the bottom, tap Agree.

In iOS 5 Apple introduced the capability to download multiple apps at once. If you choose more than one app to update instead of them downloading sequentially, all items will download simultaneously.

 If you have an iCloud account and update an app on your iPad it will also be updated on any other Apple iOS devices automatically and vice-versa.

Part III
Having Fun and Consuming Media

The 5th Wave — By Rich Tennant

©RICHTENNANT

Accessories

iPadPad

"It's a docking system for the iPad that comes with 3 bedrooms, 2 baths, and a car port."

Using Your iPad as an E-Reader

A traditional *e-reader* is a device that's used to read the electronic version of books, magazines, and newspapers. Apple has touted iPad as a great e-reader, so although it isn't a traditional e-reader device like the Barnes and Noble Nook, you won't want to miss out on this cool functionality.

Apple's free, downloadable application that turns your iPad into an e-reader is *iBooks*, which enables you to buy and download books from Apple's iBookstore. You can also use one of several other free e-reader apps — such as Kindle, Stanza, or Nook — to download books to your iPad from a variety of online bookstores and other sources such as Google so you can read to your heart's content.

 A new app that comes with iOS 5 is Newsstand. Newsstand has a similar look and feel to iBooks, but it's focus is on subscribing to and reading magazines, newspapers, and other periodicals.

In this chapter, you discover the options available for reading material and how to buy books and subscribe to publications. You also learn all about Newsstand and iBooks: how to navigate a book or periodical and adjust the brightness and type, as well as how to search books and organize your iBooks and Newsstand libraries.

Discover How iPad Differs from Other E-Readers

An *e-reader* is any electronic device that enables you to download and read books, magazines, or newspapers. These devices are typically portable and dedicated only to reading the electronic version of published materials. Most e-readers use *e-ink* technology to create a paperlike reading experience.

The iPad is a bit different: It isn't only for reading books, and you have to download an app to enable it as an e-reader (though the apps are free). Also, the iPad doesn't offer the paperlike reading experience — you read from a computer screen (though you can adjust the brightness and background color of the screen).

When you buy a book or magazine online (or get one of many free publications), it downloads to your iPad in a few seconds using a Wi-Fi or 3G connection. The iPad offers several navigation tools to move around a book, which you explore in this chapter.

Find Books at iBooks

1. In Chapter 9, I walk you through the process of downloading the iBooks application in the "Get Applications from the App Store" task, so you should go do that first, if you haven't already. To shop using iBooks, tap on the iBooks application icon to open it. (It's probably on your second Home screen, so you may have to swipe your finger to the left on the Home screen to locate it.)

2. In the iBooks library that opens (see **Figure 10-1**), you see a bookshelf; yours probably has only one free book already downloaded to it. (If you don't see the bookshelf,

tap the Library button to go there or, if no Library button is on the screen, tap the Bookshelf button in the top-right corner of the screen — it sports four small squares.) Tap the Store button and the shelf pivots around 180 degrees.

Tap the Store button

Figure 10-1

3. In the iBookstore, shown in **Figure 10-2,** featured titles are shown by default, though you can tap Release Date to see titles chronologically by release date and then do any of the following to find a book:

- Tap the Search field and type a search word or phrase using the onscreen keyboard.

- Tap the Categories button to see a list of types of books, as shown in **Figure 10-3.** Tap on a category to view those selections.

- Tap either the right or left arrow, halfway down the screen, to scroll to more suggested titles.

- Also in that area, tap See All to view more titles.

- Tap the appropriate button at the bottom of the screen to view particular categories: featured titles, the *New York Times* bestseller list, books listed on top charts, browse-worthy lists of authors or categories or only paid or free items, or titles you've already purchased.

If you go to an item by tapping a button at the bottom of the screen and you want to return to the original screen, just tap Featured again.

- Tap on a suggested selection or featured book to open more information about it.

Categories button   See All option   Featured button   Left and right arrows   Release Date button   Search field

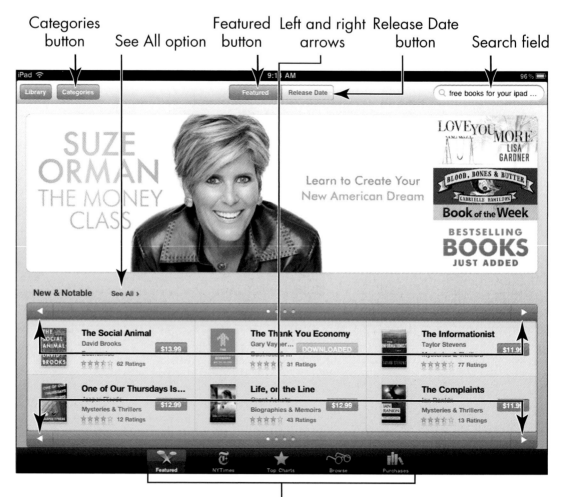

Featured, NYTimes, Top Charts, Browse, and Purchases buttons

Figure 10-2

Figure 10-3

 Download free samples before you buy. You get to read several pages of the book to see whether it appeals to you and it doesn't cost you a dime! Look for the Get Sample button when you view details about a book.

Explore Other E-Book Sources

The iPad is capable of using other e-reader apps to read book content from other bookstores, so you can get books from sources other than iBookstore. To do so, first download another e-reader application such as Kindle from Amazon or the Barnes & Noble Nook reader from the iPad App Store. (See Chapter 9 for how to download apps.) Then use their features to search for, purchase, and download content.

The Kindle e-reader application is shown in **Figure 10-4**. Any content you have already bought from Kindle is archived online and can be placed on your Kindle Home page on the iPad for you to read anytime you like. To delete a book from this reader, press the title with your finger and the Delete button appears.

 You can also get content from a variety of other sources: Project Gutenberg, Google, some publishers like Baen, and so on. Get the content using your computer if you like and then just add them to Books in iTunes and sync them to your iPad.

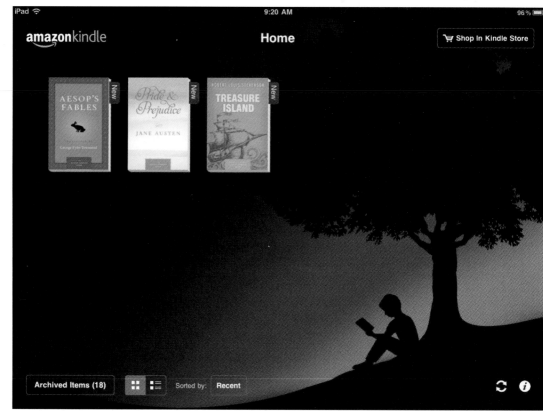

Figure 10-4

Buy Books

1. If you have set up an account with iTunes, you can buy books at the iBookstore easily. (See Chapter 3 for more about setting up an account.) When you find a book in the iBookstore that you want to buy, tap its Price button. The button changes to the Buy Book button, as shown in **Figure 10-5.** (If the book is free, these buttons are labeled Free and Get Book respectively.)

2. Tap the Buy Book or Get Book button. If you haven't already signed in, the iTunes Password dialog, shown in **Figure 10-6,** appears.

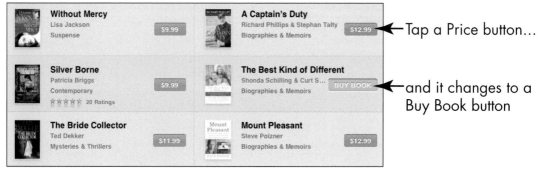

Tap a Price button...

and it changes to a Buy Book button

Figure 10-5

 If you have signed in, your purchase is accepted immediately — no returns are allowed, so tap carefully!

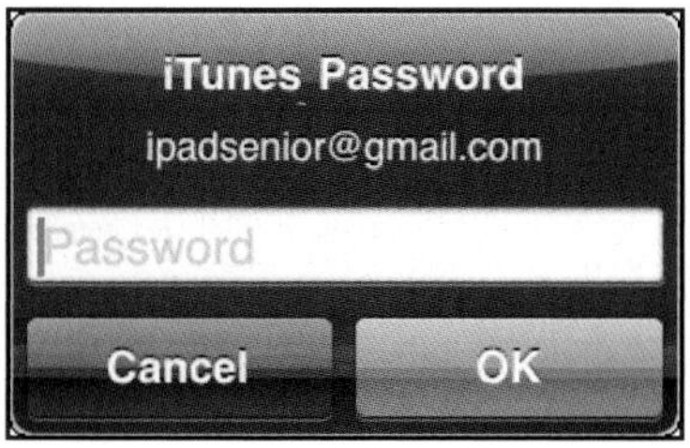

Figure 10-6

3. Enter your password and tap OK.

4. The book appears on your bookshelf and the cost is charged to whichever credit card you specified when you opened your iTunes account.

You can also sync books you've downloaded to your computer to your iPad by using the data-connection cord and your iTunes account, or by setting up iCloud and choosing to automatically sync books by tapping Settings and then Store. Using this method, you can find lots of free books from various sources online and drag them into your iTunes Book library; then simply sync them to your iPad. See Chapter 3 for more about syncing and iCloud.

Navigate a Book

1. Tap iBooks and if your Library (the bookshelf) isn't already displayed, tap the Library button.

2. Tap a book to open it. The book opens, as shown in **Figure 10-7.** (If you hold your iPad in portrait orientation, it shows one page; in landscape orientation, it shows two).

Table of Contents button

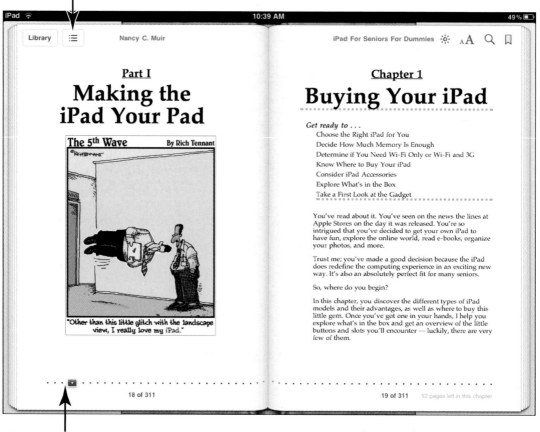

Slider to move to another page

Figure 10-7

3. Take any of these actions to navigate the book:

- **To go to the book's table of contents:** Tap the Table of Contents button at the top of the page (it looks like a little bulleted list) and then tap the name of a chapter to go to it (see **Figure 10-8**).

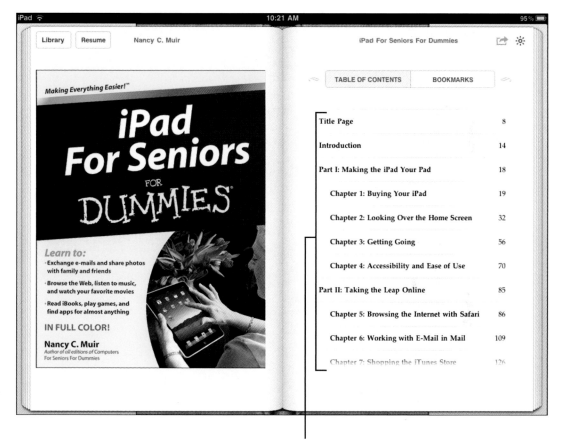

Tap any chapter to go to it

Figure 10-8

- **To turn to the next page:** Place your finger in the bottom-right or top-right corner or right edge of a page and flick to the left.

- **To turn to the preceding page:** Place your finger in the bottom-left or top-left corner or left edge of a page and flick to the right.

- **To move to another page in the book:** Tap and drag the slider at the bottom of the page to the right or left.

 To return to the Library to view another book at any time, tap the Library button. If the button isn't visible, tap anywhere on the page and the tools appear.

Adjust Brightness

1. iBooks offers an adjustable brightness setting that you can use to make your book pages comfortable to read. With a book open, tap the Brightness button, shown in **Figure 10-9.**

Tap the Brightness button...

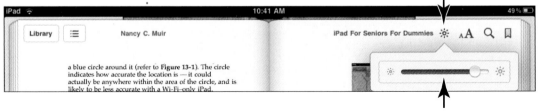

and adjust the screen brightness

Figure 10-9

2. In the Brightness dialog that appears (refer to **Figure 10-9**), tap and drag the slider to the right to make the screen brighter, or to the left to dim it.

3. Tap anywhere in the book to close the Brightness dialog.

Experiment with the brightness level that works for you, or try out the Sepia setting in the Fonts dialog. Bright white computer screens are commonly thought to be hard on the eyes, so setting the brightness halfway to its default setting (or less) is probably a good idea.

Change the Font Size and Type

1. If the type on your screen is a bit small for your taste, you can change to a larger font size or choose a different font for readability. With a book open, tap the Font button (it sports a small letter *a* and a large capital *A*, as shown in **Figure 10-10**).

Tap the Font button to change font size and type

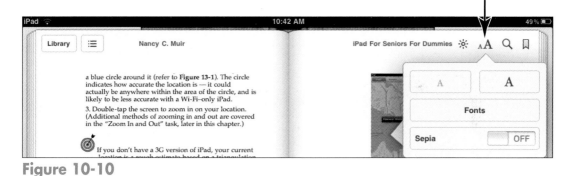

Figure 10-10

2. In the Font dialog that appears (refer to **Figure 10-10**), tap the button with a small A on the left to use smaller text, or the button with the large A on the right to use larger text.

3. Tap the Fonts button. The list of fonts shown in **Figure 10-11** appears.

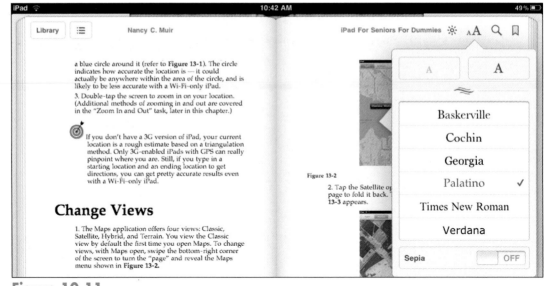

Figure 10-11

4. Tap on a font name to select it. The font changes on the book page.

5. If you want a sepia tint on the pages, which can be easier on the eye, tap the On/Off button to turn on the setting.

6. Tap outside the Fonts dialog to return to your book.

 Some fonts appear a bit larger on your screen than others because of their design. If you want the largest fonts, use Cochin or Verdana.

Search in Your Book

1. You may want to find a certain sentence or reference in your book. To do so, with the book displayed, tap the Search button shown in **Figure 10-12**. The onscreen keyboard appears.

Search button

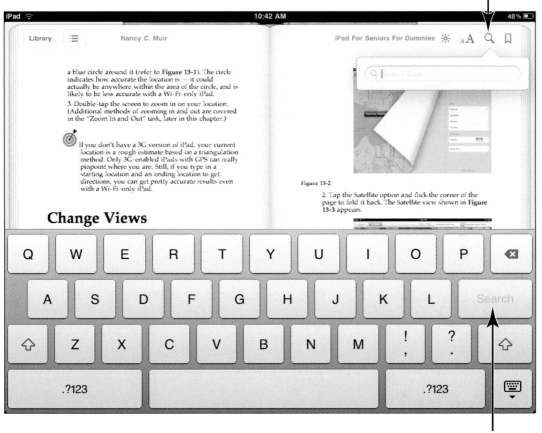

Search key

Figure 10-12

2. Enter a search term and then tap the Search key on the keyboard. iBooks searches for any matching entries.

3. Use your finger to scroll down the entries (see **Figure 10-13**).

4. You can use either the Search Google or Search Wikipedia button at the bottom of the Search dialog if you want to search for information about the search term online.

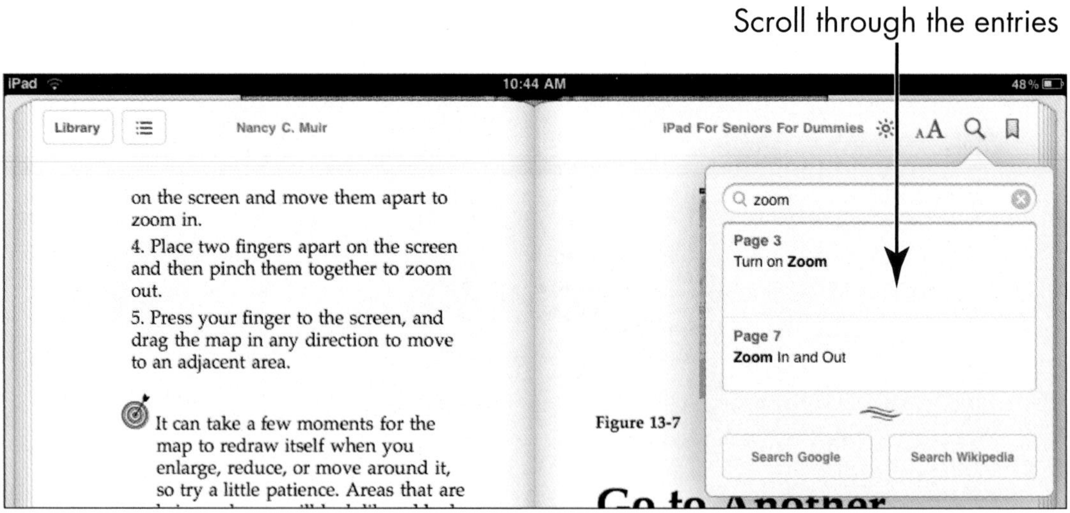

Scroll through the entries

Figure 10-13

You can also search for other instances of a particular word while in the book pages by pressing your finger on the word and tapping Search on the toolbar that appears.

Use Bookmarks and Highlights

1. Bookmarks and highlights in your e-books are like favorite sites you save in your web browser: They enable you to revisit a favorite passage or refresh your memory about a character or plot point. To bookmark a page, with that page displayed just tap the Bookmark button in the top right corner (see **Figure 10-14**).

Bookmark button

Figure 10-14

2. To highlight a word or phrase, press on a word until the toolbar shown in **Figure 10-15** appears.

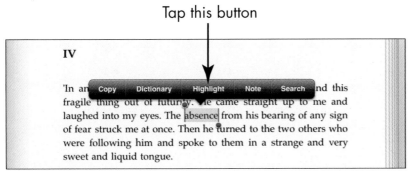

Figure 10-15

3. Tap the Highlight button. A colored highlight is placed on the word.

4. To change the color of the highlight or remove it, tap the highlighted word. The toolbar shown in **Figure 10-16** appears.

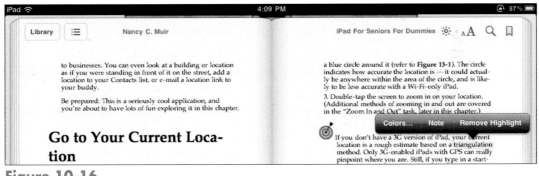

Figure 10-16

5. Tap one of these three buttons:

- *The Colors button:* Displays a menu of colors you can tap to change the highlight color.

- *The Note button:* Lets you add a note to the item.

- *The Remove Highlight button:* Removes the highlight.

6. Tap outside the highlighted text to close the toolbar.

7. To go to a list of bookmarks and highlights, tap the Table of Contents button on a book page.

8. In the table of contents, tap the Bookmarks tab. As shown in **Figure 10-17,** all bookmarks are displayed.

Bookmarks and Highlights are displayed here

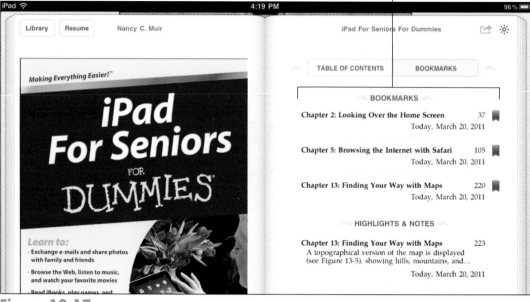

Figure 10-17

9. Tap on a bookmark or highlight in this list to go there.

 iPad automatically bookmarks where you left off reading in a book so you don't have to do it manually.

You can also highlight illustrations in a book. Display the page and press on the image until the Highlight button appears above it. Tap the button and the illustration is highlighted in yellow. As with highlighted text, you can tap on a bookmarked illustration to change the highlight color or remove its highlight.

Check Words in the Dictionary

1. As you read a book, you may come across unfamiliar words. Don't skip over them — take the opportunity to learn a word! With a book open, press your finger on a word and hold it until the toolbar shown in **Figure 10-18** appears.

Tap this button

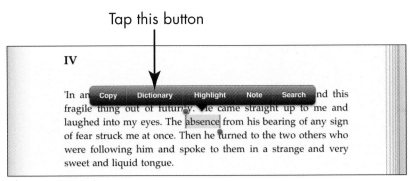

Figure 10-18

2. Tap the Dictionary button. A definition dialog appears, as shown in **Figure 10-19**.

3. Tap the definition and scroll down to view more.

4. When you finish reviewing the definition, tap anywhere on the page and the definition disappears.

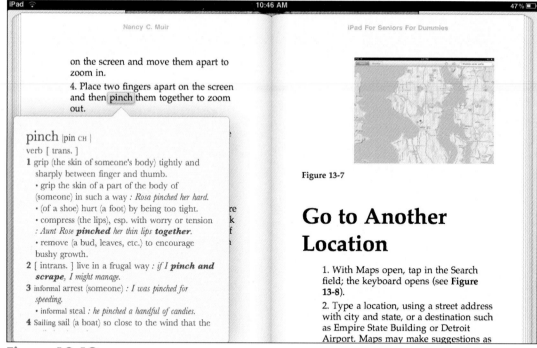

Figure 10-19

Organize Your Library

1. Your iPad's library looks like a bookshelf with books stored on it, with the most recently downloaded title in the top left corner. However, if you prefer, you can view your library in a few other ways. With the bookshelf version of the library displayed, tap the List button, shown in **Figure 10-20**.

2. Your books appear in a list, as shown in **Figure 10-21**. To organize the list alphabetically by title or author, tap the appropriate button on the bottom of the screen.

3. To organize by category, tap the Categories button on the bottom of the page. Your titles are divided by category titles such as Fiction, Mysteries & Thrillers, or Literary.

List button

Figure 10-20

Figure 10-21

 4. To return to Bookshelf view at any time, tap the Bookshelf view button.

 Tap the Bookshelf button at the bottom of the list view to remove categories and list the most recently downloaded book first.

Use the Edit button in List view to display small circles to the left of all books in the list. Tap in any of the circles and then tap the Delete button at the top of the page to delete books, and then tap the Done button to exit the Edit function.

Organize Books in Collections

1. iBooks lets you create collections of books to help you organize them by your own logic, such as Tear Jerkers, Work-related, and Great Recipes. You can only place a book in one collection, however. To create a collection from the Library bookshelf, tap Collections.

2. In the dialog that appears, tap New. On the blank line that appears, type a name (see **Figure 10-22**) and tap Done.

Enter a name for the collection...

then tap Done

Figure 10-22

3. Tap Books, which closes the dialog and returns you to the Library. To add a book to a collection from the Library, tap Edit.

4. Tap a book and then tap the Move button that appears in the top left corner of the screen. In the dialog that appears (see **Figure 10-23**), tap a Collection to move the book to.

Figure 10-23

5. To delete a book from a collection with the collection displayed, tap Edit, tap the selection circle for the book, and then tap Delete.

 To delete a collection with the Collections dialog displayed, tap Edit. Tap the minus sign to the left of any collection and then tap Delete to get rid of it. A message appears asking you to tap Remove to remove the contents of the Collection from your iPad or Don't Remove. Note that if you choose Don't Remove, all titles within a deleted collection are returned to their original collections in your library.

Download Magazines Apps to Newsstand

1. Newsstand is a new app that focuses on subscribing to and reading magazines, newspapers, and other periodicals rather than books. The app has a similar look and feel to iBooks. When you download a free publication you're actually downloading an app to Newsstand. You can then tap that app to buy individual issues, as covered in the next section. Tap the Newsstand icon on the Home screen to open Newsstand (see **Figure** 10-24).

2. Tap the Store button. The store opens offering Featured periodicals, Genius recommendations, Top Charts, and Categories for your shopping pleasure (see **Figure** 10-25).

Figure 10-24

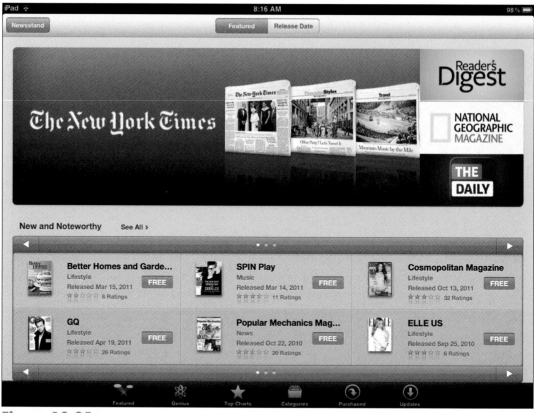

Figure 10-25

3. Tap any of the items displayed, tap the arrow buttons to move to other choices, or tap in the Search field at the top and enter a search term to locate a publication you're interested in.

> If you tap on other icons at the bottom of the screen, such as Top Charts or Categories, you're taken to other types of content than periodicals. Also if you tap Featured again after tapping one of these icons, you're taken to other kinds of apps than periodicals. Your best bet: stay on the Store screen that displays when you tap the Store button in Newsstand.

4. When you find an item, tap it to view a detailed description (see **Figure 10-26**).

5. Tap the Free button and then tap Install App. The app downloads to Newsstand.

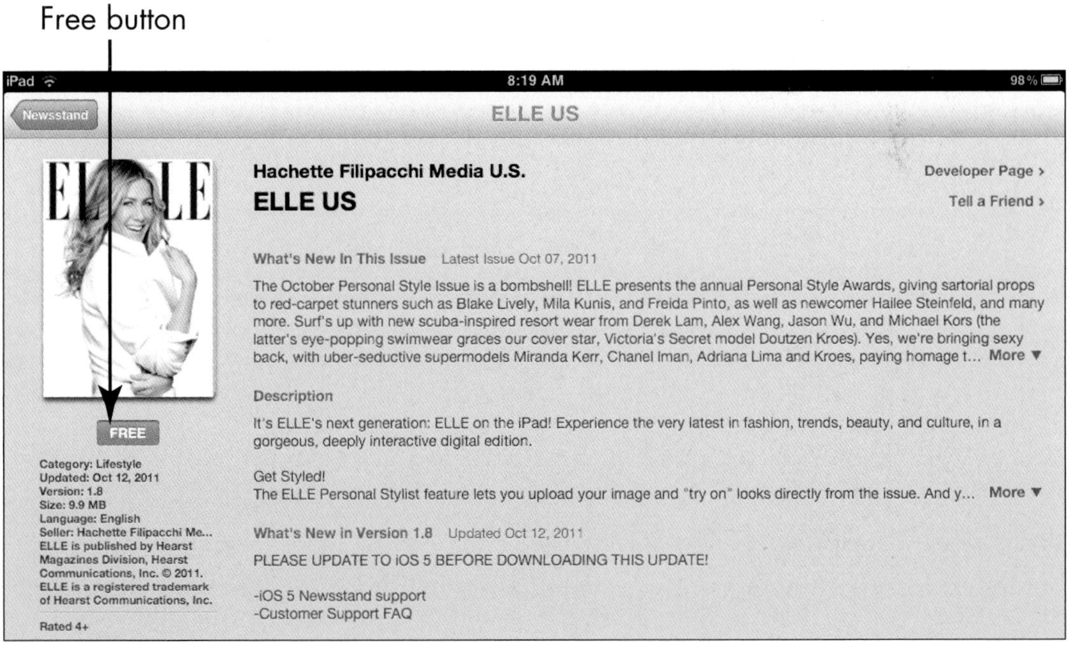

Free button

Figure 10-26

Buy Issues

1. Tap on a periodical app. The message shown in **Figure 10-27** appears, asking if you'd like to be informed of new issues. Tap OK if you would.

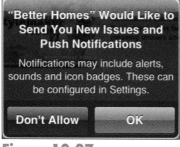

"Better Homes" Would Like to Send You New Issues and Push Notifications

Notifications may include alerts, sounds and icon badges. These can be configured in Settings.

Don't Allow   OK

Figure 10-27

2. Tap on the Preview Issue button to take a look at a description of its content, or tap the Buy button.

3. In the purchase confirmation dialog that appears, tap Buy. The issue is charged to your iTunes account.

Read Periodicals

1. If you buy a periodical or you have downloaded a free subscription preview, such as The New York Times Update shown in **Figure 10-28,** you can tap the publication in Newsstand to view it.

2. In the publication that appears use your finger to swipe left, right, or up and down to view more of the pages.

Figure 10-28

3. For many publications you can tap the Sections button shown in **Figure 10-29** to navigate to different sections of the publication.

4. To subscribe to a publication when viewing a free sample, tap the Subscribe Now button (refer to **Figure 10-29**).

 Note that different stores offer different options for subscribing, buying issues, and organizing issues. Think of Newsstand as a central collection point for apps that allow you to preview and buy content in each publication's store.

Subscribe Now button

Figure 10-29

Playing with Music on iPad

*Y*ou've probably heard of the iPod — a
small, portable, music-playing device from
Apple that's seemingly glued into the ears of
many kids and teens. iPad includes an iPod-like
app called Music that allows you to take advantage of its amazing little sound system to play
your own style of music or podcasts and audiobooks. In this chapter, you get acquainted with
the Music app and its features that allow you to
sort and find music and control playback. You
also get an overview of the Ping feature of
iTunes, to share your musical preferences with
others; Airplay features, to access and play your
music over a home network; and GarageBand,
an app that lets you be the musician, composer,
or arranger.

Get ready to . . .

View the Library Contents

1. Tap the Music app icon, located in the
   Dock on the Home screen. The Music
   library appears (the Albums view is
   shown **Figure 11-1**).

Tap a criteria to use

Figure 11-1

2. Tap the Playlists, Songs, Artists, or Albums buttons at the bottom of the library to view your music according to these criteria (refer to **Figure 11-1**).

3. Tap the More button (see **Figure 11-2**) to view music by genre or composer, or to view any audiobooks you've acquired.

Tap this button

Figure 11-2

 iTunes has several free items you can download and use to play around with the features in Music, including music and podcasts. You can also sync content stored on your computer or other Apple devices to your iPad, including iTunes Smart Playlists, and play it using the Music app. (See Chapter 3 for more about syncing and Chapter 8 for more about getting content from iTunes.)

You can tap the Store button to go to the iTunes Store to buy additional music. See Chapter 8 for more about shopping using iTunes.

 Apple offers a service called iTunes Match (www. apple.com/icloud/features/). You pay $24.99 per year for the capability to match the music you've bought from other providers (and stored on your computer) to what's in the iTunes library. If there's a match (and there usually is), that content is added to your iTunes library. Then, using iCloud, you can sync the content among all your Apple devices.

Create Playlists

1. You can create your own playlists to put tracks from various sources into collections of your choosing. Tap the Playlists button in the bottom of the iPad screen.

2. Tap New. In the dialog box that appears, enter a name for the playlist and tap Save.

3. In the list of selections that appears (see **Figure 11-3**), tap the plus sign next to each item you want to include.

Tap the plus sign to include a song in the playlist

iPad 🔋		12:32 PM		▶ 90%
◀◀ ❚❚ ▶▶ ♪	Lynne Arriale Trio Bess, You Is My Woman Now When You Listen			⚛
	0:27	-7:07 ✂		
	Add songs to the "Mellow" playlist		Add All Songs	Done
A				
After Hours	Rickie Lee Jones	Rickie Lee Jones	2:14	⊕ A
				B
Allentown	Billy Joel	Greatest Hits, Vols. 1 & 2	3:49	⊕ C
				D
Amazing Grace	Susan Boyle	I Dreamed a Dream	3:34	⊕ E
				F
American Patrol	Glenn Miller	Glenn Miller Orchestra	3:23	⊕ G
				H
As If We Never Said Goodbye	Elaine Paige	Elaine Paige LIVE - Celebrating A Life...	6:48	⊕ I
				J
As Long As You're Mine	Idina Menzel & Leo Norbert Butz	Wicked: Original Broadway Cast	3:48	⊕ K
				L
At Last	Glenn Miller	Glenn Miller Orchestra	3:07	⊕ M
B				N
				O
Baby Baby All The Time	Diana Krall	All For You: A Dedication To The Nat Ki...	3:36	⊕ P

Figure 11-3

4. Tap the Done button, and then tap Done again on the list of songs that appears.

5. Tap the Playlists button and your playlist appears in the list, and you can now play it by tapping the list name and then the Play button.

To delete a song from the playlist, swipe left to right across the name of the song you want to delete and then tap the Delete button.

Search for Audio

1. You can search for an item in your Music library by using the Search feature. With Music open, tap in the Search field in the lower-right corner (see **Figure 11-4**) to open the onscreen keyboard.

Tap here to search for audio

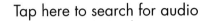

Figure 11-4

2. Enter a search term in the Search field. Results are displayed, narrowing as you type, as shown in **Figure 11-5**.

3. Tap an item to play it.

 You can enter an artist's name, an author's or a composer's name, or a word from the item's title in the Search field to find what you're looking for.

Results display as you type

Amazing Grace	Susan Boyle	I Dreamed a Dream	3:34
Boulevard Of Broken Dreams	Diana Krall	All For You: A Dedication To The Nat King...	6:28
Cry Me a River	Susan Boyle	I Dreamed a Dream	2:42
Daydream Believer	Susan Boyle	I Dreamed a Dream	3:19
The End of the World	Susan Boyle	I Dreamed a Dream	3:14
How Great Thou Art	Susan Boyle	I Dreamed a Dream	3:13
I Dreamed a Dream	Susan Boyle	I Dreamed a Dream	3:11

Figure 11-5

Play Music and Other Audio

1. Locate the song or audiobook you want to play using the methods described in previous tasks in this chapter.

2. Tap the item you want to play. Note that if you're displaying the Songs tab, you don't have to tap an album to open a song; you need only tap on a song to play it. If you're using any other tab, you have to tap items such as albums (or multiple songs from one artist) to find the song you want to hear. When you find it, you tap it.

3. Tap the item you want to play from the list that appears (see **Figure 11-6**); it begins to play.

4. Use the Previous and Next buttons at the top of the screen shown in **Figure 11-7** to navigate the audio file that's playing. The Previous button takes you back to the beginning of the item that's playing; the Next button takes you to the next item.

Tap an item to play it

1.	Piano Man	5:38
2.	Captain Jack	6:57
3.	The Entertainer	3:40
4.	Say Goodbye to Hollywood	4:37
5.	New York State of Mind	6:03
6.	The Stranger	5:08
7.	Scenes from an Italian Restaurant	7:35

Figure 11-6

5. Tap the Pause button to pause playback.

6. Tap and drag the line that indicates the current playback location on the Progress bar to the left or right to "scrub" to another location in the song.

7. If you don't like what's playing, here's how to make another selection: Tap the Back to Library arrow in the bottom-left corner to return to Library view or tap the Album List button in the bottom-right corner to show other selections in the album that's playing.

 If you play a song on an album, the album cover displays full-screen. To close the album cover and return to your Music library, place two fingers on the screen and pinch them inward.

 You can use the Genius Playlist feature in Music (enable Genius in Settings and then tap the white atom symbol on the right of the playback progress bar in **Figure 11-7**) to get lists of recommended content in your iPad library. Based on items you've purchased, iTunes suggests other purchases that would go well with your collection. Okay, it's a way to get you to buy more music, but if you're building your music collection, it might be worth a try! Visit the iTunes site at www.apple.com/itunes for more information.

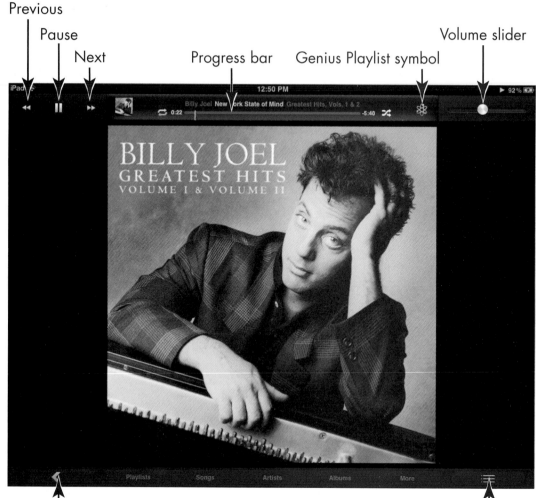

Previous
Pause
Next
Progress bar
Genius Playlist symbol
Volume slider

Back to Library arrow
Figure 11-7
Album List button

Shuffle Music

1. If you want to play a random selection of the music
you've purchased or synced to your iPad, you can use the
Shuffle feature. With Music open, tap either the Music,
Playlist, or Purchased button in the Source List and then
tap the Songs button at the bottom of the screen.

2. Tap the Shuffle button (see **Figure 11-8**). Your content
plays in random order.

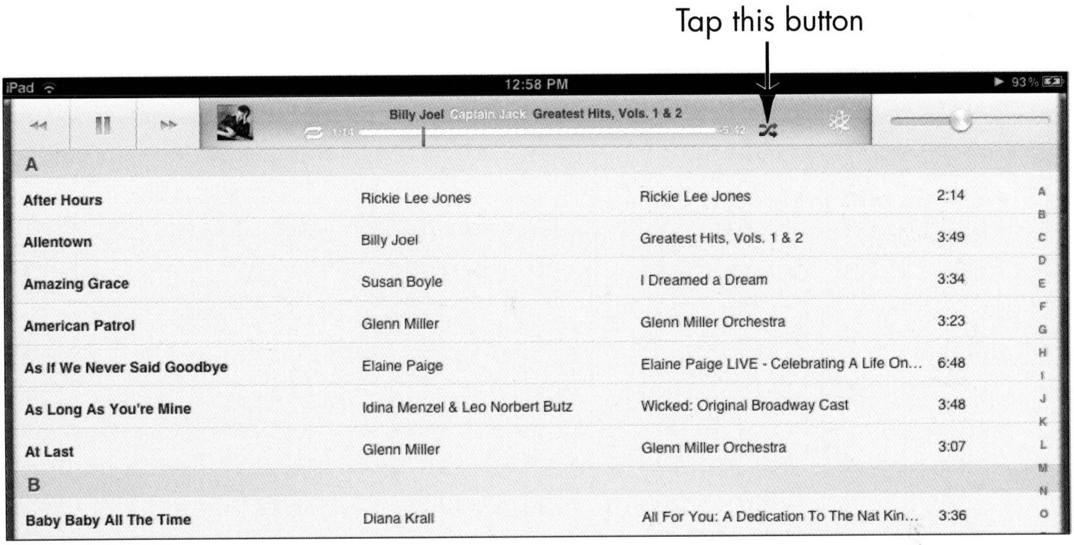

Tap this button

Figure 11-8

Adjust the Volume

1. Music offers its own volume control that you can adjust during playback. With Music open, tap on a piece of music or an audiobook to play it.

2. In the controls that appear onscreen (see **Figure 11-9**), press and drag the button on the Volume slider to the right for more volume or to the left for less volume.

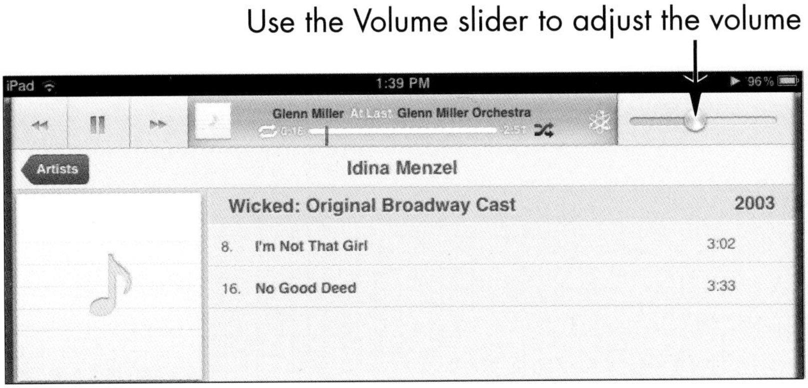

Use the Volume slider to adjust the volume

Figure 11-9

If the volume is set high and you're still having trouble hearing, consider getting a headset. It cuts out extraneous noises and may improve the sound quality of what you're listening to, as well as adding stereo to iPad's mono speaker. Preferably you should use a 3.5mm stereo headphone; insert it in the headphone jack at the top of your iPad.

Understand Ping

Ping is a social network for music lovers. If you think of Facebook or other social networking sites and imagine that they're focused around musical tastes, you have a good image of what Ping is all about.

After you join Ping, you can share the music you like with friends, take a look at the music your friends are purchasing, and follow certain artists (see **Figure 11-10**). You can also access short previews of the sounds your friends like.

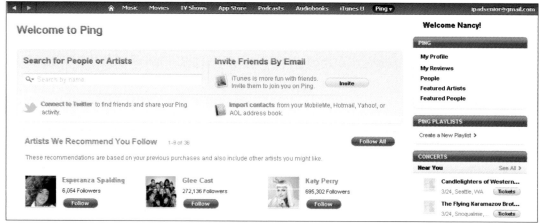

Figure 11-10

If this sounds like something your grandchildren would do, you might be right. But if you have a few musical friends with whom you want to connect, Ping can be great fun.

To use Ping, you need to activate it using iTunes on a PC or Mac by clicking the Ping link in the Source List and clicking the Turn On Ping button. You're then asked to fill in profile information, such as your name, gender, town, and musical preferences (see **Figure 11-11**). After you save this information, you have a Ping home page and can start inviting friends to share musical inspirations with you.

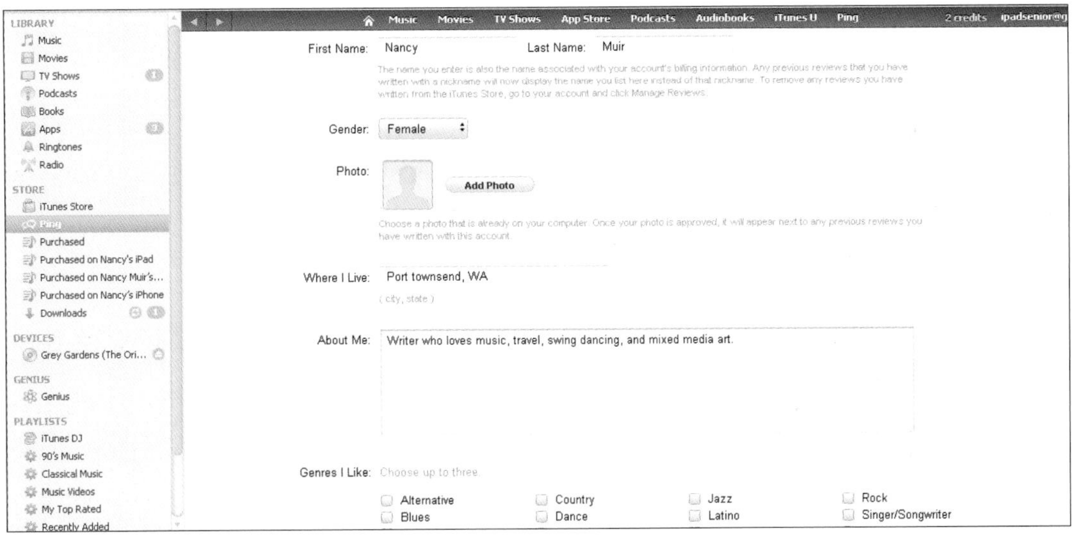

Figure 11-11

One cool feature of Ping is that, on your Ping page, a list of concerts near you is displayed. Even in my small town, Ping alerted me to some interesting events to check out.

Use AirPlay

The AirPlay streaming technology is built into the iPhone, iPod touch, and iPad. *Streaming* technology allows you to send media files from one device to be played on another. You can send (say) a movie you've purchased on your iPad or a slide show of your photos to be played on your TV — and control the TV playback from your iPad. You can also send music to be played over speakers.

You can take advantage of AirPlay in a few ways: Purchase Apple TV and stream video, photos, and music to the TV or purchase Airport Express and attach it to your speakers to play music. Finally, if you buy Airport-enabled wireless speakers, you can stream audio directly to them. Because this combination of equipment varies, my advice — if you're interested in using AirPlay — is to visit your nearest Apple Store and find out which hardware combination will work best for you.

 If you get a bit antsy watching a long movie, one of the beauties of AirPlay is that you can still use your iPad to check e-mail, browse photos or the Internet, or check your calendar while the media file is playing.

Play around with GarageBand

1. *GarageBand* is a music-playing app that has been prein-stalled on Mac computers for a while now, and now it's available for the iPad. You have to buy the app for about $5 from the App Store. After you purchase it, tap the GarageBand app on the Home screen where it appears. A list of virtual instruments appears, as shown in **Figure 11-12**. Swipe left or right to scroll through them.

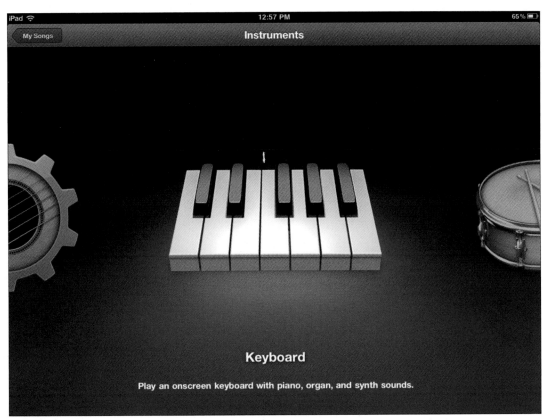

Figure 11-12

2. Tap an instrument name, such as Keyboard, to display it (see **Figure 11-13**). Each instrument has slightly different options, but all allow you to record what you play on the virtual instrument; you can also play it back, visit any songs you've saved, control volume, and return to the main menu of instruments. Tapping the Instruments button allows you to change to a different instrument.

3. Tap the Instrument Settings button to control settings such as echo and reverb (see **Figure 11-14**), or tap the Song Settings button to add sounds or adjust the tempo (see **Figure 11-15**).

My Songs button — Instruments button

Playback and recording options

Instrument Settings — Volume slider — Song Settings

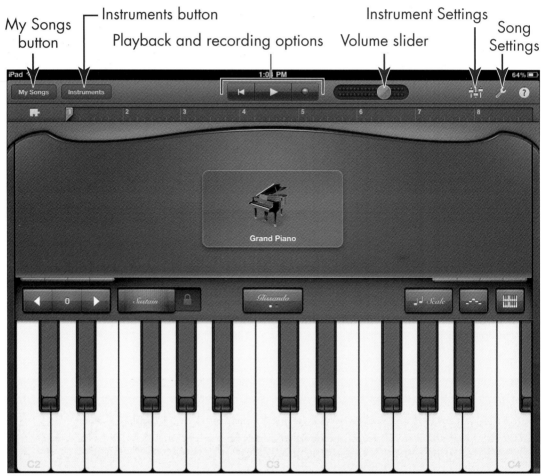

Figure 11-13

4. With the instrument displayed, tap it (whether it's a drum or keyboard) to produce sounds. If you want to record what you're playing, tap the Record button (refer to **Figure 11-15**), start playing and tap it again when you're done.

5. Play back what you've recorded by tapping My Songs, tapping an item, and then tapping the Play button (refer to **Figure 11-15**).

 I don't have enough room here for an exhaustive tutorial on using all GarageBand instruments, but feel free to play with this fun app. You can't break anything!

Figure 11-14

Play button   Record button

Figure 11-15

Playing with Photos

Chapter 12

With its gorgeous screen, the iPad is a natural for viewing photos. It supports most common photo formats, such as JPEG, TIFF, and PNG. You can shoot your photos by using the built-in cameras in iPad or sync photos from your computer, iPhone, or digital camera. You can also save images you find online to your iPad or receive them by e-mail.

When you have photos to play with, the Photos app lets you organize photos from the camera roll, view photos in albums, one by one, or in a slideshow. You can also e-mail, message, or tweet a photo to a friend, print it, or use your expensive gadget as an electronic picture frame. And, if you like to play around with photo effects, you'll enjoy the new photo-editing features as well as the pre-installed app, Photo Booth. You can read about all these features in this chapter.

Take Pictures with the iPad Cameras

1. The cameras in the iPad 2 are just begging to be used, so let's get started! Tap the Camera app icon on the Home screen to open the app.

2. If the Camera/Video slider setting at the bottom-right corner of the screen (see **Figure 12-1**) is shifted to the right, slide it to the left to choose the still camera rather than video.

 The iPad 2 introduced built-in cameras, a much-anticipated feature missing in the first-generation iPad! These front- and rear-facing cameras allow you to capture photos and video (see Chapter 13 for more about the video features) and share them with family and friends.

3. Tap the Options button and then tap the On/Off button for Grid and then tap Done. This turns on a grid that helps you position a subject within the grid and autofocus.

4. Move the camera around until you find a pleasing image. You can do a couple of things at this point to help you take your photo:

- Tap the area of the grid where you want Camera to autofocus.

- Pinch the screen to display a zoom control; drag the circle in the zoom bar to the right or left to crop the image to a smaller area.

5. Tap the Capture button at the bottom center of the screen. You've just taken a picture (see **Figure 12-1**), and it has been stored in the Photos app automatically.

 You can also use the up switch on the volume rocker on the right side of your iPad to capture a picture or start or stop video camera recording.

6. Tap the icon in the top-right corner to switch between the front camera and rear camera. You can then take pictures of yourself, so go ahead and click the Capture button to take another picture.

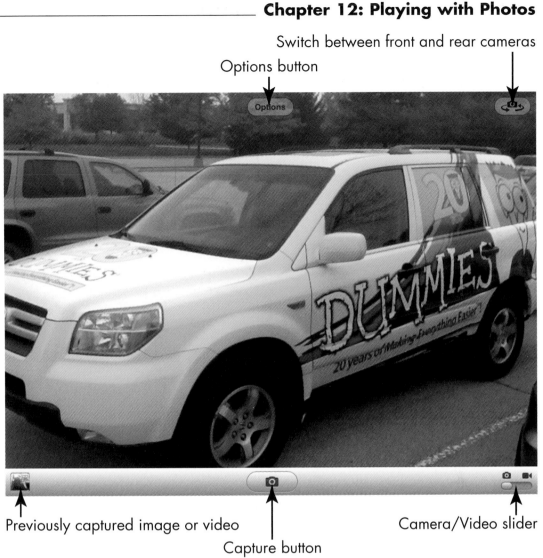

Switch between front and rear cameras

Options button

Previously captured image or video

Camera/Video slider

Capture button

Figure 12-1

7. To view the last photo taken, swipe to the left or tap the thumbnail of the latest image in the bottom-left corner of the screen; the Photos app opens and displays the photo.

8. Tap the Menu button to display a menu that allows you to e-mail, instant message, or Tweet the photo, assign it to a contact, use it as iPad wallpaper, print it, or copy it (see **Figure 12-2**).

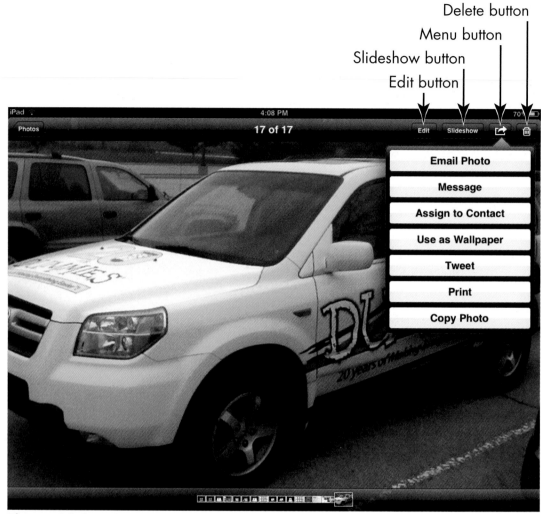

Figure 12-2

9. To delete the image, tap the Delete button.

10. Tap the Home button to close Photos and return to the Home screen.

 The iPad 2 cameras and the iPhone 4 and 4S cameras are similar but they do have differences. If you want to get more useful tips on getting the most out of Photos on your iPad, then check out *iPhone Photography and Video For Dummies* by Angelo Micheletti.

Import Photos from an iPhone, iPod, or a Digital Camera

1. You can find information in Chapter 3 about syncing your computer with your iPad through either iTunes or iCloud to port over photos. However, your computer isn't the only photo source available to you. You can also import photos from a digital camera or an iPhone if you buy the iPad Camera Connection Kit from Apple. The kit contains two adapters (see **Figure 12-3**): a USB Camera Connector to import photos from a digital camera or an iPhone and an SD Card Reader to import image files from an SD card. Start the import process by putting your iPad to sleep.

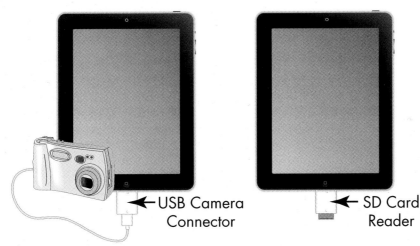

←USB Camera Connector   ← SD Card Reader

Figure 12-3

2. Insert the USB Camera Connector into the Dock connector slot of your iPad.

3. Connect the USB end of the cord that came with your digital camera or iPhone into the USB Camera Connector.

4. Connect the other end of the cord that came with your camera or iPhone into that device.

5. Wake your iPad. The Photos app opens and displays the photos on the digital camera or iPhone.

6. Tap Import All on your iPad; if you want to import only selected photos, tap individual photos and then tap Import. Finally, tap Import rather than Import All. The photos are saved to the Last Import album.

7. Disconnect the cord and the adapter and you're done!

 You can also import photos stored on a *secure digital (SD)* memory card, often used by digital cameras as a storage medium. Simply put the iPad to sleep, insert the SD Card Reader into the iPad, insert the SD card containing the photos, and then follow Steps 5 through 7 in this step list.

Save Photos from the Web

1. The web offers a wealth of images you can download to your Photo Library. Open Safari and navigate to the web page containing the image you want.

2. Press and hold the image; a menu appears, as shown in **Figure 12-4.**

3. Tap Save Image. The image is saved to your Camera Roll folder in the Photos app, as shown in **Figure 12-5.**

 For more about how to use Safari to navigate to or search for web content, see Chapter 5.

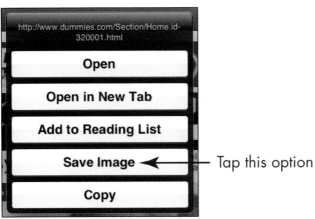

http://www.dummies.com/Section/Home.id-320001.html

Open

Open in New Tab

Add to Reading List

Save Image ◄ ———— Tap this option

Copy

Figure 12-4

The Camera Roll album

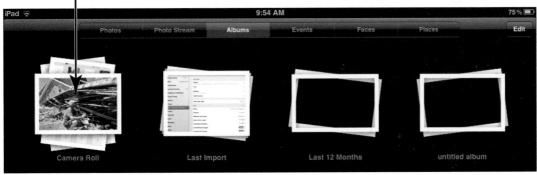

Figure 12-5

View an Album

1. The Photos app organizes your pictures into albums, using such criteria as the folder on your computer from which you synced the photos or whether you captured your photo using the iPad camera. You may also have albums for images you synced from devices such as your iPhone or digital camera. To view your albums, start by tapping the Photos app icon in the Dock on the Home screen.

2. If the Photos tab is selected when the Photos app opens, tap the Albums tab, shown in **Figure 12-6**.

Tap this tab to view albums

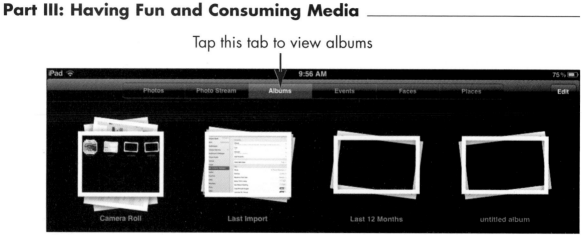

Figure 12-6

3. Tap an album. The photos in it are displayed.

View Individual Photos

1. Tap the Photos app icon in the Dock on the Home screen.

2. Tap the Photos tab, shown in **Figure 12-7**.

Tap this tab

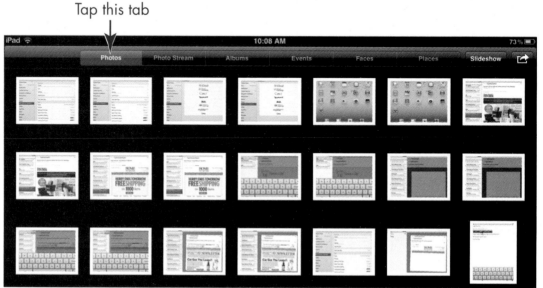

Figure 12-7

3. To view a photo, either tap the photo or pinch your fingers together, place them on the photo, and then spread your fingers apart. The picture expands, as shown in **Figure 12-8**.

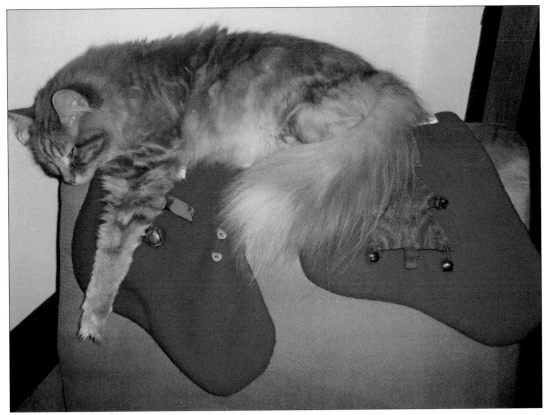

Figure 12-8

4. Flick your finger to the left or right to scroll through the album to look at the individual photos in it.

5. To reduce the size of the individual photo and return to the multi-picture view, place two fingers on the photo and then pinch them together. You can also tap the Albums button (which may display the currently open album's name) to view the album's entire contents.

You can place a photo on a person's information page in Contacts. For more about how to do it, see Chapter 18.

 You can use the Faces, Places, and Events buttons to view photos by faces included in them, by location, or by an event category, such as Wedding or Picnic.

Edit Photos

1. A new feature in iOS 5 is the ability to edit photos. Tap the Photos app on the Home screen to open it.

2. Using methods previously described in this chapter, locate a photo you want to edit.

3. Tap the Edit button; the Edit Photo screen shown in **Figure 12-9** appears.

4. At this point you can take four possible actions:

- *Rotate:* Tap the Rotate button to rotate the image 90 degrees at a time. Continue to tap the button to move another 90 degrees.

- *Enhance:* Tap Enhance to turn Auto-Enhance on or off. This feature optimizes the crispness of the image.

- *Red-Eye:* Tap Red-Eye if a person in a photo has that dreaded red-eye effect. When you activate this feature simply tap each eye that needs clearing up.

- *Crop:* To crop the photo to a portion of its original area tap the Crop button. You can then tap on any corner of the image and drag inward or outward to remove areas of the photo.

In each of the four editing features there is Cancel and a Revert to Original button. If you don't like the changes you made, use either of these to stop making changes or undo the changes you've already made.

Figure 12-9

Organize Photos in Camera Roll

1. If you want to create your own album, display the Camera Roll album (if you have an iPad first generation with no camera this album is called Saved Photos).

2. Tap the Menu button in the top-right corner, and then tap individual photos to select them. Small check marks appear on the selected photos (see **Figure 12-10**).

Checkmarks indicate selected photos

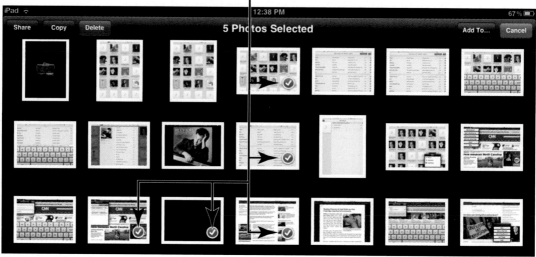

Figure 12-10

3. Tap the Menu button and tap Add to Existing Album or Add to New Album.

4. Tap an existing album or enter a name for a new album (depending on your previous selection) and tap Save. If you created a new album, it now appears in the Photos main screen with the Albums displayed.

 You can also choose the Share, Copy, or Delete buttons when you've selected photos in Step 2 of this task. This allows you to share, copy, or delete multiple photos at a time.

Share Photos

1. You can easily share photos stored on your iPad by sending them as e-mail attachments, via iMessages, or as Tweets via Twitter. First, tap the Photos app icon in the Dock on the Home screen.

2. Tap the Photos tab and locate the photo you want to share.

3. Tap the photo to select it and then tap the Menu button. (It looks like a box with an arrow jumping out of it.) The menu shown in **Figure 12-11** appears.

Tap the Menu button...

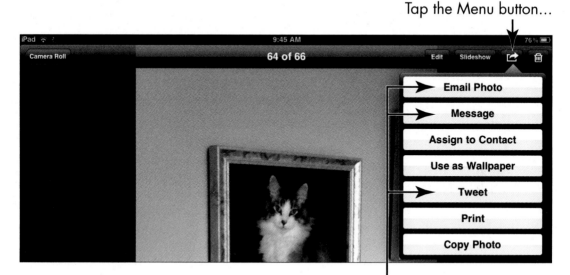

then tap one of these options

Figure 12-11

4. Tap the Email Photo, Message, or Tweet option.

5. In the message form that appears, make any modifications you want in the To, Cc/Bcc, or Subject fields and then type a message for e-mail or enter your iMessage or Tweet text.

6. Tap the Send button and the message and photo go on their way.

 You can also copy and paste a photo into documents such as those created in the available Pages word processor application. To do this, press and hold a photo in Photos until the Copy Photo command appears. Tap Copy Photo and then, in the destination application, press and hold the screen and tap Paste.

Print Photos

1. If you have a wireless printer that's compatible with Apple AirPrint technology, you can print photos. With Photos open, locate the photo you want to print and tap it to maximize it.

2. Tap the Menu button (refer to **Figure 12-11**) and then tap Print.

3. In the Printer Options dialog that appears (see **Figure 12-12**), tap Select Printer. iPad searches for any compatible wireless printers on your local network.

Figure 12-12

4. Tap the plus or minus symbols in the Copy field to set the number of copies to print.

5. Tap the Print button and your photo is on its way.

Run a Slideshow

1. You can run a slideshow of your images in Photos and even play music and choose transition effects for the show. Tap the Photos app icon to open the application.

2. Tap the Photos tab (refer to **Figure** 12-8).

3. Tap the Slideshow button to see the Slideshow Options menu, shown in **Figure 12-13**.

Tap the slideshow button

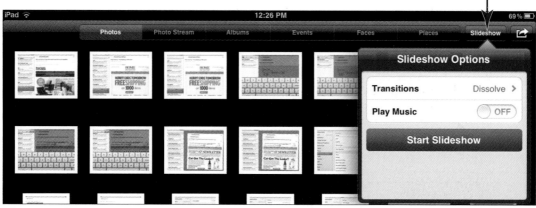

Figure 12-13

4. If you want to play music along with the slideshow, tap the On/Off button on the Play Music field.

5. To choose music to play along with the slideshow, tap Music and in the list that appears (see **Figure 12-14**), tap any selection from your Music library.

6. In the Slideshow Options dialog, tap Transitions and then tap the transition effect you want to use for your slideshow.

7. Tap the Start Slideshow button. The slideshow begins.

 To run a slideshow that includes only the photos contained in a particular album, tap the Albums tab, tap an album to open it, and then tap the Slideshow button to make settings and run a slideshow.

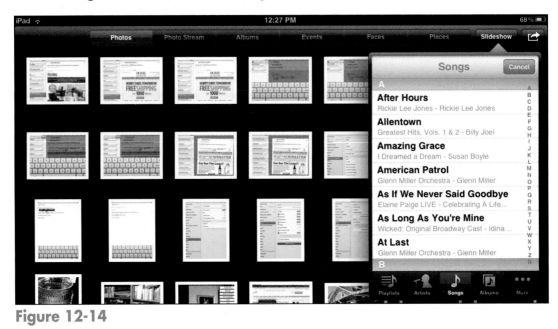

Figure 12-14

Display Picture Frame

1. You can use the slideshow settings you created in the previous task to run your slideshow while your iPad screen is locked so that you can view a continuous display of your pictures. Tap the Sleep/Wake button to lock iPad, and then tap the Home button to go to the unlock screen; the bottom of this screen looks like **Figure 12-15**.

—The Picture
Frame button

Figure 12-15

2. Tap the Picture Frame button (refer to **Figure 12-15**). The slideshow begins. To end the show, tap the Home button.

 If you don't like the effects used on the picture frame, go back to Photos and use the Slideshow button to change your slideshow's settings.

Delete Photos

1. You might find that it's time to get rid of some of those old photos of the family reunion or the last community center project. If the photos weren't transferred from your computer but instead were downloaded or captured as screenshots on the iPad, you can delete them. Tap the Photos app icon in the Dock on the Home screen.

2. Tap the Albums or Photos tab and then tap an album to open it.

3. Tap the Menu button.

4. Tap each photo you want to get rid of (a blue check mark appears; see **Figure 12-16**), and then tap the Delete button. In the confirming dialog that appears, tape the Delete Photo/Selected Photos button to finish the deletion.

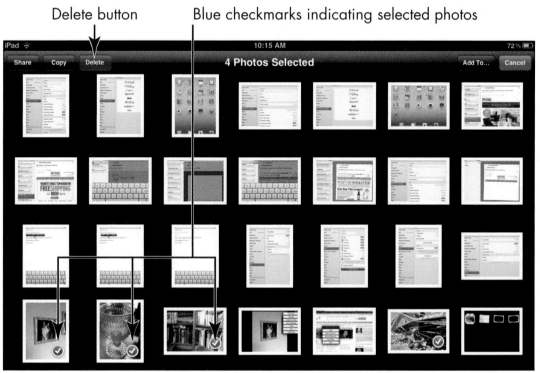

Delete button   Blue checkmarks indicating selected photos

Figure 12-16

Play around with Photo Booth

1. To open Photo Booth, tap its icon on the Home screen.

 Photo Booth is a photo manipulation app that's provided with every iPad from iPad 2 on and works with the iPad cameras. You can use this app to capture photos using various fun effects.

2. The different possible effects that can be used in the current view of the camera appear (see **Figure 12-17**).

3. Tap an effect, and then tap the Capture button (see **Figure 12-18**) to capture an image using that effect. To return to the various effects, tap the Effects button in the bottom-left corner of the screen.

Figure 12-17

Effects button   Capture button   Switch between
                                                front and rear
                                                cameras

Figure 12-18

4. The image appears, along with a filmstrip of all images
   you've captured using PhotoBooth. If you want to delete
   one, tap the photo, tap the X that appears, and then tap
   Delete Photo.

5. Tap the Home button to return to the Home screen. Your
   photos are now available in the Camera Roll folder of
   the Photos app.

Getting the Most Out of Video Features

*T*wo built-in applications on your iPad exist to help you view videos. Using the Videos app, you can watch downloaded movies or TV shows or media you've synced from iCloud or your Mac or PC. The YouTube app takes you online to the popular video-sharing site. Videos there range from professional music videos to clips from news or entertainment shows and personal videos of cats dancing (and other news-making events). If you like to view things on a bigger screen, you can even use iPad's AirPlay to send your iPad movies and photos to your TV by using the Apple Digital AV Connector, a $39.95 accessory, or Apple TV, a device that will cost you $99.

In addition, iPad 2 sports two video cameras you can use to capture your own videos, and by purchasing the iMovie app (a more limited version of the longtime mainstay on Mac computers), you add the capability to edit those videos.

In this chapter, I explain all about shooting, watching, and editing video content from a variety of sources. For practice, you might want to refer to Chapter 8 first to purchase or download one of many available free TV shows or movies.

Get ready to . . .

Capture Your Own Videos with the Built-in Cameras

1. To capture a video, tap the Camera app on the Home screen.

 In iPad 2, two video cameras that can capture video from either the front or back of the device make it possible for you to take videos that you can then share with others or edit. (See more about this topic in the next task.)

2. The Camera app opens. Use the Camera/Video slider to switch from the still camera to the video camera (see **Figure 13-1**).

3. If you want to switch between the front and back cameras, tap the icon in the top-right corner of the screen (refer to **Figure 13-1**).

4. Tap the Record button to begin recording the video. (This button flashes when the camera is recording.) When you're finished, tap the Record button again. Your new video is now listed in the bottom-left corner of the screen.

 Before you start recording, make sure you know where the camera lens is — while holding the iPad and panning, you can easily put your fingers directly over the lens!

Edit Movies with the iMovie App

1. The iMovie app has been included with (and new versions available for) Mac computers for several years, and now a version is available for the iPad. After you capture a video, you can use iMovie to edit it. If you want to edit the video you captured in the previous task, start by purchasing iMovie from the App Store (it costs $4.99), as described in Chapter 9.

Switch between front and rear cameras

Last media captured   Record button   Camera/Video slider

Figure 13-1

2. Tap the iMovie app icon on the Home screen to open it.

3. On the screen that appears, tap the New button (see **Figure 13-2**) to begin a new movie project. Any videos you've taken (see the previous task) are listed in the top-left corner of the screen; double-tap one to open it (see **Figure 13-3**).

4. To scroll through your video, tap the storyboard. Wherever the red line sits (refer to **Figure 13-3**) is where your next action, such as playing the video or adding a transition, begins.

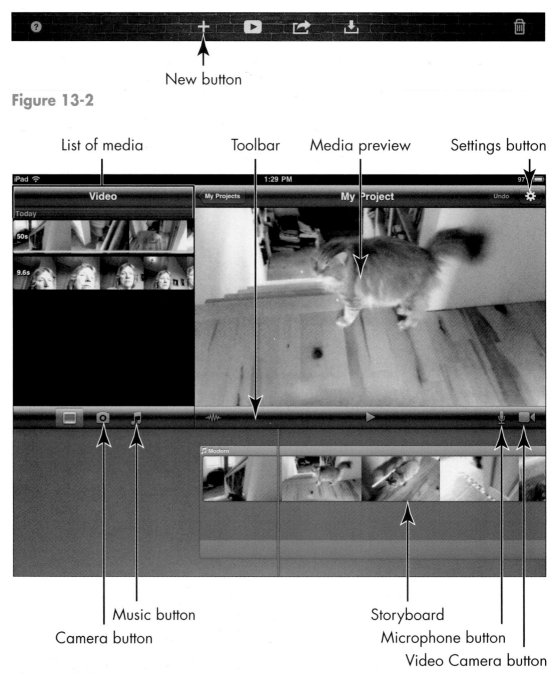

New button

Figure 13-2

List of media
Toolbar
Media preview
Settings button
iPad
1:29 PM
97
Video
Today
50s
9.6s
My Projects
My Project
Undo
Modern
Music button
Camera button
Storyboard
Microphone button
Video Camera button

Figure 13-3

5. To add one video to the end of another, double-tap another clip in the list of media. The clip appears to the right of the first one in the storyboard.

6. If you want to add music to your videos, tap the Music button (refer to **Figure 13-3**) and choose from sound effects, music in your Music library, or theme music (a quick and easy way to add a musical track to your video).

7. To record an audio narration, scroll to the point in the movie where you want it to be heard and tap the Microphone button (refer to **Figure 13-3**).

8. Tap the Record button, tap Record, and then wait for the countdown to finish, and then record. When you're done recording, tap Stop (see **Figure 13-4**).

Tap this button

Figure 13-4

9. In the options shown in **Figure 13-5,** tap Review to hear your recording, Accept to save the recording, or Discard or Retake if you're not completely happy with it. If you accept the recording, it appears below the storyboard at the point in the movie where it will play back.

Figure 13-5

You can do more things with iMovie, such as add transitions between clips or rearrange and cut segments out of clips. Play around with iMovie to see the possibilities, or check out *iLife '11 For Dummies*, by

Tony Bove, and *iPhone Photography & Video For Dummies*, by Angelo Micheletti.

 If you want to create a slideshow with still photos rather than video, tap the Camera button (refer to **Figure** 13-3) and your stored photos are listed instead.

 To quickly return from iMovie to your camera, perhaps to capture more footage, tap the Video Camera button (refer to **Figure** 13-3).

 You can tap the Settings button (refer to **Figure** 13-3) to open a menu that lets you make settings for playing theme music or not, looping the music to play continuously, and using a special effect to fade your movie in or out at the beginning and end.

Play Movies, Podcasts, or TV Shows with Videos

1. Tap the Videos app icon on the Home screen to open the application.

2. On a screen like the one shown in **Figure 13-6,** tap the Movies, TV Shows, or Podcasts tab, depending on which one you want to watch.

Tap the Movies, TV Shows, or Podcasts tab

Figure 13-6

3. Tap an item to open it. A description appears, as shown in **Figure 13-7**.

Play button

Figure 13-7

4. Tap the Play button. The movie, TV show, or podcast opens and begins playing. Note that the progress of the playback is displayed on the Progress bar (see **Figure 13-8**), showing how many minutes you've viewed and how many remain. If you don't see the bar, tap the screen once to display it briefly, along with a set of playback tools at the bottom of the screen.

5. With the playback tools displayed, take any of these actions:

- Tap the Pause button to pause playback.

- Tap either Go to Previous Chapter or Go to Next Chapter to move to a different location in the video playback.

- Tap the circular button on the Volume slider and drag the button left or right to decrease or increase the volume, respectively.

Done button   Progress bar

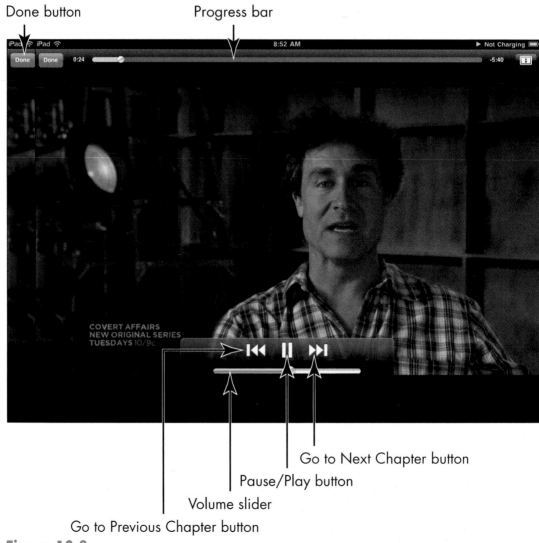

Go to Next Chapter button

Pause/Play button

Volume slider

Go to Previous Chapter button

Figure 13-8

6. To stop the video and return to the information screen, tap the Done button on the Progress bar.

 Note that if you've watched a video and stopped it partway, it opens by default to the last spot you were viewing. To start a video from the beginning, tap and drag the circular button on the Progress bar all the way to the left.

> If your controls disappear during playback, just tap near the top or bottom of the screen and they'll reappear.

Turn on Closed Captioning

1. iTunes and iPad offer support for closed captioning and subtitles. If a movie you purchased or rented has either closed captioning or subtitles, you can turn on the feature in iPad. Look for the "CC" logo on media you download to use this feature; be aware that video you record won't have this capability. Begin by tapping the Settings icon on the Home screen.

2. On the screen that appears (see **Figure 13-9**), tap Video in the Settings section on the left side of the screen.

Tap Video...   then tap here to turn on Closed Captioning

iPad 🛜		3:15 PM	66% 🔋
Settings		**Video**	
✈️ **Airplane Mode** OFF		**Start Playing**	Where Left ▾ ❯
🛜 **Wi-Fi** earland nancy		**Closed Captioning**	⬭ OFF
🔘 **Notifications**		**Home Sharing**	
🧭 **Location Services** On		**Apple ID** example@me.com	
🖼️ **Brightness & Wallpaper**		**Password** Required	
🖼️ **Picture Frame**		An Apple ID is required to use Home Sharing.	
⚙️ **General**			
☁️ **iCloud**			
✉️ **Mail, Contacts, Calendars**			
🐦 **Twitter**			
📷 **FaceTime**			
🧭 **Safari**			
💬 **Messages**			
🎵 **Music**			
🎬 **Video**			

Figure 13-9

3. On the menu that displays on the right side of the screen (refer to **Figure 13-9**), tap the Closed Captioning On/Off button to turn on the feature. Now when you play a movie with closed captioning, you can click the Audio and Subtitles button to the left of the playback controls to manage these features.

Go to a Movie Chapter

1. Tap the Videos app icon on the Home screen.

2. Tap the Movie tab, if it isn't already displayed.

3. Tap the title of the movie you want to watch. Information about the movie is displayed (refer to **Figure 13-7**).

4. Tap the Chapters tab. A list of chapters is displayed, as shown in **Figure 13-10**.

Chapters tab

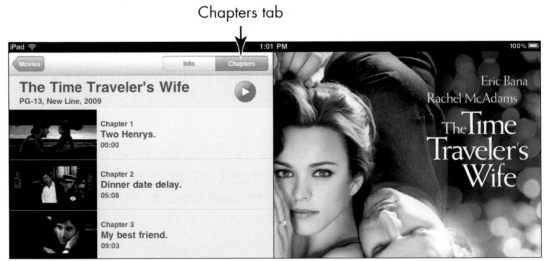

Figure 13-10

5. Tap a chapter to play it.

You can also use the playback tools to go back one chapter or forward one chapter. See the "Play Movies,

Podcasts, or TV Shows with Videos" task, earlier in this chapter, for more information.

Delete an Item from the iPad

1. Tap the Videos app icon on the Home screen.

2. Locate the item you want to delete on the Movies, Podcasts, or TV Shows tab.

3. Press and hold the item; the Delete button appears, as shown in **Figure 13-11**.

—The Delete button

Figure 13-11

4. Tap the Delete button. The item is deleted.

 If you buy a video using iTunes, sync to download it to your iPad, and then delete it from your iPad, it's still saved in your iTunes library. You can sync your computer and iPad again to download the video once more. Remember, however, that rented movies, once deleted, are gone with the wind.

 iPad has much smaller storage capacity than your typical computer, so downloading lots of TV shows or movies can fill its storage area quickly. If you don't want to view an item again, delete it to free up space.

Find Videos on YouTube

1. Although you *can* go to YouTube and make use of all its features using iPad's Safari browser, there's an easier way: using the dedicated YouTube application that's preinstalled on your iPad. This app provides buttons you can tap to display different content and features using your touchscreen. Tap the YouTube icon on the Home screen to open the app.

2. Tap the Featured button at the bottom of the screen, if it's not already selected (see **Figure** 13-12).

Featured button

Figure 13-12

3. To find videos, tap in the Search field in the top-right corner of the screen; the keyboard opens.

4. Type a search term and tap the Search key on the keyboard.

5. Use your finger to scroll down the screen to see additional results.

6. To display the top-rated or most-viewed videos, tap the Top Rated or Most Viewed button at the bottom of the screen.

7. When you find a movie you want to view, tap it to display it. The movie begins loading; see the next task for details about how to control the playback.

 When you load a movie, you can use the Related and More From tabs in the playback window to find additional content related to the topic, or find more videos posted on YouTube by the same source.

If you find a movie you like, tap the More From tab and you can then tap the Subscribe button to subscribe to all movies from this source. View your subscriptions by tapping the Subscriptions button at the bottom of the YouTube screen.

Control Video Playback

1. With a video displayed (see the previous task), tap the Play button. The video plays (see **Figure 13-13**).

Playback progress bar

Play/Pause button   Full Screen button

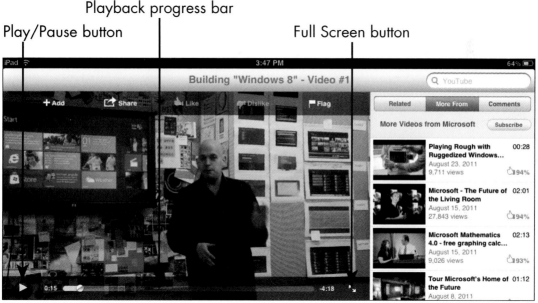

Figure 13-13

2. Tap the Pause button to pause playback. (If the button isn't visible, tap the screen once to display it.)

3. To move forward or backward in the movie, tap the circular button on the Playback progress bar and drag the button to the right or left.

 When the video is finished, you can replay it from the beginning by tapping the Play button again.

Change Widescreen Media Views

 1. In the previous task, you watched a video in one of three available views for widescreen content. To change to another view, tap the Full Screen button (a two-headed arrow at the far right of the playback controls; refer to **Figure 13-13**) and the video displays in a full-screen version with a black border.

 2. To return the movie to its smallest size, tap the button on the right side of the playback controls. Tap the button in the upper-right corner to return to the medium view.

> You can use the double-tap method of enlarging the playback in either of the two larger screen formats. Double-tapping the smaller of the two moves you to the largest full-screen view. Double-tapping the largest full-screen view zooms in further. Depending on the quality of the video, the largest zoom factor can produce a rather grainy image.

Flag Content as Inappropriate

1. If there's a chance your grandkids can get hold of your iPad, you might appreciate the capability to flag inappropriate content on YouTube. First you have to set a restriction in your YouTube account using your computer and then set a flag using the iPad YouTube app, which causes a passcode to be required in order to access that content. With a video open in the YouTube application in the smaller view, tap in the black area near the top of the screen to display tools, as shown in **Figure 13-14**.

2. Tap the Flag option.

3. Tap the Flag As Inappropriate button that appears.

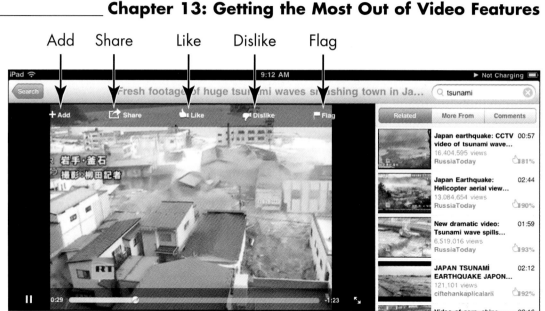

Figure 13-14

Rate Videos

1. Display a video you want to rate in the small view.

2. Tap the Like or Dislike button (refer to **Figure 13-14**).

3. You're asked to sign in to your YouTube account. After you sign in, your Like or Dislike rating is accepted.

 You can view the highest-rated videos on YouTube by tapping the Top Rated button at the bottom of the screen.

Share Videos

1. Display a video you want to share in the small view.

2. Tap the Share button (refer to **Figure 13-14**). Tap either Mail Link to this Video or Tweet.

3. In the e-mail form shown in **Figure 13-15**, enter a recipient in the To field and add to the message, if you like. If you chose to post a tweet, enter your message in the Tweet form.

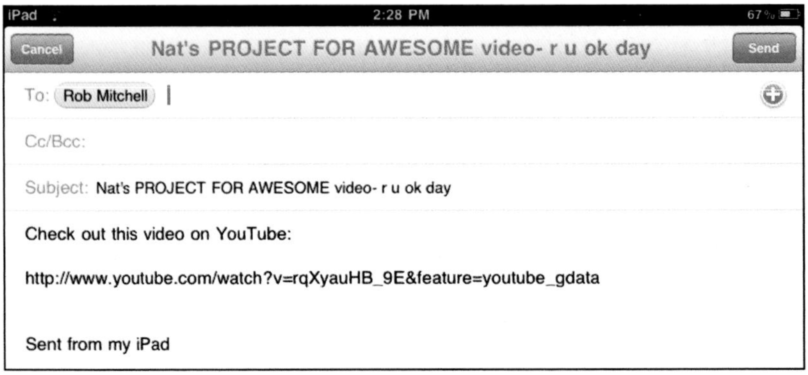

iPad	2:28 PM	67%
Cancel	Nat's PROJECT FOR AWESOME video- r u ok day	Send

To: Rob Mitchell |

Cc/Bcc:

Subject: Nat's PROJECT FOR AWESOME video- r u ok day

Check out this video on YouTube:

http://www.youtube.com/watch?v=rqXyauHB_9E&feature=youtube_gdata

Sent from my iPad

Figure 13-15

4. Tap the Send button to send a link to the video or post your tweet.

Add to Video Favorites

1. Display a video you want to add to Favorites in the small view.

2. Tap the Add button (refer to **Figure 13-14**).

3. On the menu that appears, tap Favorites.

4. To view your favorite movies, tap the Favorites button at the bottom of the YouTube screen. Your favorite videos are displayed.

 To delete a favorite while on the Favorites screen, tap the Edit button. Delete buttons appear on each movie. Tap the movie-specific Delete button to remove that movie. Tap the Done button to leave Editing mode.

Playing Games

The iPad is super for playing games, with its bright screen, great sound system, and ability to rotate the screen as you play and track your motions. You can download game apps from the App Store and play them on your device. You can also use the preinstalled Game Center app to help you find and buy games, add friends to play against, and track scores.

In this chapter, you get an overview of game playing on your iPad, including opening a Game Center account, adding a friend, purchasing and downloading games, and playing basic games solo or against friends.

 Of course, you can also download games from the App Store and play them on your iPad without having to use Game Center. What Game Center provides is a place where you can create a gaming profile, add a list of gaming friends, keep track of your scores and perks, and shop for games (and only games) in the App Store, along with listings of top-rated games and game categories to choose from.

Get ready to . . .

Open an Account in Game Center

1. Using the Game Center app, you can search for and buy games, add friends with whom you can play those games, and keep records of your scores for posterity. From the Home screen, tap the Game Center icon. If you've never used Game Center, you're asked whether to allow *push* notifications: If you want to receive these notices alerting you that your friends want to play a game with you, tap OK. You should, however, be aware that push notifications can drain your iPad's battery.

2. On the Game Center opening screen (see **Figure 14-1**), tap Create New Account.

Tap this button

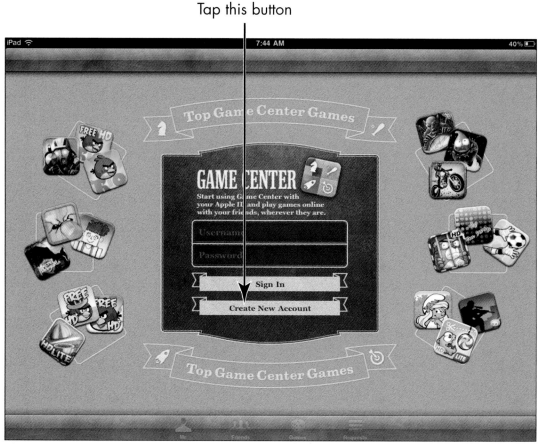

Figure 14-1

3. If the correct country isn't listed in the New Account dialog, tap in the Location field and select another location. If the correct location is already showing, tap Next to confirm it.

4. In the next dialog you see, tap the Month, Day, and Year fields, enter your date of birth, and then then tap Next.

5. In the Game Center Terms & Conditions dialog, swipe to scroll down (and read) the conditions, and then tap Agree if you want to continue creating your account. A confirmation dialog appears; tap Agree once more to accept for real!

6. In the next dialog that opens, tap each field or the Next button above the onscreen keyboard and enter your name, e-mail address, and password information. Tap the Question field to select a security question to identify yourself, and tap the Answer field and type in an answer to the question. Be sure to scroll to the bottom of this dialog and choose to turn off the e-mail notification subscription if you don't want to have Game Center send you messages. Tap Next to proceed. See the following task, "Create a Profile," to create your Game Center profile in subsequent dialogs.

 When you first register for Game Center, if you use an e-mail address other than the one associated with your Apple ID, you may have to create a new Apple ID and verify it using an e-mail message that's sent to your e-mail address. See Chapter 3 for more about creating an Apple ID when opening an iTunes account.

Create a Profile

1. When you reach the last dialog in Step 6 of the previous task, you're ready to create your profile and specify some account settings. You can also make most of these settings after you've created your account, by tapping your Account name on the Game Center Home screen. In the Create Profile dialog that appears (see **Figure 14-2**), in the Nickname field, enter the "handle" you want to be known by when playing games.

Figure 14-2

2. If you don't want other players to be able to invite you to play games when Game Center is open, tap the Game Invites On/Off slider to turn off the feature.

3. If you don't want other players to be able to see your real name, tap the Public Profile On/Off slider to turn this feature off.

4. If you want your friends to be able to send you requests for playing games via e-mail check to see if the e-mail address listed in this dialog is the one you want them to

use. If not, tap Add Another Email and enter another e-mail address.

5. To use your contacts saved in the iPad Contacts app to get friend recommendations tap the Use My Contacts On/Off slider to turn this feature on. Gaming Center can now recommend friends from that list.

6. Tap Done when you're finished with the settings. You return to the Game Center Home screen, already signed in to your account with information displayed about friends, games, and gaming achievements (all at zero initially.)

7. To add a picture to your profile tap on Change Photo. You see a message that your photo will be shared with all other Game Center players. Tap OK.

8. The two options of Take Photo (on iPad 2 only) or Choose Photo appear. Tap Choose Photo to select a photo from your camera roll or a photo library. Tap the library you want to use and scroll to locate the photo.

9. Tap the photo and it appears in a Choose Photo dialog. You can use your finger to move the photo around or scale it, and then tap Use. The photo now appears on your Game Center home screen (see **Figure 14-3**).

 After you create an account and a profile, whenever you go to the Game Center, you log in by entering your e-mail address and password and then tapping Sign In.

 You can change account settings from the Game Center Home screen: Tap your account name and then View Account, make changes to your settings, and then tap Done.

Your photo appears here

Figure 14-3

Add Friends

1. If you want to play Game Center games with others who
   have an Apple ID and an iPhone, iPod touch, or iPad,
   add them as friends so that you can invite them to play.
   From the Game Center Home screen, tap the Friends button at the bottom of the screen.

2. On the Friends page, tap Add Friends.

3. Enter an e-mail address in the To field and edit the invitation, if you like.

4. Tap the Send button. A confirmation message tells you that your invitation has been sent. Tap OK. After your friend accepts your invitation, his or her name is listed on the Friends screen.

 With iOS 5 Game Center gained a Friend Recommendations feature. Tap the Friends tab, and then tap the A-Z button in the top-left corner. A Recommendations section appears above the list of your current friends. These are people who play the same or similar games, so if you like, try adding one or two as friends.

 You will probably also receive requests from friends who know you're on Game Center. When you get these e-mail invitations, be sure that you know the person sending it before you accept it — especially if you've allowed e-mail access in your account settings — otherwise you could be putting a stranger in communication with you.

Purchase and Download Games

1. Time to get some games to play! Open Game Center and sign in to your account.

2. Tap the Games button at the bottom of the screen, and then tap Find Game Center Games (see **Figure** 14-4).

3. In the list of games that appears, scroll through the list of featured games. To view different games, tap either the Top Charts or Categories button at the bottom of the screen. *Note:* Accessing these from the Game Center displays only game apps, as opposed to accessing apps from the App Store which shows you all categories of apps.

Tap here to find more games

Figure 14-4

4. To search for a particular title, tap the Search field and enter the name by using the onscreen keyboard.

5. Tap a game title to view information about it. To buy a game, tap the button labeled with either the word *free* or the price (such as $1.99). Then tap the button again, which is now labeled Install App. A dialog appears, asking for your Apple ID and password. Enter these and tap OK. Another verification dialog appears, asking you to sign in. Follow the instructions on the next couple of screens to enter your password and verify your payment information if this is the first time you've signed in to your account from this device.

6. When the verification dialog appears, tap Buy. The game downloads.

 If you have added friends to your account, you can go to the Friends page and view games your friends have downloaded. To purchase one of these games, just tap it in your friend's list.

 You may see buttons labeled Buy It Now or Available at the App Store while you're exploring game recommendations in the Games section of Game Center. Tapping such a button takes you from Game Center directly to the App Store to buy the game.

Master iPad Game-Playing Basics

It's almost time to start playing games, but first let me give you an idea of iPad's gaming strengths. For many reasons, iPad may be the ultimate gaming device, because of the following strengths:

⟹ **Fantastic-looking screen:** First, the high-resolution, 9.7-inch screen has a backlit LED display that Apple describes as "remarkably crisp and vivid." It's no lie: See the *Haunted Manor* game in **Figure 14-5,** for example. In-plane switching (IPS) technology lets you hold your iPad at almost any angle (it has a 178-degree viewing angle) and still see good color and contrast.

⟹ **Faster processor:** The superfast A5 processor chip in your iPad 2 can run rings around your iPhone, making the iPad ideal for gaming.

⟹ **Game play in full-screen mode:** Rather than play on a small iPhone screen, you can play most games designed for the iPad in full-screen mode. Seeing the full screen brings the gaming experience to you in an even more engaging way than a small screen ever could.

Figure 14-5

 Ability to drag elements onscreen: Though the Multi-Touch screen in the iPad may be based on the same technology that's in the iPhone, it has been redone from the ground up for the iPad. The newer screen is responsive — and when you're about to be zapped by virtual aliens in a fight to the death, responsiveness counts.

➥ **Ten-hour battery life:** A device's long battery life means that you can tap energy from it for many hours of gaming fun.

➥ **Specialized game-playing features:** Some newer games have features that take full advantage of the iPad's capabilities. For example, *Nova* (from

Gameloft) features Multiple Target Acquisition, which lets you target multiple bad guys in a single move to blow them out of the water with one shot. In *Real Racing Game* (Firemint), for example, you can look in your rearview mirror as you're racing to see what's coming up behind you, a feature made possible by the iPad's larger screen.

➡ **Stellar sound:** The built-in iPad speaker is a powerful little item, but if you want an experience that's even more up close and personal, you can plug in a headphone, some speaker systems, or microphone using the built-in jack.

The iPad has a built-in motion sensor — the *three-axis accelerometer* — as well as a gyroscope. These features provide lots of fun for people developing apps for the iPad as they use the automatically rotating screen to become part of the gaming experience. For example, a built-in compass device reorients itself automatically as you switch your iPad from landscape to portrait orientation. In some racing games, you can grab the iPad as though it were a steering wheel and rotate the device to simulate the driving experience.

Play against Yourself

Many games allow you to play a game all on your own. Each has different rules and goals, so you'll have to study a game's instructions and help to learn how to play it, but here's some general information about these types of games:

➡ Often a game can be played in two modes: with others or in a 'solitaire' version, where you play yourself or the computer.

⇒ Many games you may be familiar with in the offline world, such as Carcassone or Scrabble, have online versions. For these you already know the rules of play, so you simply need to figure out the execution. For example, in the online Carcassone solitaire game you tap to place a tile on the board, tap the placed tile to rotate it, and tap the check mark to complete your turn and reveal another tile.

⇒ All the games you play on your own will record your scores in Game Center so you can see how you're progressing in building your skills.

Play Games with Friends in Game Center

1. After you have added a friend and both of you have downloaded the same games, you're ready to play. The rules of play are different for each game, but here are the basic steps for getting a game going. Tap the Game Center app icon on the Home screen and sign in, if necessary.

2. Tap Friends. The Friend page (see **Figure 14-6**) appears.

3. Tap the name of the friend you want to play and then tap the name of a game you have in common. At this point, some games offer you an invitation to send to the friend — if so, wait for your friend to respond, which he does by tapping Accept or Decline on his device.

4. The game should appear, and you can tap Play to start playing according to whatever rules the game has. Your scores mount up as you play.

5. When you're done playing, tap either Friend or Game in Game Center to see your score and your friend's score listed. Game Center tracks your achievements, including points and perks that you've earned along the way. You can also compare your gaming achievements to those of top-ranking players across the Internet — and check your friends' scores by displaying the Friends page with the Points portion showing (refer to **Figure 14-6**).

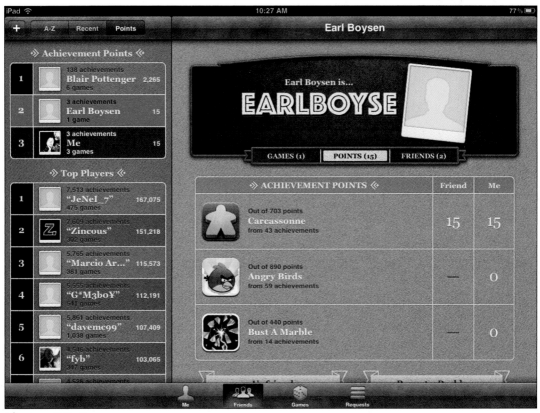

Figure 14-6

 If your friends aren't available, you can play a game by tapping its title on the Games page and then tapping Play. You can then compare your scores with others around the world who have also played the game recently.

Finding Your Way with Maps

*I*f you own an iPhone, the Google Maps app on iPad should look familiar to you. The big difference with iPad is its large screen, on which you can view all the beautiful map visuals and terrain and street views as long as you have an Internet connection. In the iPad version you can also display the map and written directions simultaneously.

If you're new to the Maps app, it has lots of useful functions. You can find directions with suggested alternative routes from one location to another. You can bookmark locations to return to them again. And, the Maps app makes it possible to get information about locations, such as the phone numbers and web links to businesses. You can even look at a building or location as though you were standing in front of it on the street, add a location to your Contacts list, or e-mail a location link to your buddy.

Be prepared: This application is seriously cool, and you're about to have lots of fun exploring it in this chapter.

Chapter 15

Get ready to . . .

Go to Your Current Location

1. iPad can figure out where you are at any time and display
your current location. From the Home screen, tap the
Maps icon. Tap the Current Location icon (the small, blue
arrow to the left of the Search field; see **Figure 15-1**).

Current Location icon

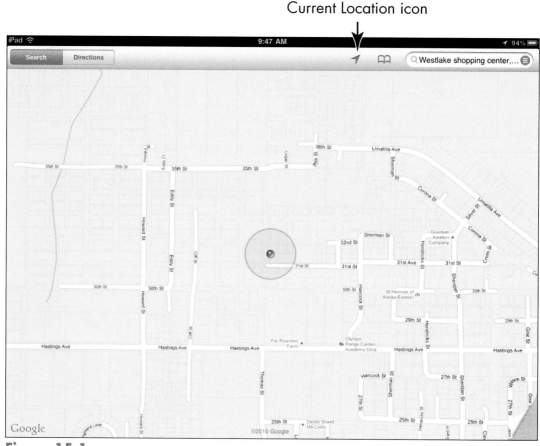

Figure 15-1

2. Your current location is displayed with a blue pin in it
and a blue circle around it (refer to **Figure 15-1**). The circle indicates how accurate the location is — it can be
anywhere within the area of the circle, and it's likely to
be less accurate on a Wi-Fi–only iPad.

3. Double-tap the screen to zoom in on your location. (Additional methods of zooming in and out are covered in the "Zoom In and Out" task, later in this chapter.)

> If you don't have a 3G version of iPad, your current location is a rough estimate based on a triangulation method. Only 3G-enabled iPads with the global positioning system (GPS) can pinpoint where you are. Still, if you type a starting location and an ending location to get directions, you can get pretty accurate results even with a Wi-Fi–only iPad.

Change Views

1. The Maps application offers four views: Standard, Satellite, Hybrid, and Terrain. iPad displays the Standard view (see the top-left image in **Figure 15-2**) by default the first time you open Maps. To change views, with Maps open, swipe the bottom-right corner of the screen to turn the "page" and reveal the Maps menu, shown in **Figure 15-3**.

2. Tap the Satellite option. The Satellite view (refer to the top-right image in **Figure 15-2**) appears.

3. Swipe to reveal the menu again and then tap Hybrid. Satellite view is displayed with street names superimposed (refer to the bottom-left image in **Figure 15-2**).

4. Finally, swipe to reveal the menu one more time and then tap Terrain. A topographical version of the map is displayed (refer to the bottom-right image in **Figure 15-2**), showing hills, mountains, and valleys. This view is helpful if you want to walk around San Francisco (for example) and avoid those steep streets!

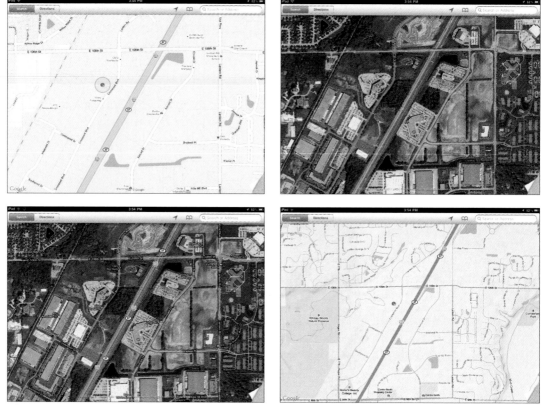

Figure 15-2

 On the Maps menu, there's also a Traffic overlay feature. If you live in a larger metropolitan area (this feature doesn't really work in small towns), turn on this feature by tapping the On/Off button. The traffic overlay shows different colors on roads indicating accidents or road closures to help you navigate your rush hour commute or trip to the mall. Green tells you you're good to go, yellow indicates slowdowns, and red means avoid at all costs.

 You can drop a pin to mark a location on a map that you can return to. See the task "Drop a Pin," later in this chapter, for more about this topic.

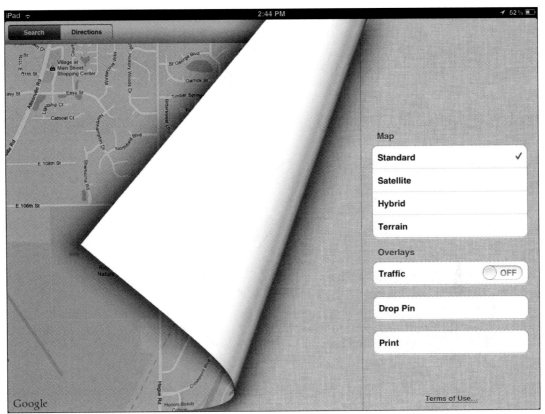

Figure 15-3

 To print any displayed map to an AirPrint-compatible wireless printer, just tap the Print button on the Maps menu.

Zoom In and Out

1. You'll appreciate the Zoom application because it gives you the capability to zoom in and out to see more or less detailed maps and to move around a displayed map. With a map displayed, double-tap with a single finger to zoom in (see **Figure 15-4**).

2. Double-tap to zoom out, revealing less detail.

3. Place two fingers positioned together on the screen and move them apart to zoom in.

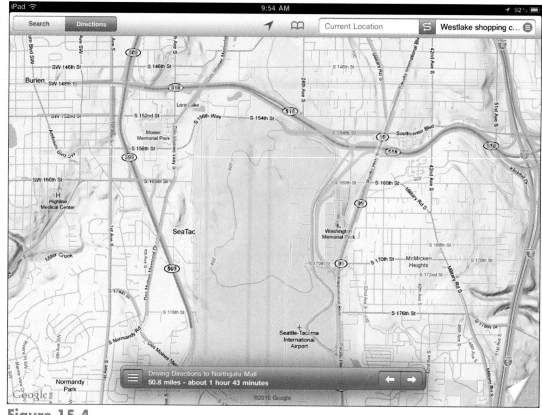

Figure 15-4

4. Place two fingers apart on the screen and then pinch them together to zoom out.

5. Press your finger to the screen and drag the map in any direction to move to an adjacent area.

 It can take a few moments for the map to redraw itself when you enlarge, reduce, or move around it, so try a little patience. Areas that are being redrawn look like blank grids but are filled in eventually. Also, if you're in Satellite view or Hybrid view, zooming in may take some time; wait it out because the blurred image resolves itself.

Go to another Location

1. With Maps open, tap in the Search field (see **Figure 15-5**); the keyboard opens.

Search field

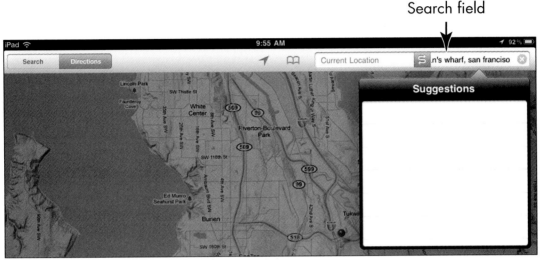

Figure 15-5

2. Type a location, using a street address with city and state, or a destination such as *Empire State Building* or *Detroit airport*. Maps may make suggestions as you type if it finds any logical matches. Tap the Search key on the keyboard and the location appears with a red pin inserted in it and a label with the location, an Information icon, and in some cases, the Street view icon (see **Figure 15-6**). Note that if several locations match your search term, several pins may be displayed.

 Try asking for a type of business or location by zip code. For example, if you crave something with pepperoni, enter **99208 pizza**.

The information bar

Bookmark icon

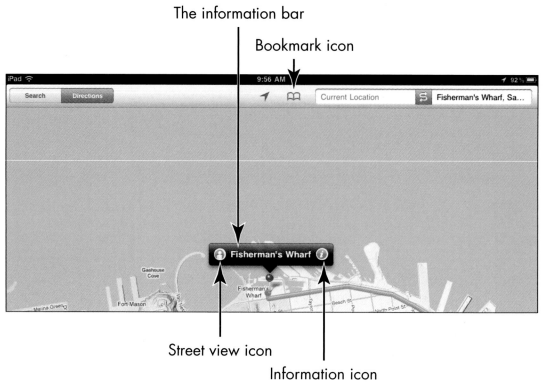

Street view icon

Information icon

Figure 15-6

3. You can also tap the screen and drag in any direction to move to a nearby location.

4. Tap the Bookmark icon (the little book symbol to the left of the Search field; refer to **Figure 15-6**), and then tap the Recents tab to reveal recently visited sites. Tap a bookmark to go there.

 As you discover later in this chapter, in the "Add and View a Bookmark" task, you can also quickly go to any location you've previously visited and saved using the Bookmarks feature.

 If you enter a destination such as *Bronx Zoo*, you might want to also enter its city and state. Entering *Bronx Zoo* landed me in the Woodland Park Zoo in Tacoma, because Maps look for the closest match to your geographical location in a given category.

Drop a Pin

1. Pins are markers: A green pin marks a start location, a red pin marks a search result, and a blue pin (referred to as the *blue marker*) marks your iPad's current location. If you drop a pin yourself, it appears in a lovely purple. Display a map that contains a spot where you want to drop a pin to help you find directions to or from that site.

2. If you need to, you can zoom in to a more detailed map to see a better view of the location you want to pin.

3. Press and hold your finger on the screen at the location where you want to place the pin. The pin appears, together with an information bar (refer to **Figure 15-6**).

4. Tap the Information icon (refer to **Figure 15-6**) on the information bar to display details about the pin location (see **Figure 15-7**).

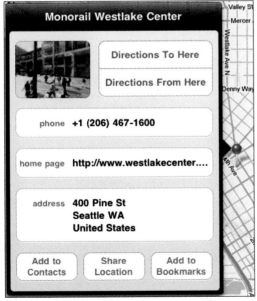

Figure 15-7

To delete a pin you've dropped, tap the pin to display the information bar and then tap the Information icon. In the Information dialog that opens, tap Remove Pin. This method works only with pinned sites that aren't bookmarked.

Add and View a Bookmark

1. A *bookmark* provides a way to save a destination so you can display a map or directions to it quickly. To add a bookmark to a location, first place a pin on it, as described in the preceding task.

2. Tap the Information icon to display the Information dialog.

3. Tap the Add to Bookmarks button (refer to **Figure 15-7**).

4. The Add Bookmark dialog (see **Figure 15-8**) and the keyboard appear. If you like, you can modify the name of the bookmark.

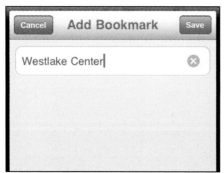

Figure 15-8

5. Tap Save.

6. To view your bookmarks, tap the Bookmark icon (it looks like a little open book; refer to **Figure 15-6**) at the top of the Maps screen. Be sure that the Bookmarks tab is selected; a list of bookmarks is displayed.

7. Tap on a bookmark to go to the location.

 You can also view recently viewed locations, even if you haven't bookmarked them. Tap the Bookmark icon and then, at the bottom of the Bookmarks dialog that appears, tap Recents. Locations you've visited recently are listed there. Tap on one to return to it.

Delete a Bookmark

1. Tap the Bookmark icon and then tap the Bookmarks tab at the bottom of the dialog that appears, to be sure you're viewing Bookmarks.

2. Tap the Edit button. A red minus icon appears to the left of your bookmarks, as shown in **Figure 15-9.**

Red minus icons

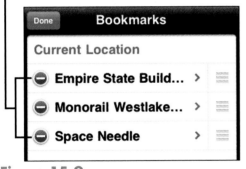

Figure 15-9

3. Tap a red minus icon.

4. Tap Delete. The bookmark is removed.

 You can also use a touchscreen shortcut after you've displayed the Bookmarks in Step 1 above. Simply swipe across a bookmark and then tap the Delete button.

You can also clear out all recent locations stored by Maps to give yourself a clean slate. Tap the Bookmark icon and then tap the Recents tab. Tap Clear and then confirm by tapping Clear All Recents.

Find Directions

1. You can get directions in a couple of different ways. With at least one pin on your map in addition to your current location, tap the Directions tab. A line appears, showing the route between your current location and the closest pin for the currently selected transportation method: by car, on foot, or by using public transit (see **Figure 15-10**).

Line indicating your route

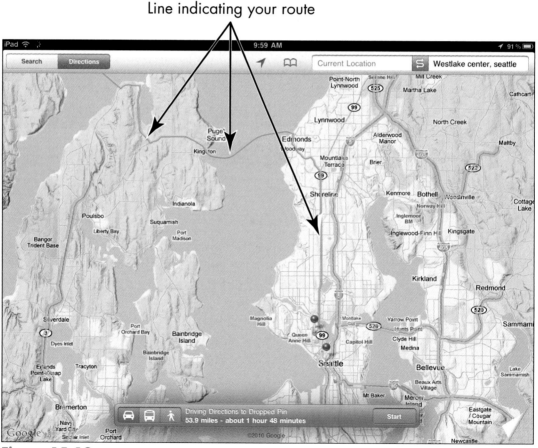

Figure 15-10

2. To show directions from your current location to another pin, tap the other pin and the route is redrawn.

3. You can also enter two locations to get directions from one to the other. With the Directions tab selected in Maps, tap in the field labeled *Current Location* (see **Figure 15-11**). The keyboard appears.

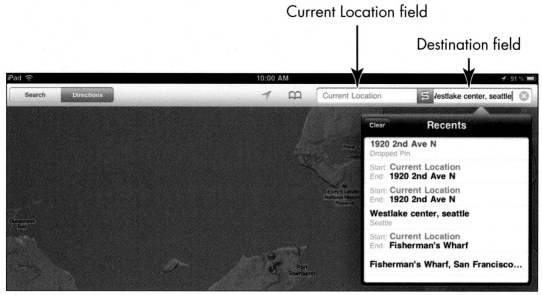

Figure 15-11

4. Enter a different starting location.

5. Tap in the Destination field, enter a destination location, and then press the Search button on the keyboard. The route between the two locations is displayed.

6. You can also tap the Information icon on the information bar that appears above any selected pin and use the Directions To Here or Directions From Here button to generate directions (refer to **Figure 15-7**).

7. When a route is displayed, a blue bar appears along the bottom of the Maps screen (refer to **Figure 15-10**) with information about the distance and time it takes to travel between the two locations. Here's what you can do with this informational display:

- Tap the car, bus, or pedestrian logo to get driving, public transportation, or walking directions.

- Tap Start to change the tools offered: The icon on the left, showing several lines of text from a small document, takes you to step-by-step directions (see **Figure 15-12**); the arrow keys take you through the directions one step at a time.

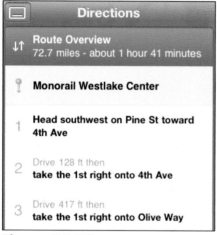

Figure 15-12

8. If there are alternate routes, Maps notes the number of alternate routes in the informational display and shows the routes on the map. Tap a route number to make it the active route (See **Figure 15-13**).

In Directions view in Maps, notice the button with a zigzag line between the Current Location and Destination fields (refer to **Figure 15-10**). After you generate directions from one location to another, tap this button to generate reverse directions. Believe me: They aren't always the same — especially when one-way streets are involved!

Tap a route number to select it

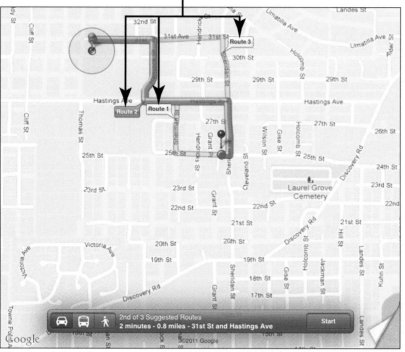

Figure 15-13

View Information about a Location

1. You've displayed the Information dialog for locations to add a bookmark or get directions in previous tasks. Now you focus on the useful information displayed there. Go to a location and tap the pin.

2. On the information bar that appears above the pinned location, tap the Information icon (refer to **Figure 15-6**).

3. In the Information dialog (refer to **Figure 15-7**), tap the web address listed in the Home Page field to be taken to the location's web page, if it has one associated with it.

4. You can also press and hold either the Phone or Address field and use the Copy button to copy the phone number, for example, so that you can place it in a Notes document for future reference.

5. Tap outside the Information dialog to close it.

Rather than copy and paste information, you can easily save all information about a location in your Contacts address book. See the "Add a Location to a Contact" task, later in this chapter, to find out how it's done.

View a Location from Street Level

1. You can view only certain locations from street level, so you have to explore to try out this feature. On the Search tab of Maps, tap in the Search field and enter a location, such as your favorite local shopping mall.

2. When the location appears, tap the Street view icon on its information bar. Street view appears.

3. When you're in Street view (see **Figure 15-14**), you can tap and drag the screen to look around you in all directions. Remember the view is a moment frozen in time, perhaps from a few years ago.

4. Tap the small circular map in the bottom-right corner (refer to **Figure 15-14**) to return to the standard map view.

You can also drag the screen down to get a better look at tall skyscrapers or drag up to view the street and its manhole covers. The small, circular map in the bottom-right corner highlights what you're looking at in the specific moment. In addition, street names are displayed down the center of streets.

Tap here to
return to the
standard map
view

Figure 15-14

Use the Compass

1. The Compass feature works from only your current location, so start by tapping the Current Location icon at the
top of the Maps screen (refer to **Figure 15-1**).

2. Tap the icon again to turn on the Compass. A small compass appears in the top-right corner of the screen (see **Figure 15-15**).

Compass

Figure 15-15

3. Move your iPad around in different directions and note that the compass symbol moves as well, indicating which direction you're facing.

4. To turn off the Compass, tap the Current Location icon one more time.

 A message may appear indicating that the Compass needs resetting because of interference. To do so, move away from any electronic equipment that might be causing the problem and move the iPad around in what Apple describes as a figure-eight motion.

A message may appear indicating that the Compass needs resetting because of interference. To do so, move away from any electronic equipment that might be causing the problem and move the iPad around in what Apple describes as a figure-eight motion.

Location Services has to be turned on in iPad Settings for the Compass feature to be available.

Add a Location to a Contact

1. Tap on a pin to display the information bar.

2. Tap on the Information icon.

3. In the Information dialog that appears (refer to **Figure 15-7**), tap Add to Contacts.

4. In the resulting dialog, tap Create New Contact. The New Contact dialog appears (see **Figure 15-16**).

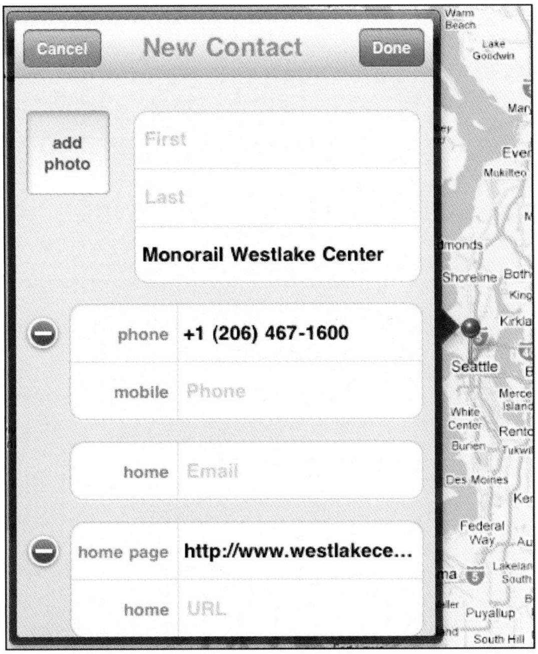

Figure 15-16

5. Whatever information was available about the location has already been entered. Enter any additional information you need, such as name, phone, or e-mail address.

6. Tap Done. The information is stored in your Contacts address book.

 You can choose a distinct ringtone or text tone for a new contact. Just tape the Ringtone or Text Tone field in the New Contact form to see a list of options. When that person calls via FaceTime or texts you via iMessage, you will recognize him or her from the type of tone that plays.

Share Location Information

1. Tap a pin to display the information bar.

2. Tap the Information icon.

3. In the Information dialog that appears, tap Share Location. In the dialog that appears you can choose to share via text message, Tweet, or e-mail. Tap Email to see how this option works.

4. On the e-mail form that appears (see **Figure 15-17**), use the onscreen keyboard to enter a recipient's e-mail address and any Cc/Bcc addresses, and add or change the subject or message as you like.

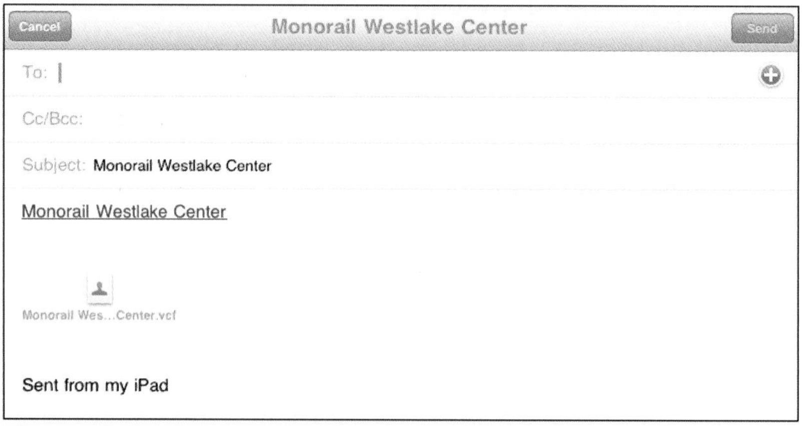

Cancel	Monorail Westlake Center	Send

To: |

Cc/Bcc:

Subject: Monorail Westlake Center

Monorail Westlake Center

Monorail Wes...Center.vcf

Sent from my iPad

Figure 15-17

5. Tap Send. A link to the location information in Google Maps is sent to your designated recipients.

 If you choose Tweet in Step 3, you have to have installed the Twitter app and have a Twitter account set up using iPad Settings. Tapping Message in Step 3 displays a new message form; just enter an e-mail address or phone number in the To: field, enter your text message, and then tap Send.

Part IV

Managing Your Life and Your iPad

The 5th Wave   By Rich Tennant

iPad

"In fact it does come with a compass."

Keeping On Schedule with Calendar

Chapter 16

Whether you're retired or still working, you have a busy life full of activities (even busier if you're retired, for some unfathomable reason). You may need a way to keep on top of all those activities and appointments. The Calendar app on your iPad is a simple, elegant, electronic daybook that helps you do just that.

In addition to being able to enter events and view them by the day, week, month, or year, you can set up Calendar to send alerts to remind you of your obligations and search for events by keywords. You can even set up repeating events, such as weekly poker games, monthly get-togethers with the girls or guys, or weekly babysitting appointments with your grandchild. To help you coordinate calendars on multiple devices, you can also sync events with other calendar accounts.

In this chapter, you master the simple procedures for getting around your calendar, entering and editing events, setting up alerts, syncing, and searching.

View Your Calendar

1. Calendar offers several ways to view your schedule. Start
by tapping the Calendar app icon on the Home screen to
open it.

2. Tap the Day button at the top of the screen to display Day
view (if it's not already displayed). This view, shown in
Figure 16-1, displays your daily appointments with times
listed on the left page, along with a calendar for the month,
and an hourly breakdown of the day on the right page. Tap
a day on the monthly calendar displayed in the top-right
corner of the left page to change days in this view.

List of the day's appointments   Hourly breakdown of the day

Calendar for the month

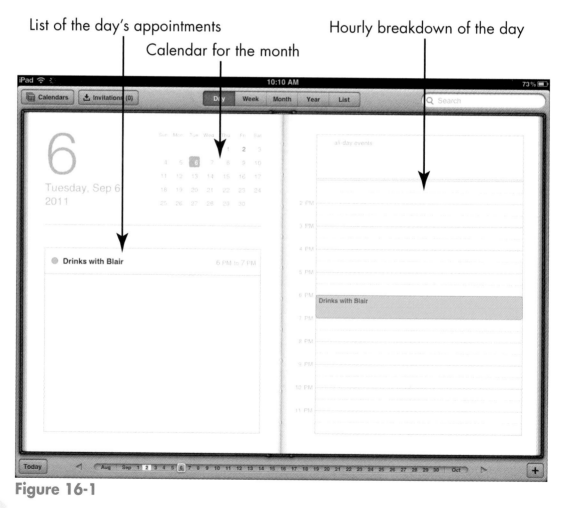

Figure 16-1

3. Tap the Week button to view all events for the current
week, as shown in **Figure 16-2**. In this view, appointments appear with times listed along the left side of the
screen.

Week button
↓

Figure 16-2

4. Tap the Month button to get an overview of your busy
month (see **Figure 16-3**). In this view, you don't see the
timing of each event, but you can spot your busiest days
and see which ones have room to squeeze in one more
event.

Month button

Figure 16-3

5. Tap the Year button to see your entire year of commitments, as shown in **Figure 16-4.**

Year button

Figure 16-4

6. Tap the List button to see List view, which displays your daily calendar with a list of all commitments for the month to the left of it, as shown in **Figure 16-5**.

7. To move from one day or week or month or year to another, use the Timeline displayed along the bottom of every view. Tap a day to move to it, or press the Forward

or Backward button to move forward or backward one
increment at a time: a day at a time in Day view, a week
at a time in Week view, and so on.

Figure 16-5

8. To jump back to today, tap the Today button in the bottom-left corner of Calendar.

 For the feel of a paper calendar book, rotate your screen to landscape orientation when in the Calendar app. This orientation provides a nice book-like experience, especially in Day view.

Add Calendar Events

1. With any view displayed, tap the Add button (refer to **Figure 16-5**) to add an event. The Add Event dialog, shown in **Figure 16-6**, appears.

Figure 16-6

2. Enter a title for the event and, if you want, a location.

3. Tap the Starts/Ends field; the Start & End dialog, shown in **Figure 16-7,** is displayed.

Cancel	**Start & End**	Done

Starts	Wed, Aug 24, 2011 3:00 PM
Ends	4:00 PM
All-day	OFF
Time Zone	Cupertino >

Mon **Aug 22**	1	50	
Tue **Aug 23**	2	55	AM
Today	3	00	PM
Thu **Aug 25**	4	05	
Fri **Aug 26**	5	10	

Figure 16-7

4. Place your fingertip on the date, hour, minute, or AM/PM column and move your finger to scroll up or down. If you want to change the Time Zone tap that field, begin to enter a new location, and then tap on the location in the suggestions that appear. When each item is set correctly, tap Done. (Note that, if the event will last all day, you can simply tap the All-Day On/Off button and forget about setting start and end times.)

5. If you want to add notes, use your finger to scroll down in the Add Event dialog and tap in the Notes field. Type your note, and then tap the Done button to save the event.

 You can edit any event at any time by simply tapping it in any view of your calendar. The Edit Event dialog appears, offering the same settings as the Add Event dialog (shown earlier, in **Figure 16-6**). Tap the Done button to save your changes after you've made them.

Create Repeating Events

1. If you want an event to repeat, such as a weekly or monthly appointment, you can set a repeating event. With any view displayed, tap the Add button to add an event. The Add Event dialog (refer to **Figure 16-6**) appears.

2. Enter a title and location for the event and set the start and end dates and times, as shown in the earlier task "Add Calendar Events."

3. Tap the Repeat field; the Repeat Event dialog, shown in **Figure 16-8,** is displayed.

4. Tap on a preset time interval: Every Day, Week, 2 Weeks, Month, Or Year.

5. Tap Done. You return to the Add Event dialog.

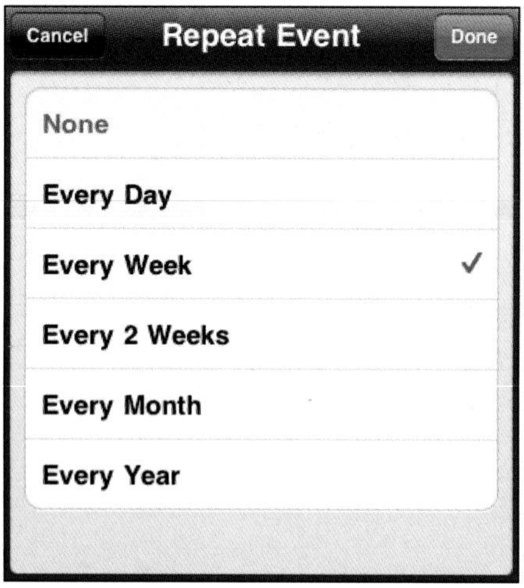

Figure 16-8

6. Tap Done again to save your repeating event.

> Other calendar programs may seem to give you more control over repeating events; for example, you might be able to make a setting to repeat an event every Tuesday. If you want a more robust calendar feature you might consider setting up your appointments in iCal or Outlook and syncing them to iPad. But, if you want to create a repeating event in iPad's Calendar app, simply add the first event on a Tuesday and make it repeat every week. Easy, huh?

Add Alerts

1. If you want your iPad to alert you when an event is coming up, you can use the Alert feature. First tap the Settings icon on the Home screen and choose General, and then choose Sounds.

2. Tap on Calendar Alerts and then tap on any Alert Tone, which plays the tone for you. When you've chosen the alert tone you want, tap Sounds to return to Sounds settings.

3. Tap the Home button and then tap Calendar and create an event in your calendar or open an existing one for editing, as covered in earlier tasks in this chapter.

4. In the Add Event or Edit dialog (refer to **Figure 16-6**), tap the Alert field. The Event Alert dialog appears, as shown in **Figure 16-9**. Note that if you want two alerts — say, one a day before and one an hour before — you can repeat this procedure using Second Alert instead.

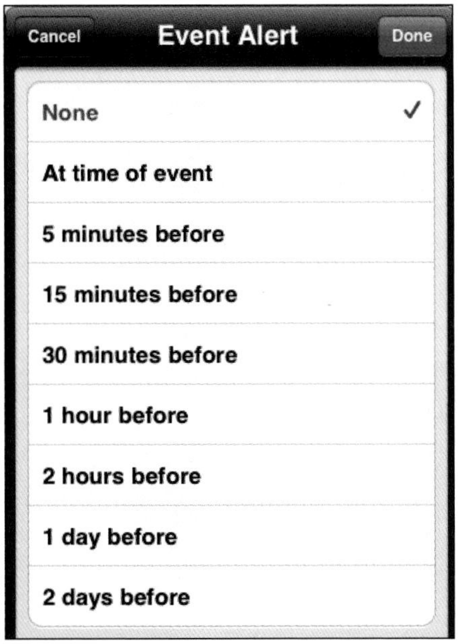

Cancel	**Event Alert**	Done
None		✓
At time of event		
5 minutes before		
15 minutes before		
30 minutes before		
1 hour before		
2 hours before		
1 day before		
2 days before		

Figure 16-9

5. Tap any preset interval, from 5 Minutes to 2 Days Before or at the time of the event. (Remember that you can scroll down in the dialog to see more options.)

6. Tap Done to save the alert, and then tap Done in the Add Event dialog to save all settings.

7. Tap the Day button to display Day view of the date of your event; note that the alert and timeframe are listed under the event in that view, as shown in **Figure 16-10**.

An event's alert and timeframe

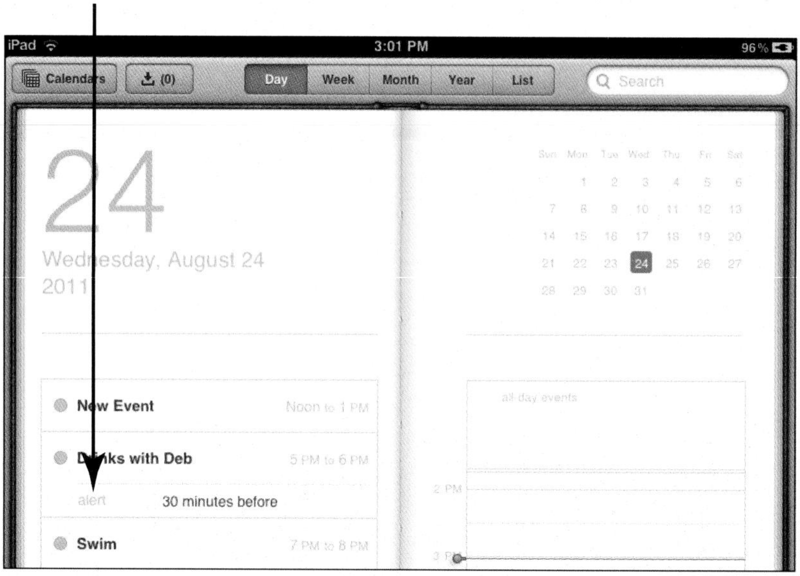

Figure 16-10

 If you work for an organization that uses a Microsoft Exchange account, you can set up your iPad to receive and respond to invitations from colleagues in your company. When somebody sends an invitation that you accept, it appears on your calendar. Check with your company network administrator (who will jump at the chance to get her hands on your iPad) or the *iPad User Guide* to set up this feature if it sounds useful to you. Or you can check into the MobileMe subscription service — which pretty much does the same thing minus the IT person.

Search Calendars

1. With Calendar open in any view, tap the Search field in the top-right corner (refer to **Figure 16-5**). The onscreen keyboard appears.

2. Type a word or words to search by and then tap the Search key on the onscreen keyboard. As you type, the Results dialog appears, as shown in **Figure 16-11**.

Figure 16-11

3. Tap on any result to display it in the view you were in when you started the search. The Edit dialog appears; there you can edit the event if you want.

Subscribe to and Share Calendars

1. If you use a calendar available from an online service such as Yahoo! or Google, you can subscribe to that calendar to read events saved there on your iPad. Note that you can only read, not edit, these events. Tap the Settings icon on the Home screen to get started.

2. Tap the Mail, Contacts, Calendars option on the left.

3. Tap Add Account. The Add Account options, shown in **Figure 16-12,** appear.

4. Tap an e-mail choice, such as Gmail or Yahoo! Mail.

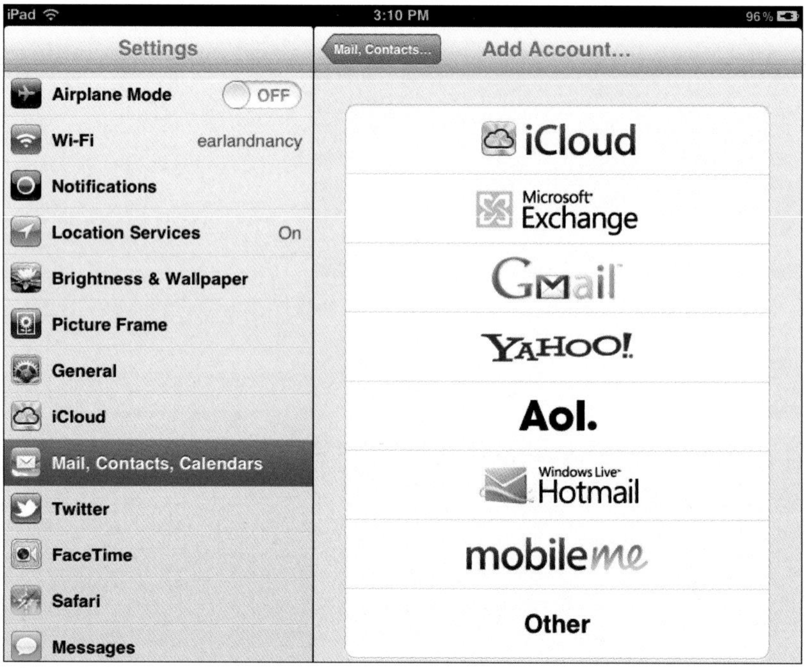

Figure 16-12

5. In the dialog that appears (see **Figure 16-13**), enter your name, e-mail address, and e-mail account password.

6. Tap Save. iPad verifies your address.

7. Your iPad retrieves data from your calendar at the interval you have set to fetch data. To review these settings, tap the Fetch New Data option in the Mail, Contacts, Calendars dialog.

8. In the Fetch New Data dialog that appears (see **Figure 16-14**), be sure that the Push option's On/Off button reads *On* and then choose the option you prefer for how frequently data is pushed to your iPad.

Cancel	Gmail	Save

Name	Helen Marks
Address	ipadsenior@gmail.com
Password	••••••••
Description	ipadsenior@gmail.com

Figure 16-13

Make sure this is set to On

iPad ᚦ	3:11 PM	96%

Settings | ‹ Mail, Contacts... **Fetch New Data**

- **Airplane Mode**   OFF
- **Wi-Fi**   earlandnancy
- **Notifications**
- **Location Services**   On
- **Brightness & Wallpaper**
- **Picture Frame**
- **General**
- **iCloud**
- **Mail, Contacts, Calendars**
- **Twitter**
- **FaceTime**

Push   ON

New data will be pushed to your iPad from the server.

Fetch

The schedule below is used when push is off or for applications which do not support push. For better battery life, fetch less frequently.

Every 15 Minutes	
Every 30 Minutes	
Hourly	
Manually	✓

| **Advanced** | › |

Figure 16-14

 If you use Microsoft Outlook's calendar or iCal on your main computer, you can sync it to your iPad calendar to avoid having to re-enter event information. To do this, use iCloud settings to sync automatically (see Chapter 3) or connect your iPad to your computer with the Dock Connector to USB Cable and use settings in your iTunes account to sync with calendars. Click the Sync button and your calendar settings will be shared between your computer and iPad (in both directions). Read more in Chapter 3 about working with iTunes to manage your iPad content.

If you store birthdays for people in the Contacts app the Calendar app then displays these when the day comes around so you won't forget to pass on your congratulations!

You can also have calendar events sent if you subscribe to a push service such as MobileMe. It can sync calendars from multiple e-mail accounts with your iPad calendar. If you choose to have data pushed to your iPad, your battery may drain faster.

Delete an Event

1. When an upcoming luncheon or meeting is canceled, you should delete the appointment. With Calendar open, tap an event. Then tap the Edit button on the information bar that appears (see **Figure 16-15**). The Edit dialog opens.

● Anniversary party   7 PM to 10 PM   Edit   ←————Tap this button

Figure 16-15

2. In the Edit Event dialog, tap the Delete Event button (see **Figure 16-16**).

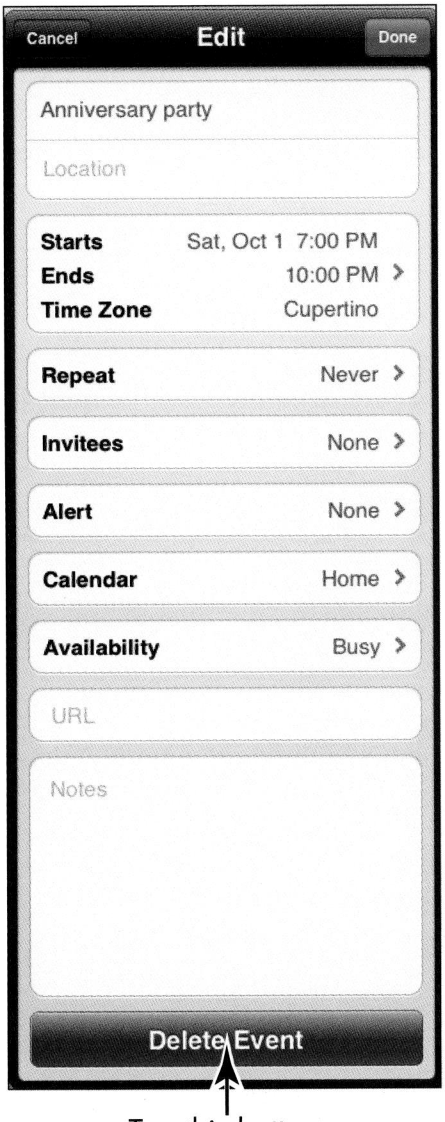

Cancel	Edit	Done

Anniversary party

Location

Starts	Sat, Oct 1 7:00 PM
Ends	10:00 PM ›
Time Zone	Cupertino

Repeat — Never ›

Invitees — None ›

Alert — None ›

Calendar — Home ›

Availability — Busy ›

URL

Notes

Delete Event

Tap this button

Figure 16-16

3. Confirming options appear; if this is a repeating event, you have the option to delete this instance of the event or this and all future instances of the event (see **Figure 16-17**). Tap the button for the option you prefer. The event is deleted and you return to Calendar view.

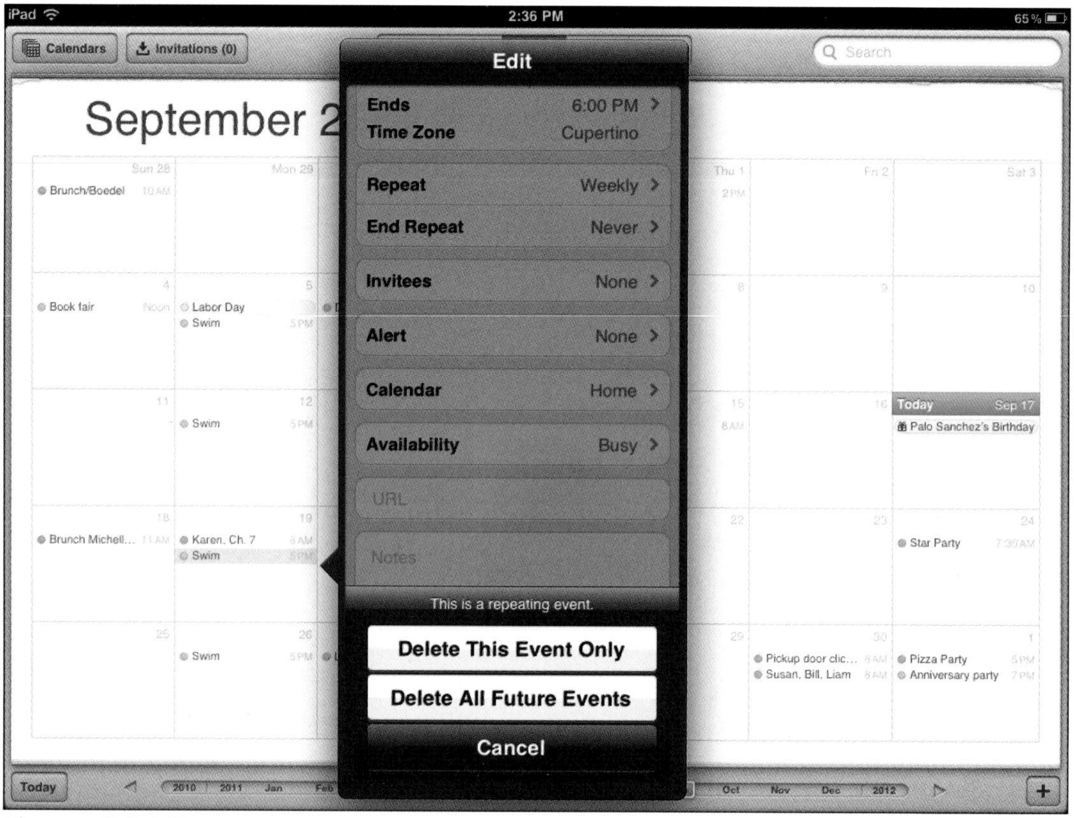

iPad
2:36 PM
65 %
Calendars
Invitations (0)
Search
Edit
September 2
Ends
6:00 PM
Time Zone
Cupertino
Repeat
Weekly
End Repeat
Never
Invitees
None
Alert
None
Calendar
Home
Availability
Busy
URL
Notes
This is a repeating event.
Delete This Event Only
Delete All Future Events
Cancel
Brunch/Boedel
Book fair
Labor Day
Swim
Brunch Michell...
Karen, Ch. 7
Today
Sep 17
Palo Sanchez's Birthday
Star Party
Pickup door clic...
Susan, Bill, Liam
Pizza Party
Anniversary party
Today
2010
2011
Jan
Oct
Nov
Dec
2012

Figure 16-17

If an event is moved but not canceled, you don't have to delete the old one and create a new one: Simply edit the event to change the day and time in the Event dialog.

Working with Reminders and Notifications

*W*ith the arrival of iOS 5, the Reminders app and the Notification Center feature appeared, warming the hearts of those who need help remembering every detail of their lives.

Reminders is a kind of to do list that lets you create tasks and set reminders so you don't forget them.

Notifications allows you to review all the things you should be aware of in one place, such as mail messages, text messages, calendar appointments, and alerts. You can also display weather and stock reports in the Notification Center.

In this chapter, you discover how to set up and view tasks in Reminders and how the new Notification Center can centralize all your alerts in one easy-to-find place.

Create a Task in Reminders

1. Creating a task in Reminders is pretty darn simple. Tap Reminders on the Home screen.

2. In the screen that appears (see **Figure 17-1**) tap the plus sign to add a task. The onscreen keyboard appears.

Tap here to create a new task

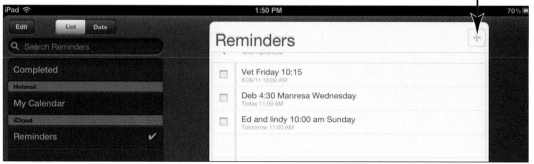

Figure 17-1

3. Enter a task name or description using the onscreen keyboard and tap the Return button. The new task is added to the Reminders list.

 You can't add details about a task when you enter it, only a descriptive name. To add details about timing and so forth, see the next task.

Edit Task Details

1. Tap a task to open the Details dialog. To see all the available options, tap Show More to display the choices shown in **Figure 17-2**. (Note that I deal with reminder settings in the following task.)

2. Tap Priority, choose None, Low, Medium, or High from the choices that appear, and then tap Done.

3. Tap List and then, from the options displayed (see **Figure 17-3**), choose My Calendar or Reminders to choose whether to display the task in the Calendar or Reminder app; then tap Done.

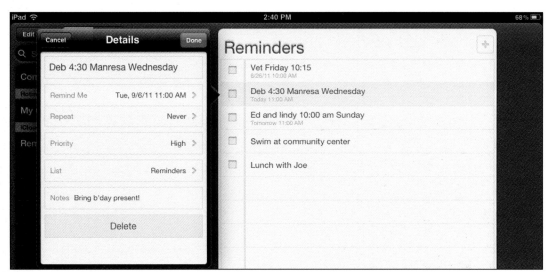

Figure 17-2

Choose where to display the task

Figure 17-3

4. Tap Notes and then, using the onscreen keyboard, enter a note about the task.

 With this version of the app, priority settings don't do much: They don't set a flag of any kind on a task in a list, nor do they reorder tasks to show priority tasks first. You can only see the priority of a task by displaying its details.

Schedule a Reminder

1. One of the major features of Reminders is to remind you of upcoming tasks. To set a reminder, tap a task.

2. In the dialog that appears tap Remind Me and in the dialog that appears, tap the On/Off field for the On a Day field to turn it on.

3. Tap the date field to display the settings shown in **Figure 17-4.**

Make date settings here

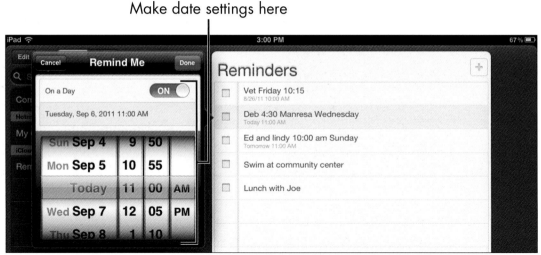

Figure 17-4

4. Tap and flick the day, hour, and minutes fields to scroll to the date and time for the reminder.

5. Tap Done to save the settings for the reminder.

 If you want a task to repeat with associated reminders, tap the Repeat field, and from the dialog that appears tap Every Day, Week, 2 Weeks, Month, or

Year (for those annual meetings or great holiday get-togethers with the gang). Tap Done twice to save the setting.

Display Tasks as a List or by Date

1. You can display various lists of reminders (these include Reminders, tasks that come from My Calendar, Completed tasks, and lists you create yourself, as explained later in this chapter), or display reminders by date alongside a panel display of monthly calendars, which is a great help in planning your schedule. Tap Reminders and then tap the List button. A list of reminders appears, as shown in **Figure 17-5**.

Figure 17-5

2. Tap the Date tab and you see the tasks for the current date and a set of calendars displayed, as shown in **Figure 17-6**.

 You can scroll the monthly calendar display to show months in the past or future, and tap any date to show its tasks in the daily list on the right.

Figure 17-6

Create a List

1. You can create your own lists of tasks to help you keep different parts of your life organized. Tap Reminders on the Home screen to open it.

2. Tap the List tab to display that view if it's not already selected, and then tap the Edit button.

3. Tap Create New List (see **Figure 17-7**) and enter the name of the list using the onscreen keyboard, and then tap Done.

Tap this option

Figure 17-7

4. You return to the Edit dialog. Tap Done again to save the list. If you tap on the list in the List view now a new blank sheet appears on the right with that title. Tap the plus sign to add new tasks to the list (see **Figure 17-8**).

Tap this button to add a new task to the list

Figure 17-8

Sync with Other Devices and Calendars

 Note that to make all these settings work you should set up your default Calendar in the Calendar settings, and set up your iCloud account under Accounts in the Mail, Contacts, Calendar settings.

1. To determine which tasks are brought over from other devices or calendars such as Outlook or iCal, tap the Settings button on the Home screen.

2. Tap iCloud and be sure that in the list that appears in the right pane, make sure that Reminders is set to On (see **Figure 17-9**).

Tap this option

Settings	Mail, Contacts, Calendars	
Airplane Mode	OFF	
Wi-Fi	earlandnancy	
Notifications	**Default Account**	iCloud >
Location Services	On	
Brightness & Wallpaper	Messages created outside of Mail will be sent from the default account.	
Picture Frame	**Contacts**	
General	**Sort Order**	Last, First >
iCloud	**Display Order**	First, Last >
Mail, Contacts, Calendars	**My Info**	None >
Twitter	**Calendars**	
FaceTime	**New Invitation Alerts**	ON
Safari	**Sync**	Events 1 Month Back >
Messages	**Time Zone Support**	Off >
Music	**Default Alert Times**	>
Video	**Default Calendar**	Home >
Photos	New events created outside of a specific calendar will default to this calendar.	
	Reminders	
	Sync	Reminders 1 Month Back >
	Default List	Reminders >
	New reminders created outside of a specific list will default to this list.	

Figure 17-9

3. Also make sure that Calendars is set to On in the right pane.

4. Tap Mail, Contacts, Calendars and scroll down to the Reminders category.

5. Tap the Sync field and then choose how far back to sync Reminders (see **Figure 17-10**).

Figure 17-10

Mark as Complete or Delete a Reminder

1. You may want to mark a task as completed or just delete it entirely. With Reminders open, tap a task to display the Details dialog shown in **Figure 17-11**.

2. Tap Delete. In the confirming dialog, tap Delete again.

3. To mark a task as complete tap in the check box to the left of it in List view, and then tap the Completed category. The task moves to that category and is removed from the My Calendar category.

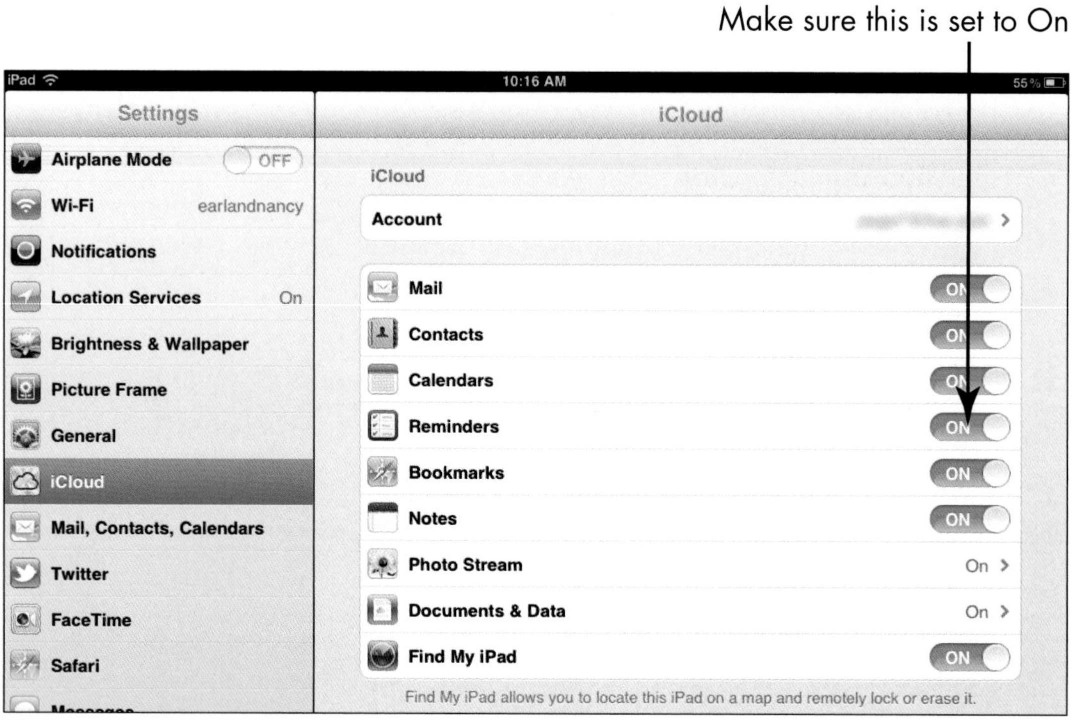

Make sure this is set to On

Figure 17-11

Set Notification Types

1. Notification Center is on by default, but there are some settings you can make to control what types of notifications are included in it. Tap Settings, and then tap Notifications.

2. In the settings that appear (see **Figure 17-12**), note that there is a list of items included in Notification Center and a list of items not included. For example, Messages and Reminders may be included, but alerts in game apps may not.

3. Tap any item, and in the settings that appear (see **Figure 17-13**) tap the On/Off button to have that item included or excluded from Notification Center.

Figure 17-12

4. Tap on an Alert Style to have no alert, a banner across the top of the screen, or a boxed alert appear. If you choose Banner it will appear and then disappear automatically. If you choose Alert you have to take an action to dismiss the alert when it appears.

5. Badge App Icons is a feature that places a red circle and number on icons on your Home screens representing alerts associated with those apps. To turn this feature off, Tap the On/Off button for Badge App Icon.

6. If you want to be able to view alerts when the Lock Screen is displayed, turn on the View in Lock Screen setting. When you've finished making settings for an individual app, tap the Notifications button to go back to the Notifications settings.

Include or exclude from Notification Center

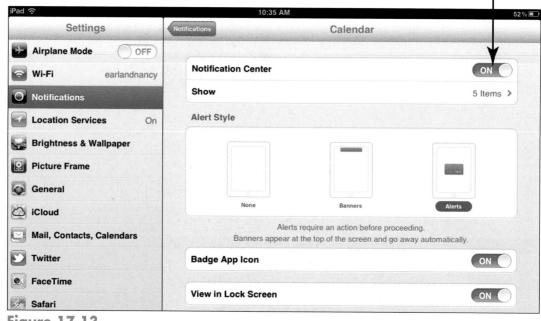

Figure 17-13

View Notification Center

1. Once you've made settings for what should appear in Notification Center, you'll regularly want to take a look at those alerts and reminders. From any screen, tap the black status bar on top and drag down to display Notification Center (see **Figure 17-14**).

2. Note that items are divided into lists by type, for example Reminders, Mail, Calendar, and so on.

3. To close Notification Center tap the three lines in the bottom center of the center and drag up towards the status bar.

 To determine what is displayed in Notification Center, see the previous task.

Notification Center

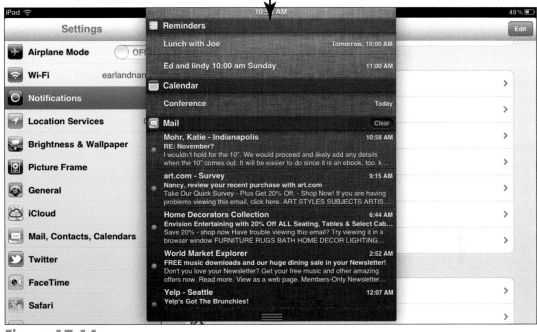

Figure 17-14

Go to an App from Notification Center

1. You can easily jump from Notification Center to any app that caused an alert or reminder to be displayed. Tap the status bar and drag down to display Notification Center.

2. Tap any item; it opens in its originating app. If you've tapped on a message such as an e-mail, you can then reply to the message using the procedure described in Chapter 6.

Clear Notifications

1. To get rid of old notifications for an app, tap the status bar and drag down to display Notification Center.

2. Tap the pale gray X to the right of a category of notifications, such as Mail. The button changes to read Clear (see **Figure 17-15**).

Tap this option

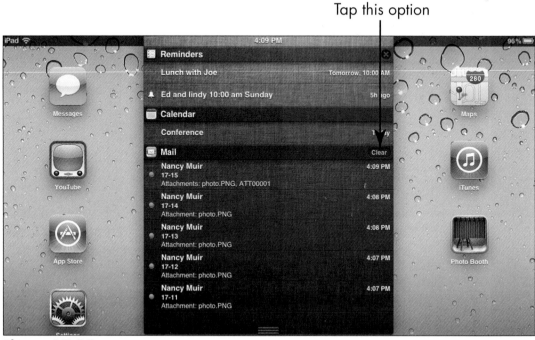

Figure 17-15

3. Tap the Clear button and all items for that category are removed.

 If you change your mind about clearing all items in a group after you tap the Clear button, just close Notification Center.

Managing Contacts

*C*ontacts is the iPad equivalent of the dog-eared address book that sits by your phone. The Contacts app is simple to set up and use, and it has some powerful features beyond simply storing names, addresses, and phone numbers.

For example, you can pinpoint a contact's address in iPad's Maps application. You can use your contacts to address e-mail and Facebook messages and tweets quickly. If you store a contact record that includes a website, you can use a link in Contacts to view that website instantly. And, of course, you can easily search for a contact by a variety of criteria, including people related to you by family ties or mutual friends.

In this chapter, you discover the various features of Contacts, including how to save yourself from having to spend time entering contact information by syncing a Google or Yahoo! contacts list to your iPad.

Chapter
18

Get ready to . . .

Add a Contact

1. Tap the Contacts app icon on the Home screen to open
the application. If you haven't entered any contacts yet,
you see a blank address book, like the one shown in
Figure 18-1.

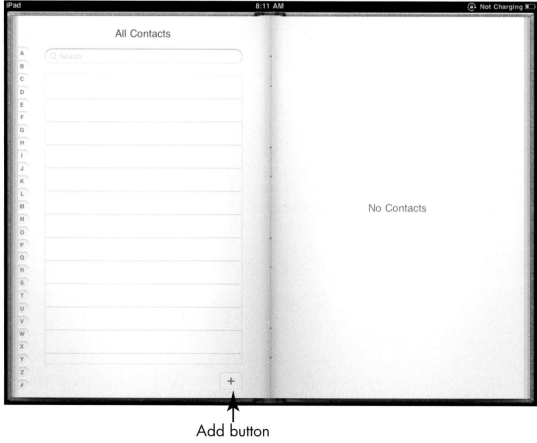

Add button

Figure 18-1

2. Tap the Add button, the button with the small plus sign (+) on it. A blank Info page opens (see **Figure 18-2**) and the onscreen keyboard is displayed.

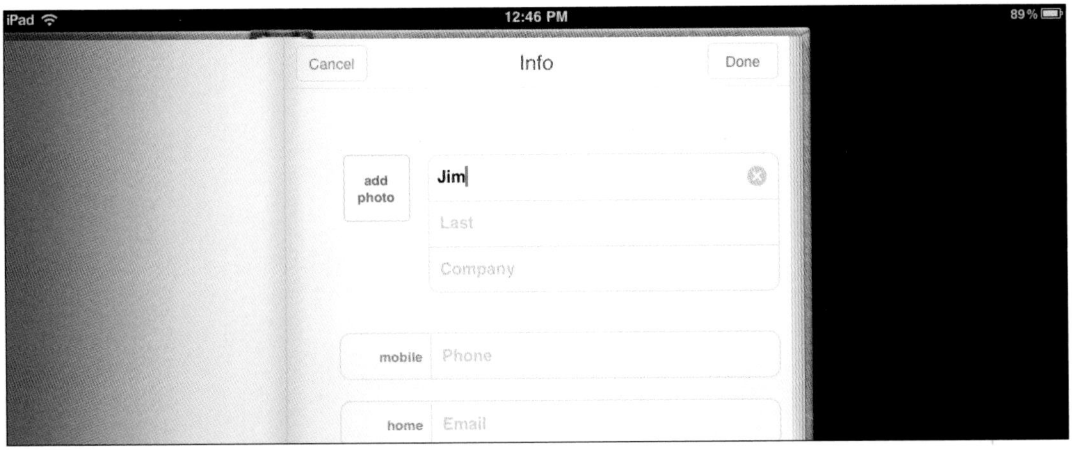

Figure 18-2

3. Enter any contact information you want. (Only a first name in the First field is required.)

4. To scroll down the contact page and see more fields, flick up on the page with your finger.

5. If you want to add a mailing or street address, you can tap Add New Address, which opens additional entry fields.

6. To add an information field such as Nickname or Job Title, tap Add Field. In the Add Field dialog that appears (see **Figure 18-3**), choose a field to add. (You may have to flick the page up with your finger to view all the fields.)

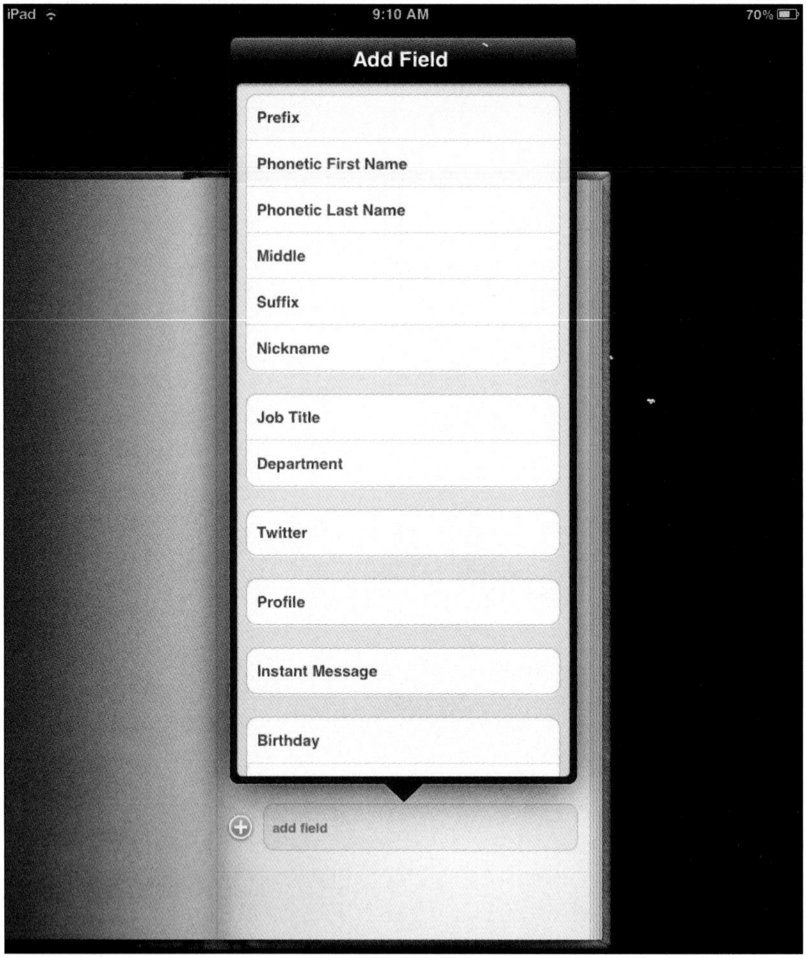

iPad 📶   9:10 AM   70% 🔋

Add Field

Prefix

Phonetic First Name

Phonetic Last Name

Middle

Suffix

Nickname

Job Title

Department

Twitter

Profile

Instant Message

Birthday

⊕   add field

Figure 18-3

7. Tap the Done button when you finish making entries.
The new contact appears in your address book. (**Figure
18-4** shows an address book with several entries added.)

 If your contact has a name that's difficult for you to
pronounce, consider adding the Phonetic First Name
or Phonetic Last Name field, or both, to that person's
record (refer to Step 6).

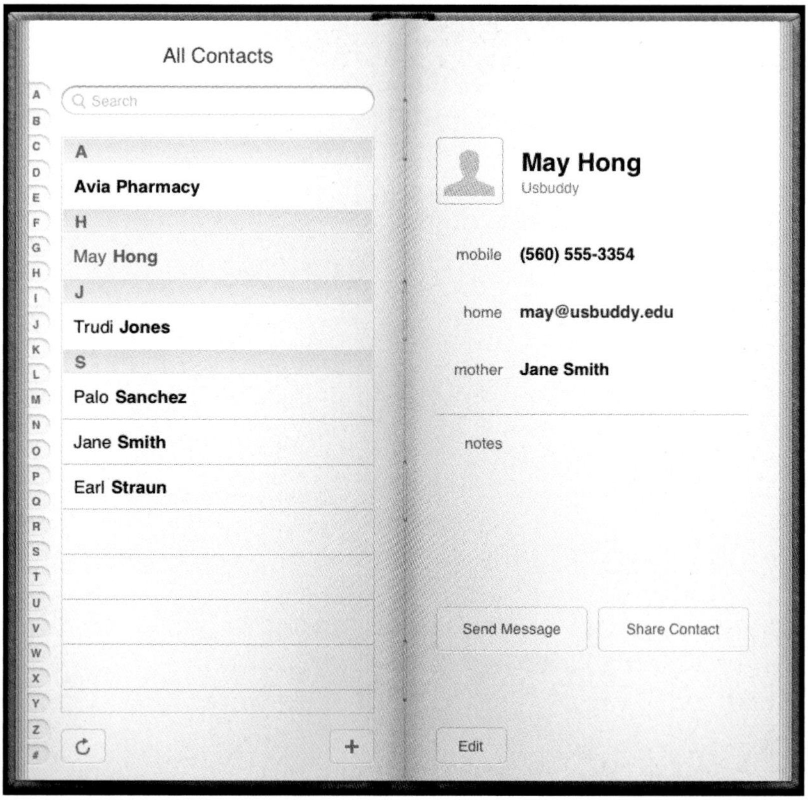

All Contacts

A
Avia Pharmacy

H
May Hong

J
Trudi Jones

S
Palo Sanchez

Jane Smith

Earl Straun

May Hong
Usbuddy

mobile   (560) 555-3354

home   may@usbuddy.edu

mother   Jane Smith

notes

Send Message   Share Contact

Edit

Figure 18-4

Sync Contacts Using iTunes

1. You can use your iTunes account, accessed from your computer, to sync contacts between your Yahoo! or Gmail e-mail account (such as the one shown in **Figure 18-5**), for example, and your iPad Contacts application. This sync works in both directions: Contacts from the iPad are sent to your e-mail account, and contacts from your e-mail account are sent to the iPad. First connect your iPad to your computer using the Dock Connector to USB Cable.

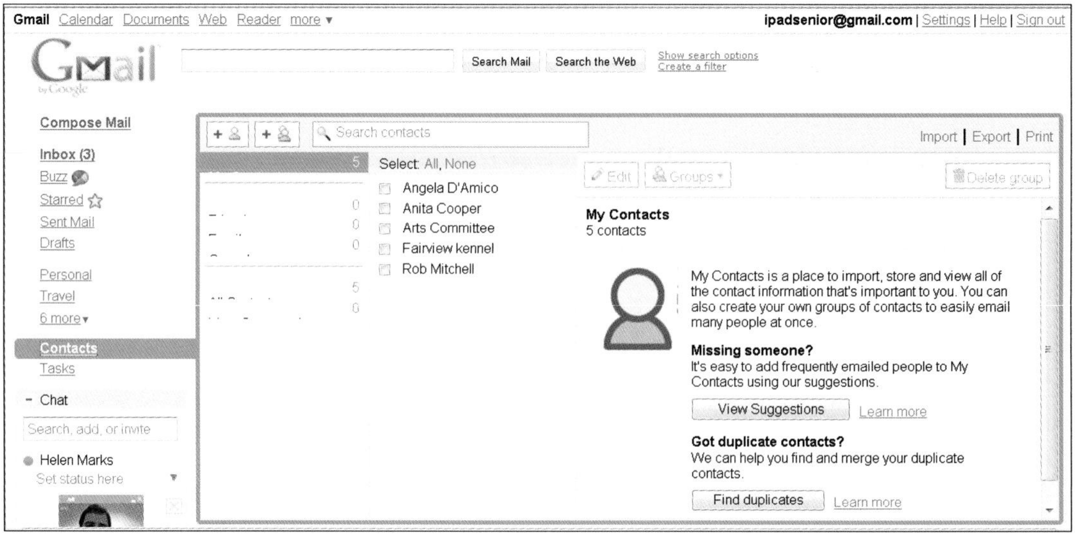

Figure 18-5

2. In the iTunes application that opens on your computer, click the name of your iPad (such as Nancy's iPad), which is now listed in the left navigation area of iTunes.

3. Click on the Info tab, shown in **Figure 18-6**.

4. Click to select the Sync Contacts check box, and then select your e-mail provider.

5. Enter your account information in the dialog that appears.

6. Click the Sync button and your iPad screen changes to show that syncing is in progress.

7. When the sync is complete, open Contacts on your iPad. All contacts have been brought over to it.

8. Unplug the Dock Connector to USB Cable.

 You can also use iCloud to automatically sync contacts among all your Apple devices. See Chapter 3 for more about making iCloud settings to choose whether your contacts are synced through the cloud.

Click this tab...

then select this option

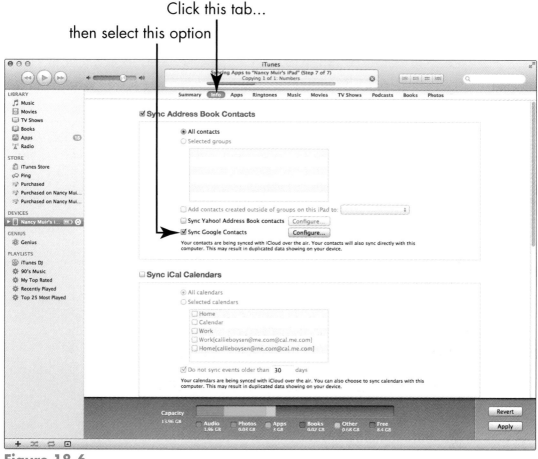

Figure 18-6

Assign a Photo to a Contact

1. With Contacts open, tap on a contact to whose record you want to add a photo.

2. Tap the Edit button.

3. On the Info page that appears (see **Figure 18-7**), tap Add Photo.

Tap here...

then select a photo option

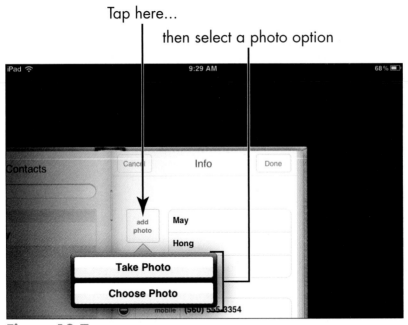

Figure 18-7

4. In the dialog that appears (refer to **Figure 18-7**), tap Choose Photo to choose an existing photo in the Photos app's Camera Roll (called the Saved Photos album on a first generation iPad). You could also choose Take Photo to take that contact's photo on the spot.

5. In the Photo Albums dialog that appears, choose a source for your photo (such as Camera Roll or Photo Library) or categories such as Last Import, Last 12 Months, or Flags.

6. In the photo album that appears, tap a photo to select it. The Choose Photo dialog, shown in **Figure 18-8,** appears.

7. Tap the Use button to use the photo for this contact. The photo appears on the contact's Info page (see **Figure 18-9**).

8. Tap Done to save changes to the contact.

Figure 18-8

Figure 18-9

While in the Choose Photo dialog in Step 6, you can modify the photo before saving it to the contact information. You can unpinch to expand the photo and move it around the space to focus on a particular section and then tap the Use button to use the modified version.

Add Twitter or Facebook Information

1. New with iOS 5, you can add Twitter information so you can quickly tweet (send a short message) others using Twitter or post a message to your contact's Facebook account. With Contacts open, tap a contact.

2. Tap the Edit button.

3. Scroll down and tap Add Fields.

4. In the list that appears (refer to **Figure 18-3**) tap on Twitter.

5. Both Twitter and Facebook fields open (see **Figure 18-10**). Tap in either field and enter the contact's user name information for an account.

Twitter and Facebook fields

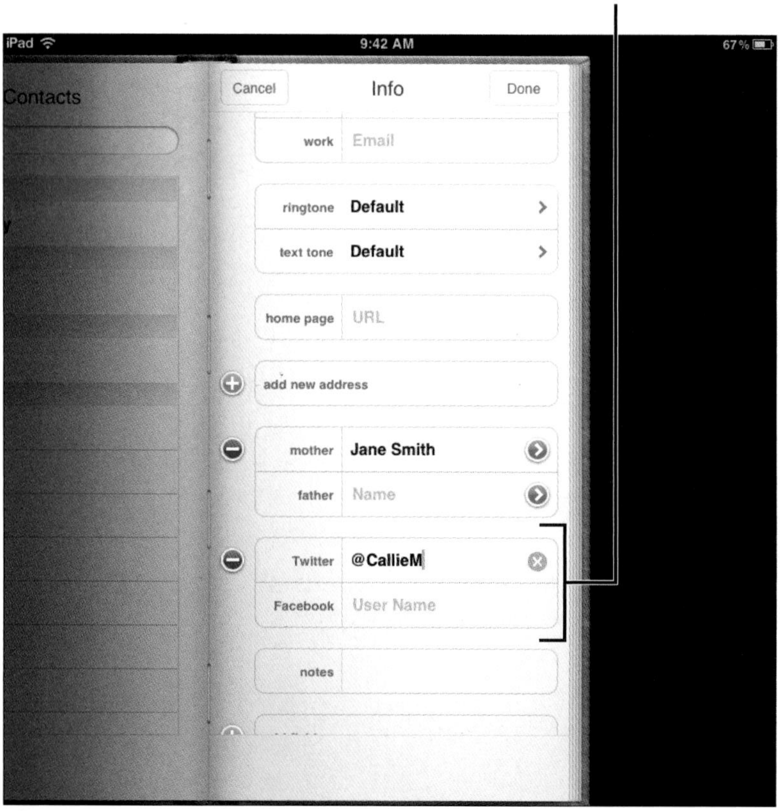

Figure 18-10

6. Tap Done and the information is saved. The account is now displayed when you select the contact and you can send a tweet or Facebook message by simply tapping on the user name and choosing the appropriate command (such as Tweet, as shown in **Figure 18-11**).

Figure 18-11

Designate Related People

1. You can quickly designate family relations in a contact record if those people are saved to Contacts. Tap a contact and then tap Edit.

2. Scroll down the record and tap Add Field.

3. Tap Related People (see **Figure 18-12**). A new field labeled Mother now appears.

Tap this option

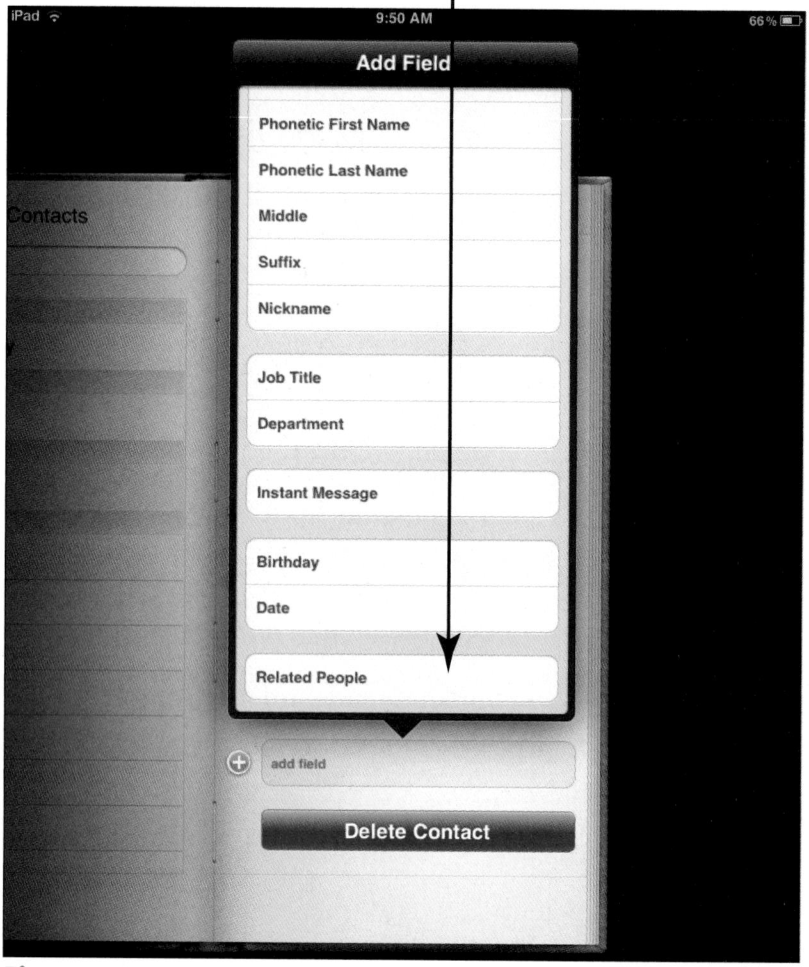

iPad 📶   9:50 AM   66% 🔋

Add Field

Phonetic First Name

Phonetic Last Name

Middle

Suffix

Nickname

Job Title

Department

Instant Message

Birthday

Date

Related People

➕ add field

Delete Contact

Contacts

Figure 18-12

4. Tap the word 'mother' and a list of other possible relations appears. Tap one to change the label if you wish.

5. Tap the blue arrow in the field and your contact list appears. Tap the person's name and it appears in the field. A new blank field also appears (see **Figure 18-13**).

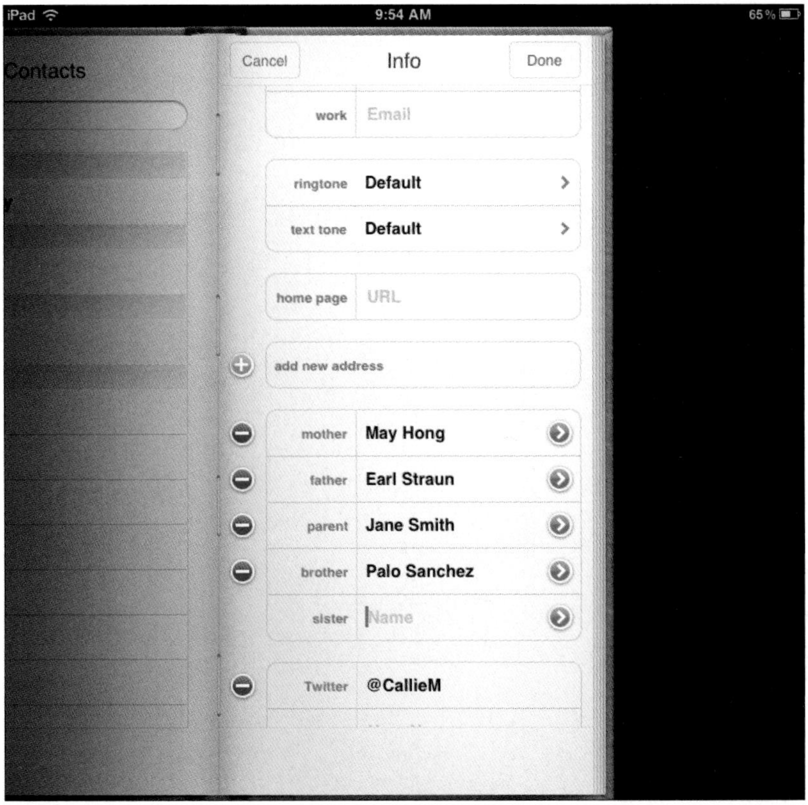

Figure 18-13

> After you add relations to a contact record, when you select the person in the Contacts main screen, all the related people for that contact are listed there.

Set Ringtones

1. If you want to hear a unique tone when you receive a FaceTime call from a particular contact, you can set this up in Contacts. For example, if you want to be sure you know instantly if your spouse, sick friend, or boss is calling, set a unique tone for that person. Tap to add a new contact or select a contact in the list of contacts and tap Edit.

2. Tap the Ringtone field and a list of tones appears (see **Figure 18-14**).

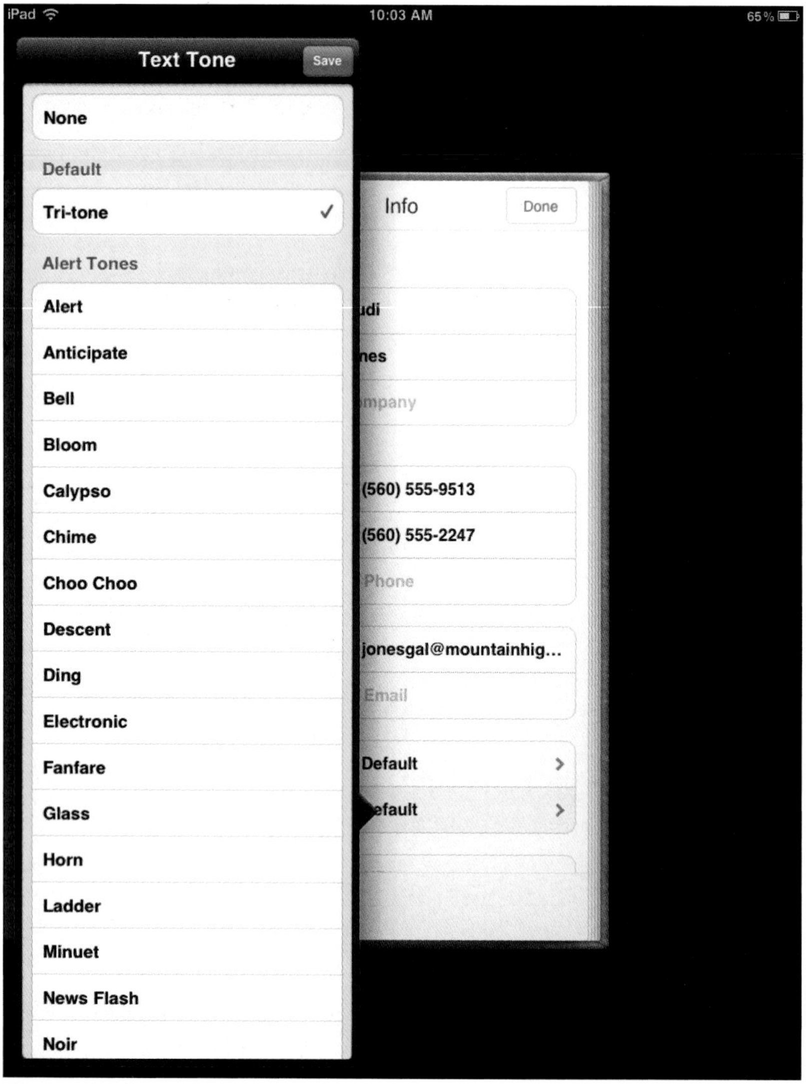

iPad 🛜	10:03 AM	65% 🔋

Text Tone Save

None

Default

Tri-tone ✓

Alert Tones

Alert

Anticipate

Bell

Bloom

Calypso

Chime

Choo Choo

Descent

Ding

Electronic

Fanfare

Glass

Horn

Ladder

Minuet

News Flash

Noir

Info Done

udi

nes

mpany

(560) 555-9513

(560) 555-2247

Phone

jonesgal@mountainhig...

Email

Default ›

efault ›

Figure 18-14

3. Tap on a tone and it previews. When you hear one you like, tap Save.

4. Tap Done to save the new tone setting.

 You can set a custom tone for FaceTime calls and text messages through Settings, General, Sounds.

If your Apple devices are synced via iCloud, setting a unique ringtone for an iPad contact will also set it for your iPhone. See Chapter 3 for more about iCloud.

Search for a Contact

1. With Contacts open, tap in the Search field at the top of the left page (see **Figure 18-15**). The onscreen keyboard opens.

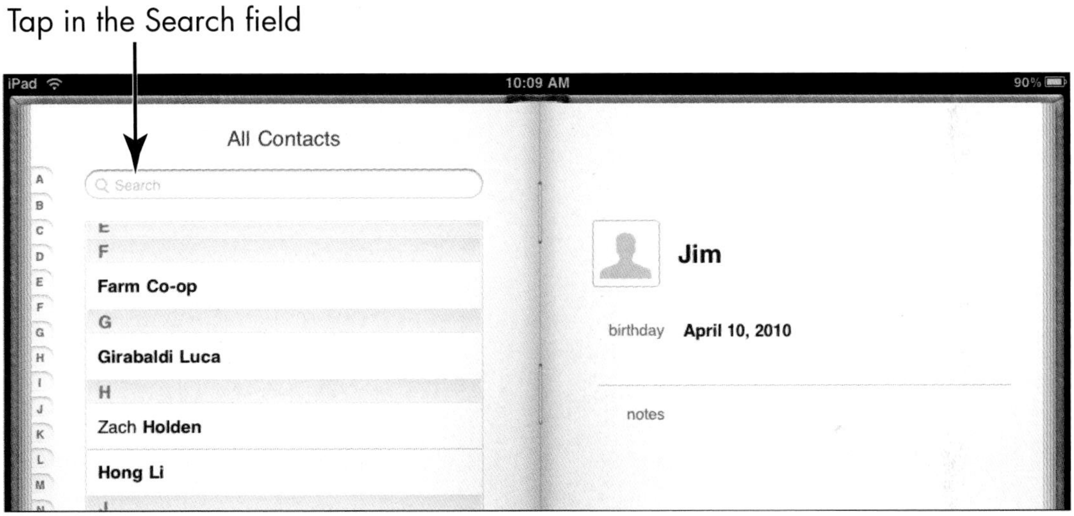

Tap in the Search field

Figure 18-15

2. Type the first letter of either the first or last name or company; all matching results appear, as shown in **Figure 18-16**. In the example, pressing *N* displays *Nancy Boysen*, *Nettie Dillon*, and *Space Needle* in the results, all of which have *N* as the first letter of the first or last part of the name.

3. Tap a contact in the results to display that person's information on the page on the right (refer to **Figure 18-16**).

 You can't search by phone number, website, or address in Contacts at the time of this writing, though you can search by these criteria using

Spotlight Search. We can only hope that Apple adds this functionality in future versions of the app!

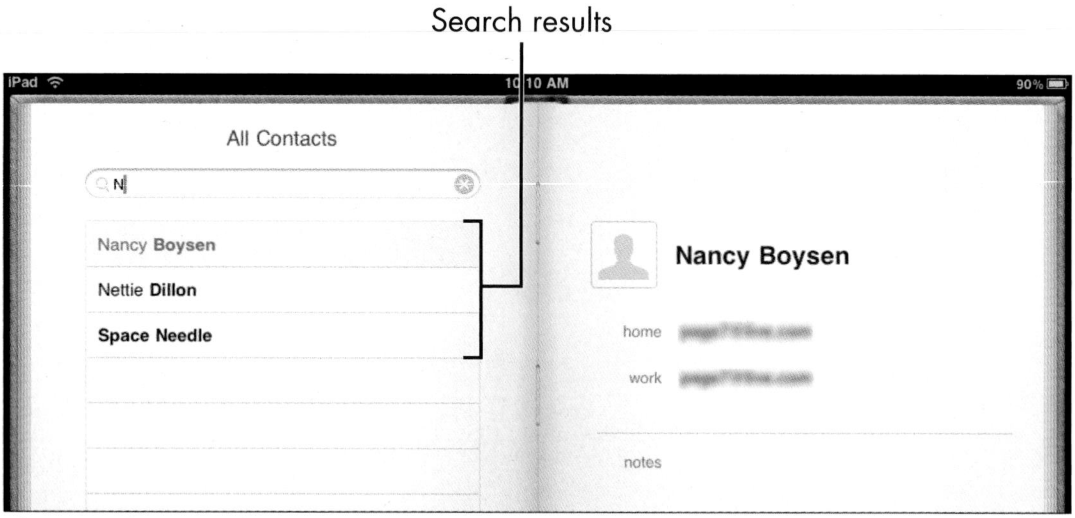

Search results

| iPad 🔋 | | 10:10 AM | | 90% 🔋 |

All Contacts

🔍 N

Nancy **Boysen**

Nettie **Dillon**

Space **Needle**

Nancy Boysen

home ▓▓▓▓▓▓

work ▓▓▓▓▓▓

notes

Figure 18-16

You can also use the alphabetical listing to locate a contact. Tap and drag to scroll down the list of contacts on the All Contacts page on the left. You can also tap on any tabbed letter along the left side of the page to scroll quickly to the entries starting with that letter.

Go to a Contact's Website

1. If you entered website information in the Home Page field, it automatically becomes a link in the contact's record. Tap the Contacts app icon on the Home screen to open Contacts.

2. Tap on a contact's name to display the person's contact information on the page at the right, and then tap the link in the Home Page field (see **Figure 18-17**).

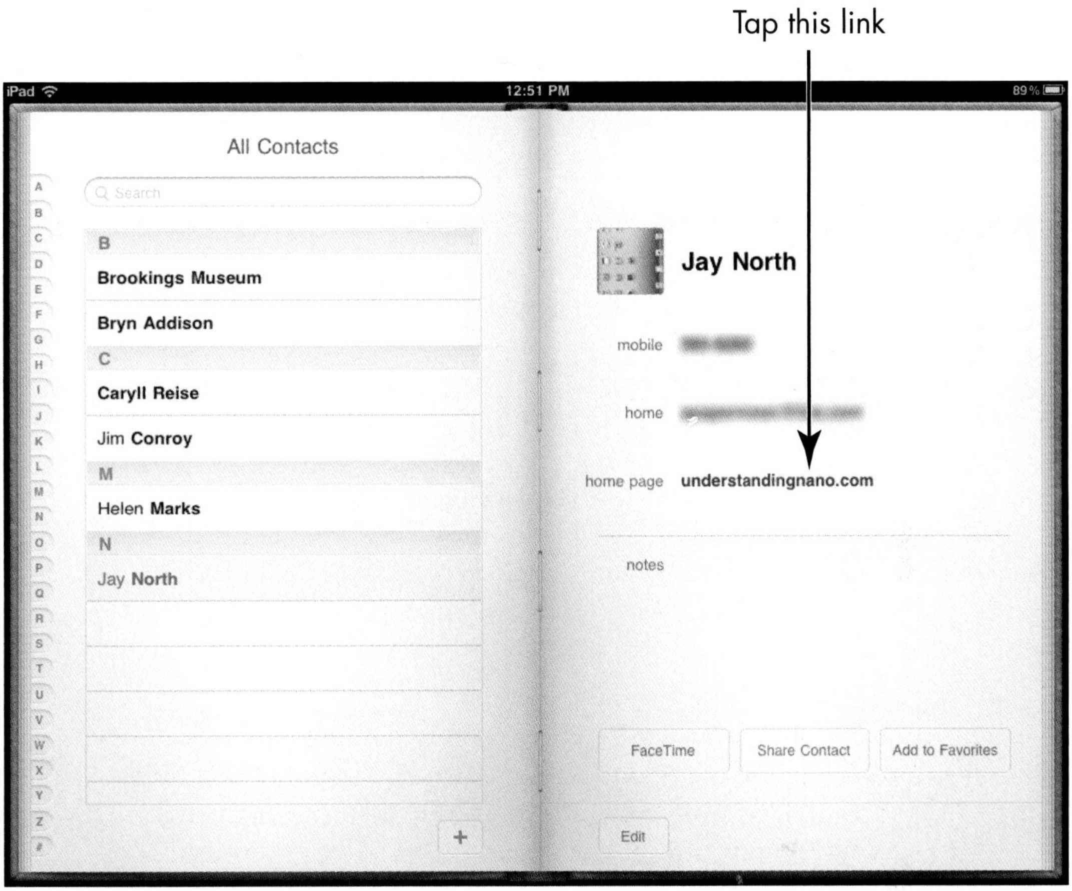

Tap this link

Figure 18-17

3. The Safari browser opens with the web page displayed (see **Figure 18-18**).

You cannot go directly back to Contacts after you follow a link to a website. You have to tap the Home button and then tap the Contacts app icon again to re-enter the application or use the multitasking feature by double-tapping the Home button and choosing Contacts from the icons that appear along the bottom of the screen.

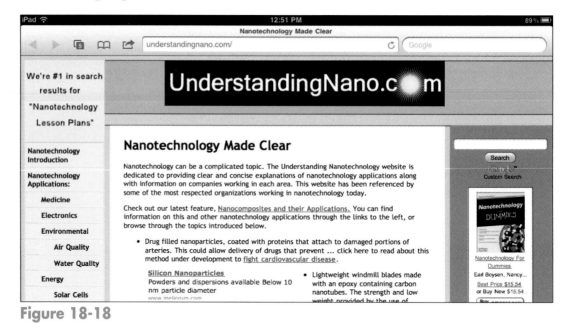

Figure 18-18

Address E-Mail Using Contacts

1. If you entered an e-mail address for a contact, the address automatically becomes a link in the contact's record. Tap the Contacts app icon on the Home screen to open Contacts.

2. Tap a contact's name to display the person's contact information on the page at the right, and then tap on the e-mail address link labeled Home (see **Figure 18-19**).

3. The New Message dialog appears, as shown in **Figure 18-20**. Initially the title bar of this dialog reads New Message but as you type a Subject, New Message changes to the specific title as shown in this example.

4. Use the onscreen keyboard to enter a subject and message.

5. Tap the Send button. The message goes on its way!

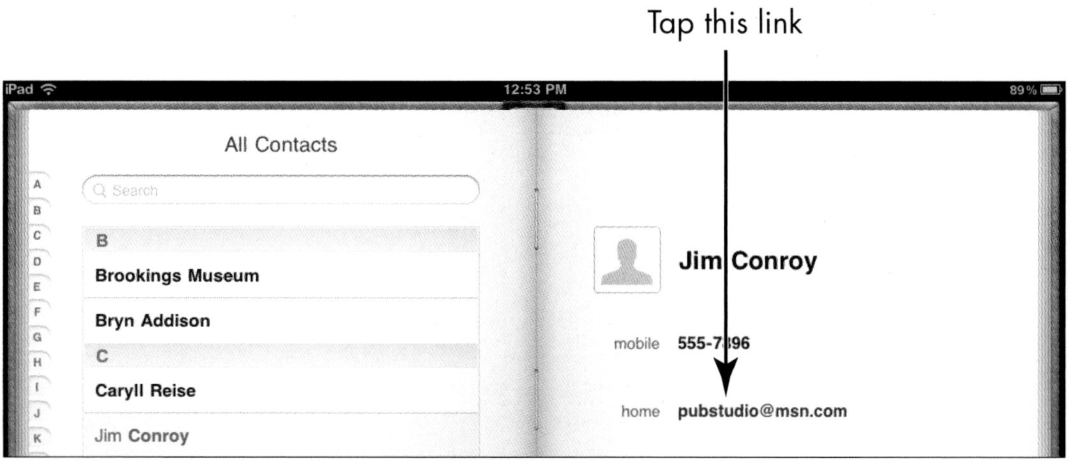

Tap this link

Figure 18-19

Figure 18-20

Share a Contact

1. After you've entered contact information, you can share it with others via an e-mail message. With Contacts open, tap a contact name to display its information.

2. On the information page, tap the Share Contact button (refer to **Figure 18-4**). In the dialog that appears tap either Email or Message. A New Message form appears.

3. In the New Message form, shown in **Figure 18-21**, use the onscreen keyboard to enter the recipient's e-mail address. Note if the person is saved in Contacts, just type his or her name here.

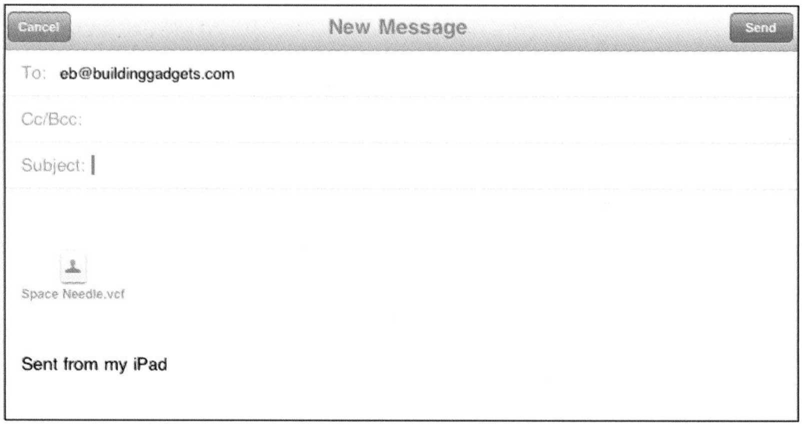

Cancel	New Message	Send

To: eb@buildinggadgets.com

Cc/Bcc:

Subject: |

Space Needle.vcf

Sent from my iPad

Figure 18-21

4. Enter information in the Subject field.

5. If you like, enter a message and then tap the Send button. The message goes to your recipient with the contact information attached as a `.vcf` file. (This *vCard* format is commonly used to transmit contact information.)

 When somebody receives a vCard containing contact information, he or she needs only to click the attached file to open it. At this point, depending on the the e-mail or contact management program, the recipient can perform various actions to save the content. Other iPhone, iPod touch, or iPad users can easily import `.vcf` records into their own Contacts apps.

View a Contact's Location in Maps

1. If you've entered a person's address in Contacts, you have a shortcut for viewing that person's location in the Maps application. Tap the Contacts app icon on the Home screen to open it.

2. Tap the contact you want to view to display his information.

3. Tap the address. Maps opens and displays a map to the address (see **Figure 18-22**).

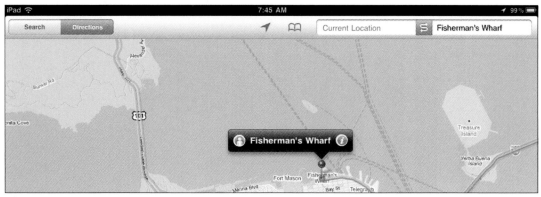

Figure 18-22

This task works with more than your friends' addresses. You can save information for your favorite restaurant or movie theater or any other location and use Contacts to jump to the associated website in the Safari browser or to the address in Maps. For more about using Safari, see Chapter 5. For more about the Maps application, see Chapter 17.

Delete a Contact

1. When it's time to remove a name or two from your Contacts, it's easy to do. With Contacts open, tap the contact you want to delete.

2. On the information page on the right (refer to **Figure 18-4**), tap the Edit button.

3. On the Info page that displays, drag your finger upward to scroll down and then tap the Delete Contact button at the bottom (see **Figure 18-23**).

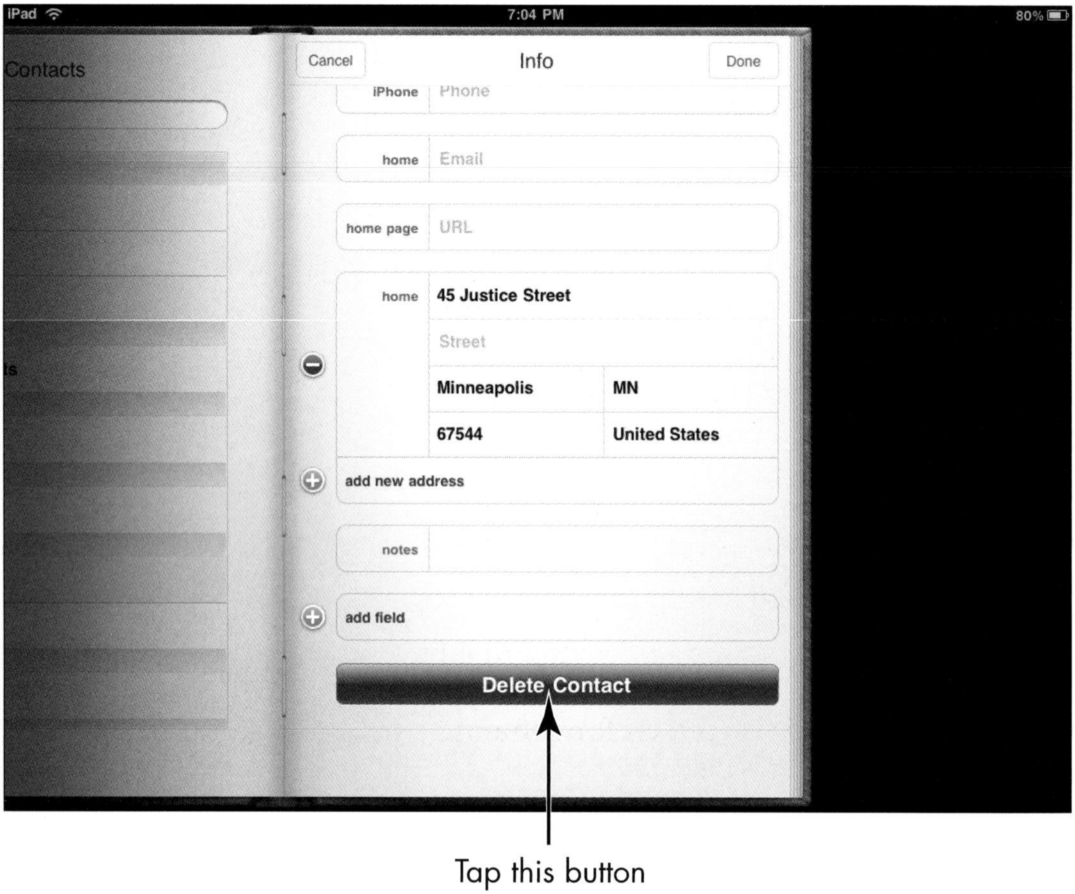

Tap this button

Figure 18-23

4. The confirming dialog shown in **Figure 18-24** appears; tap the Delete button to confirm the deletion.

Delete Contact

Delete ◁ Cancel ——— Tap this button

Figure 18-24

 During this process, if you change your mind before you tap Delete, tap the Cancel button in Step 4. But be careful: After you tap Delete, there's no going back!

Making Notes

*N*otes is the built-in application that you can use to do everything from jotting down notes at meetings to keeping to-do lists. It isn't a robust word processor (such as Apple Pages or Microsoft Word) by any means, but for taking notes on the fly, jotting down to-do lists, or writing a few pages of your novel-in-progress while you sit and sip a cup of tea on your deck, it's a great option.

In this chapter, you see how to enter and edit text in Notes and how to manage notes by navigating among them, search for content, e-mail notes, or delete notes.

Open a Blank Note

1. To get started with Notes, tap the Notes app icon on the Home screen. If you've never used Notes, it opens with a new, blank note displayed. (If you have used Notes, it opens to the last note you were working on. If that's the case, you might want to jump to the next task to create a new, blank note.) Depending on how your iPad is oriented, you see the view shown in **Figure 19-1** (portrait) or **Figure 19-2** (landscape).

Get ready to . . .

Figure 19-1

2. Tap the blank page. The onscreen keyboard, shown in
Figure 19-3, appears.

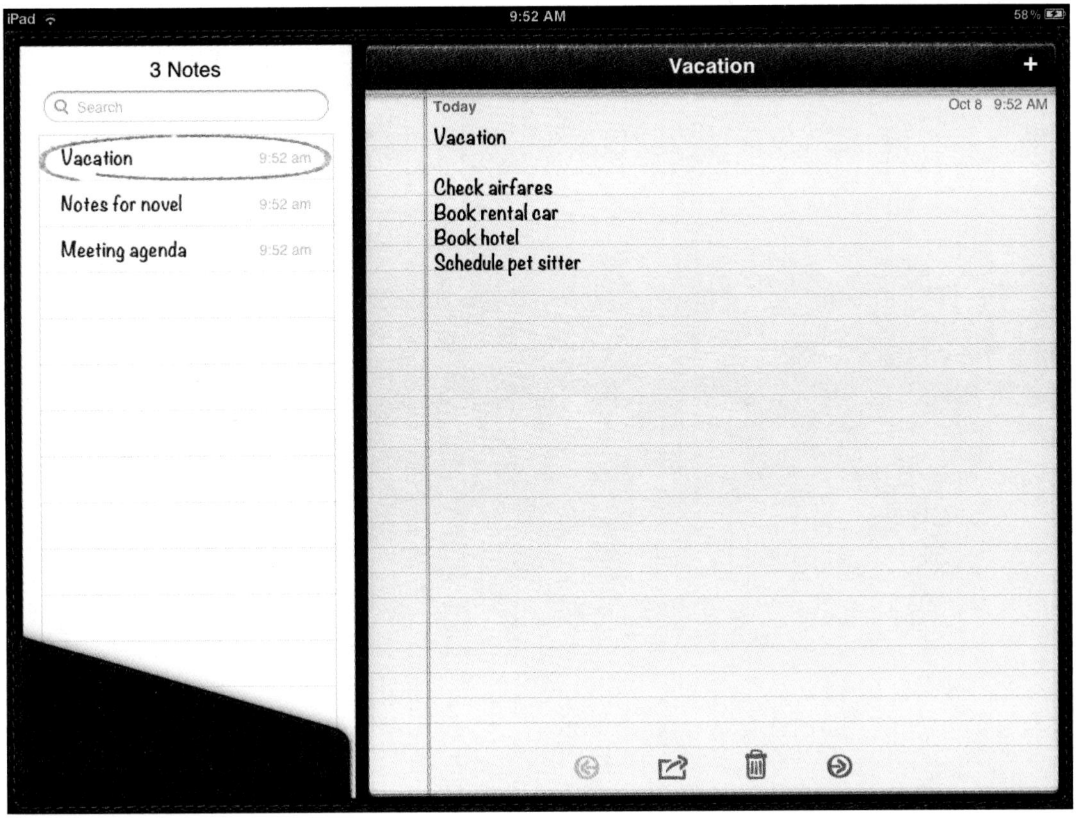

Figure 19-2

Figure 19-3

.?123 **3.** Tap keys on the keyboard to enter text. If you want to enter numbers or symbols, tap either of the keys labeled .?123 on the keyboard. The numerical keyboard, shown in **Figure 19-4,** appears. Whenever you want to return to the alphabetic keyboard, tap either of the keys labeled ABC.

Figure 19-4

4. To capitalize a letter, tap a Shift key (one with the upward-pointing arrow on it) at the same time as you tap the letter. If you enable the Enable Caps Lock feature in Settings, you can also turn caps lock on by double-tapping one the Shift key; tap the key once to turn the feature off.

5. When you want to start a new paragraph or a new item in a list, tap the Return key.

6. To edit text, tap the text you want to edit and either use the Delete key to delete text to the left of the cursor or type new text.

When you have the numerical keyboard displayed (refer to **Figure 19-4**), you can tap either of the keys labeled #+= to access more symbols, such as the percentage sign or the euro symbol, or additional bracket styles. Pressing and holding certain keys displays alternative characters.

No need to save a note — it's kept automatically until you delete it.

Create a New Note

 1. With one note open, to create a new note, tap the New Note button — the one with the plus sign (+) on it — in the top-right corner.

2. A new, blank note appears (refer to **Figure 19-1**). Enter and edit text as described in the previous task.

If your iPad is in portrait orientation and you want to see the list of saved notes beside the current note, switch to landscape orientation. You can also tap the Notes button in portrait orientation to see a drop-down list of notes.

Use Copy and Paste

1. The Notes app includes two essential editing tools you're probably familiar with from other word processors: copy and paste. With a note displayed, press and hold your finger on a word. The toolbar shown in **Figure 19-5** appears.

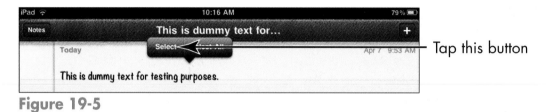

Tap this button

Figure 19-5

2. Tap the Select button. The toolbar shown in **Figure 19-6** appears.

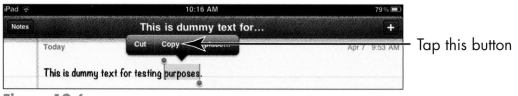

Tap this button

Figure 19-6

3. Tap the Copy button.

4. Press and hold your finger in the document at the spot where you want to place the copied text.

5. On the toolbar that appears (see **Figure 19-7**), tap the Paste button. The copied text appears.

Tap this option

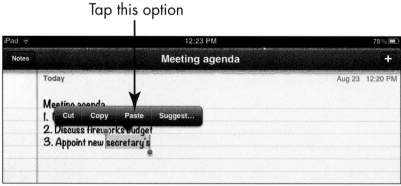

Figure 19-7

If you want to select all text in a note to either delete or copy it, tap the Select All button on the toolbar shown in **Figure 19-5**. The Cut/Copy/Paste/Suggest toolbar appears, which you can use to deal with the selected text. To extend a selection to adjacent words, press one of the little handles that extent from the selection and drag to the left or right. To get an alternate spelling suggestion you can tap Suggest.

To delete text, you can use the Select or Select All command and then press the Delete key on the onscreen keyboard.

Display the Notes List

1. Tap the Notes app icon on the Home screen to open Notes.

2. In landscape orientation, a list of notes appears by default on the left side of the screen (refer to **Figure 19-2**). In portrait orientation, you can display this list by tapping the Notes button in the top-left corner of the screen; the notes list appears, as shown in **Figure 19-8**.

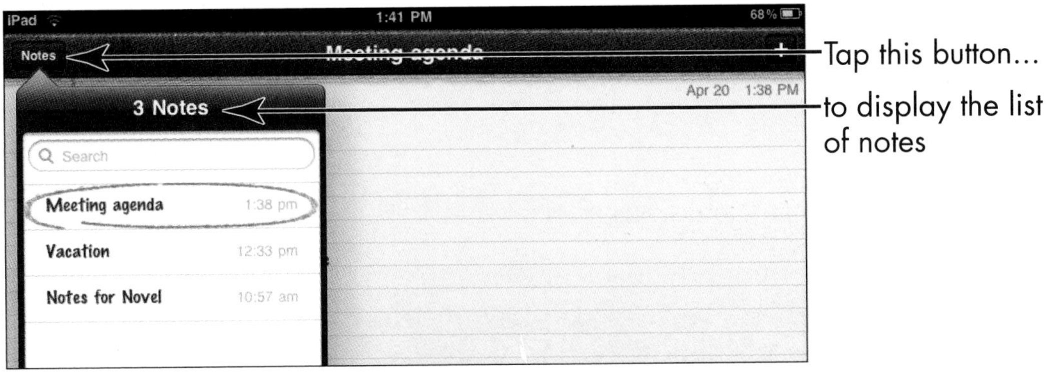

iPad	1:41 PM	68%
Notes	Meeting agenda	+
		Apr 20 1:38 PM

3 Notes

Q Search

Meeting agenda	1:38 pm
Vacation	12:33 pm
Notes for Novel	10:57 am

Tap this button...

to display the list of notes

Figure 19-8

3. Tap any note on the list to display it.

 Notes names your note, using the first line of text. If you want to rename a note, first display the note, tap at the end of the first line of text, and then tap the Delete key on your onscreen keyboard to delete the old title. Enter a new title; it's reflected as the name of your note in the notes list.

Move among Notes

1. You have a couple of ways to move among notes you've created. Tap the Notes app icon on the Home screen to open Notes.

2. With the notes list displayed (you can either turn your iPad to landscape orientation or tap the Notes button in portrait orientation; see the previous task for more on viewing the notes list), tap a note to open it.

3. To move among notes, tap the Next or Previous button (the right- or left-facing arrow at the bottom of the Notes pad, as shown in **Figure 19-9**).

Tap either of these buttons

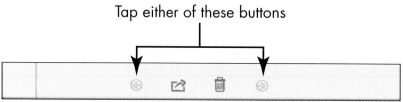

Figure 19-9

 Even though Notes lets you enter multiple notes with the same title — which causes confusion — name your notes uniquely!

Search for a Note

1. You can search to locate a note that contains certain text. The Search feature lists only notes that contain your search criteria; it doesn't highlight and show you every instance of the word or words you enter. Tap the Notes app icon on the Home screen to open Notes.

2. Either hold the iPad in landscape orientation or tap the Notes button in portrait orientation to display the notes list (refer to **Figure 19-8**).

3. Tap in the Search field at the top of the notes list (see **Figure 19-10**). The onscreen keyboard appears.

Tap here to display the onscreen keyboard

Figure 19-10

4. Begin to enter the search term. All notes that contain matching words appear on the list, as shown in **Figure 19-11**.

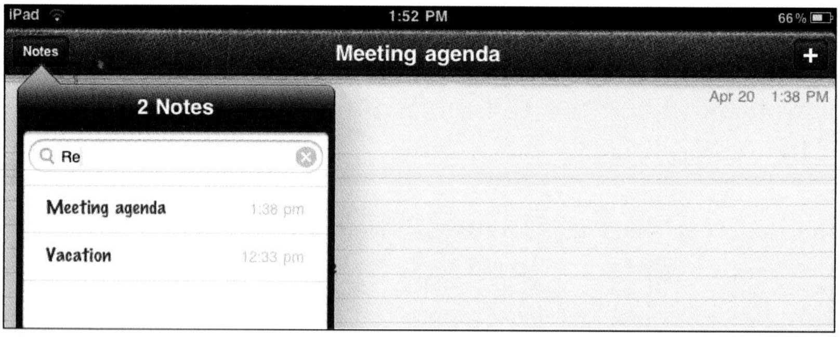

Figure 19-11

5. Tap a note to display it and then locate the instance of the matching word the old-fashioned way — by skimming to find it.

> If you want to look for a note based on how long ago you created it, you should know that notes are stored with the most recently created or modified notes — at the top of the notes list. Older notes fall toward the bottom of the list. The date you last modified a note is also listed in the notes list to help you out.

E-Mail a Note

1. If you want to share what you wrote with a friend or colleague, you can easily e-mail the contents of a note. With a note displayed, tap the E-Mail button at the bottom of the screen, as shown in **Figure 19-12**.

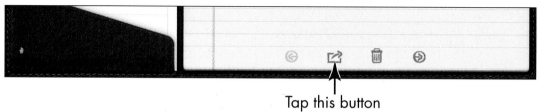

Tap this button

Figure 19-12

2. Tap Email. In the e-mail form that appears (see **Figure 19-13**), type one or more e-mail addresses in the appropriate fields. At least one e-mail address must appear in the To field.

iPad	2:03 PM	65%
Cancel	**Meeting agenda**	Send

To: ipadsenior@gmail.com ⏐   ⊕   Enter e-mail
                                                                    addresses here
Cc/Bcc:

Subject: Meeting agenda

Meeting agenda

1. Review committee report
2. Discuss fireworks budget
3. Appoint new secretary
4. Appoint new member-at-large

Sent from my iPad

Figure 19-13

3. If you need to make changes to the subject or message, tap in either area and make the changes.

4. Tap the Send button and your e-mail is on its way.

 If you want to print a note in Step 2, choose Print rather than Email. Complete the Printer Options dialog by designating an AirPrint-enabled wireless printer (or shared printer on a printer on a network that you can access using AirPrint) and how many copies to print, and then tap Print.

 You can tap the button with a plus sign (+) on it in the top-right corner of the e-mail message form to display your contacts list and choose recipients from it. This method works only with contacts for whom you have added an e-mail addresses. See Chapter 18 for more about using the Contacts app.

To cancel an e-mail message and return to Notes
without sending it, tap the Cancel button in the
e-mail form and then tap Don't Save on the menu
that appears. To leave a message but save a draft so
that you can finish and send it later, tap Cancel and
then tap Save. The next time you tap the e-mail
button with the same note displayed in Notes, your
draft appears.

Delete a Note

1. There's no sense in letting your notes list get cluttered,
making it harder to find the ones you need. When you're
done with a note, it's time to delete it. Tap the Notes app
icon on the Home screen to open Notes.

2. With the iPad in landscape orientation, tap a note in the
notes list to open it.

3. Tap the Trash Can button, shown in **Figure 19-14**.

Tap this button

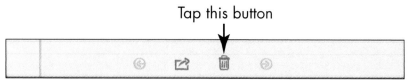

Figure 19-14

4. Tap the Delete Note button that appears (see
Figure 19-15). The note is deleted.

Tap this button

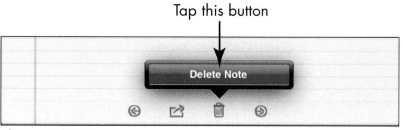

Figure 19-15

Notes is a nice little application, but it's limited. It offers no formatting tools or ways to print the content you enter. You can't paste pictures into Notes (you can try, but it won't work: only the filename appears, not the image). So, if you've made some notes and want to graduate to building a more robust document in a word processor, you have a couple of options. One way is to buy the Pages word processor application for iPad, which costs about $9.99, and copy your note (using the copy-and-paste feature discussed earlier in this chapter). Alternatively, you can send the note to yourself in an e-mail message. Open the e-mail and copy and paste its text into a full-fledged word processor, and you're good to go.

Troubleshooting and Maintaining Your iPad

*i*Pads don't grow on trees — they cost a pretty penny. That's why you should learn how to take care of your iPad and troubleshoot any problems it might have so that you get the most out of it.

In this chapter, I provide some advice about the care and maintenance of your iPad, as well as tips about how to solve common problems, update iPad system software, and even reset the iPad if something goes seriously wrong. In case you lose your iPad, I even tell you about a new feature that helps you find it — or even disable it if it has fallen into the wrong hands. Finally, you get information about backing up your iPad settings and content using iCloud.

Keep the iPad Screen Clean

If you've been playing with your iPad, you know (despite Apple's claim that the iPad has a fingerprint-resistant screen) that it's a fingerprint magnet. Here are some tips for cleaning your iPad screen:

➡️ **Use a dry, soft cloth:** You can get most fingerprints off with a dry, soft cloth such as the one you use to clean your eyeglasses or a cleaning tissue that's lint- and chemical-free. Or try products used to clean lenses in labs such as Kimwipes or Kaydry, which you can get from several major retailers such as Amazon.

➡️ **Use a slightly dampened soft cloth:** To get the surface even cleaner, slightly dampen the soft cloth. Again, make sure that whatever cloth material you use is free of lint.

➡️ **Remove the cables:** Turn off your iPad and unplug any cables from it before cleaning the screen with a moistened cloth.

➡️ **Avoid too much moisture:** Avoid getting too much moisture around the edges of the screen, where it can seep into the unit.

➡️ **Never use household cleaners:** They can degrade the coating that keeps the iPad screen from absorbing oil from your fingers.

 Do *not* use premoistened lens-cleaning tissues to clean your iPad screen. Most brands of wipe contain alcohol, which can damage the screen's coating.

Protect Your Gadget with a Case

Your screen isn't the only element on the iPad that can be damaged, so consider getting a case for it so you can carry it around the house or around town safely. Besides providing a bit of padding if you drop the device, a case makes the iPad less slippery in your hands, offering a better grip when working with it.

Several types of cases were available the first day the iPad shipped, and more are showing up all the time. You can choose the Smart Cover, from Apple, for example ($39 for polyurethane or $69 for leather), or a cover from another manufacturer, such as Tuff-Luv (www.Tuff-Luv.com) or Griffin (www.griffintechnology.com) that come in materials ranging from leather to silicone (see **Figure 20-1** and **Figure 20-2**).

Figure 20-1

←A silicone "skin" case

Figure 20-2

Cases range from a few dollars to $70 or more for leather (with some outrageously expensive designers cases upward of $500). Some provide a cover for the screen and back (refer to **Figure 20-1**), and others protect only the back and sides (refer to **Figure 20-2**) or, in the case of Smart Cover, only the screen. If you carry your iPad around much, consider a case with a screen cover to provide better protection for the screen or use a screen overlay, such as InvisibleShield from Zagg (www.Zagg.com).

Extend Your iPad's Battery Life

The much-touted 10-hour battery life of the iPad is a wonderful feature, but you can do some things to extend it even further. Here are a few tips to consider:

➡ **Keep tabs on remaining battery life:** You can estimate the amount of remaining battery life by looking at the Battery icon on the far-right end of the Status bar, at the top of your screen.

➡ **Use standard accessories to charge your iPad most effectively:** When connected to a Mac computer for charging, the iPad can slowly charge; charging the iPad on certain PC connections, on the other hand, slowly *drains* the battery. Even so, the most effective way to charge your iPad is to plug it into the wall outlet using the Dock Connector to USB Cable and the 10W USB Power Adapter that come with your iPad (see **Figure 20-3**).

➡ The fastest way to charge the iPad is to turn it off while charging it.

➡ Your battery may *lose* power if you leave it connected to the USB port on an external keyboard.

➡ The Battery icon on the Status bar lets you know when the charging is complete.

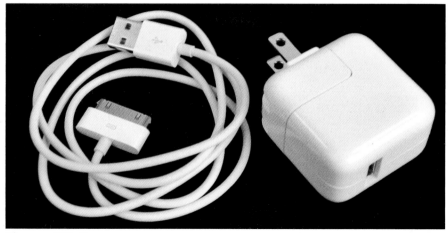

Figure 20-3

 Your iPad battery is sealed in the unit, so you can't replace it, as you can with many laptops or cellphone batteries. If the battery is out of warranty, you have to fork over more than $100, possibly, to get a new one. See the "Get Support" section, later in this chapter, to find out where to get a replacement battery.

Find Out What to Do with a Nonresponsive iPad

If your iPad goes dead on you, it's most likely a power issue, so the first thing to do is to plug the Dock Connector to USB Cable into the 10W USB Power Adapter, plug the 10W USB Power Adapter into a wall outlet, plug the other end of the Dock Connector to USB Cable into your iPad, and charge the battery.

Another thing to try — if you believe that an app is hanging up the iPad — is to press the Sleep/Wake button for a couple of seconds. Then press and hold the Home button. The app you were using should close.

You can always try the old reboot procedure, too: On the iPad, you press the Sleep/Wake button on top until the red slider appears. Drag the slider to the right to turn off your iPad. After a few moments, press the Sleep/Wake button to boot up the little guy again.

If the situation seems drastic and none of these ideas works, try to reset your iPad. To do this, press the Sleep/Wake button and the Home button at the same time until the Apple logo appears onscreen.

Make the Keyboard Reappear

When you're using a Bluetooth keyboard, your onscreen keyboard doesn't appear. The physical keyboard has, in essence, co-opted keyboard control of your device. To use your onscreen keyboard after connecting a Bluetooth keyboard, you can turn off the Bluetooth keyboard by turning off Bluetooth in the iPad's General settings, or by moving the keyboard out of range or switching the keyboard off. Your onscreen keyboard should reappear.

Update Software

1. Apple occasionally updates the iPad system software to fix problems or offer enhanced features. You should occasionally check for an updated version (say, every month). Start by connecting your iPad to your computer.

2. On your computer, open the iTunes software you installed. (See Chapter 3 for more about this topic.)

3. Click on your iPad in the iTunes source list on the left.

4. Click the Summary tab, shown in **Figure 20-4**.

5. Click the Check for Update button. iTunes displays a message telling you whether a new update is available.

6. Click the Update button to install the newest version.

 If you're having problems with your iPad, you can use the Update feature to try to restore the current version of the software. Follow the preceding set of steps, and then click the Restore button instead of the Update button in Step 6.

Click on your iPad... then click the Summary tab

Figure 20-4

 If you've chosen to back up and restore iPad via iCloud when you first set up the device, restoring and updating your device happens automatically.

Restore the Sound

On the morning I wrote this chapter, as my husband puttered with our iPad, its sound suddenly (and ironically) stopped working. We gave ourselves a quick course in sound recovery, so now I can share some tips with you. Make sure that

⟹ **You haven't touched the volume control keys on a physical keyboard connected to your iPad via Bluetooth:** They're on the right side of the top row (see **Figure 20-5**). Be sure not to touch one and inadvertently mute the sound.

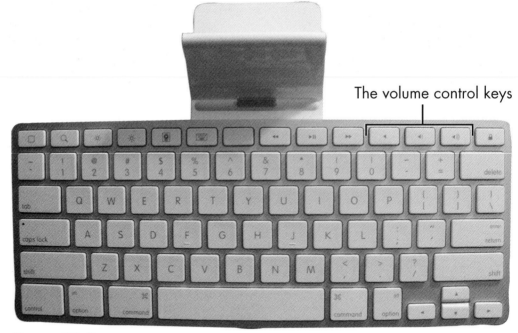

The volume control keys

Figure 20-5

⟼ **You haven't flipped the Silent switch:** If you have the Screen Rotation/Silent switch set up to the Silent feature, moving the switch mutes sound on the iPad.

⟼ **The speaker isn't covered up:** It may be covered in a way that muffles the sound.

⟼ **A headset isn't plugged in:** Sound doesn't play over the speaker and the headset at the same time.

⟼ **The volume limit is set to Off:** You can set up the volume limit in the Music settings to control how loudly your music can play (which is useful if you have teenagers around). Tap the Settings icon on the Home screen and then, on the left side of the screen that displays, tap Music and use the Volume Limit control (see **Figure 20-6**) to turn off the volume limit.

Make sure this is set to Off

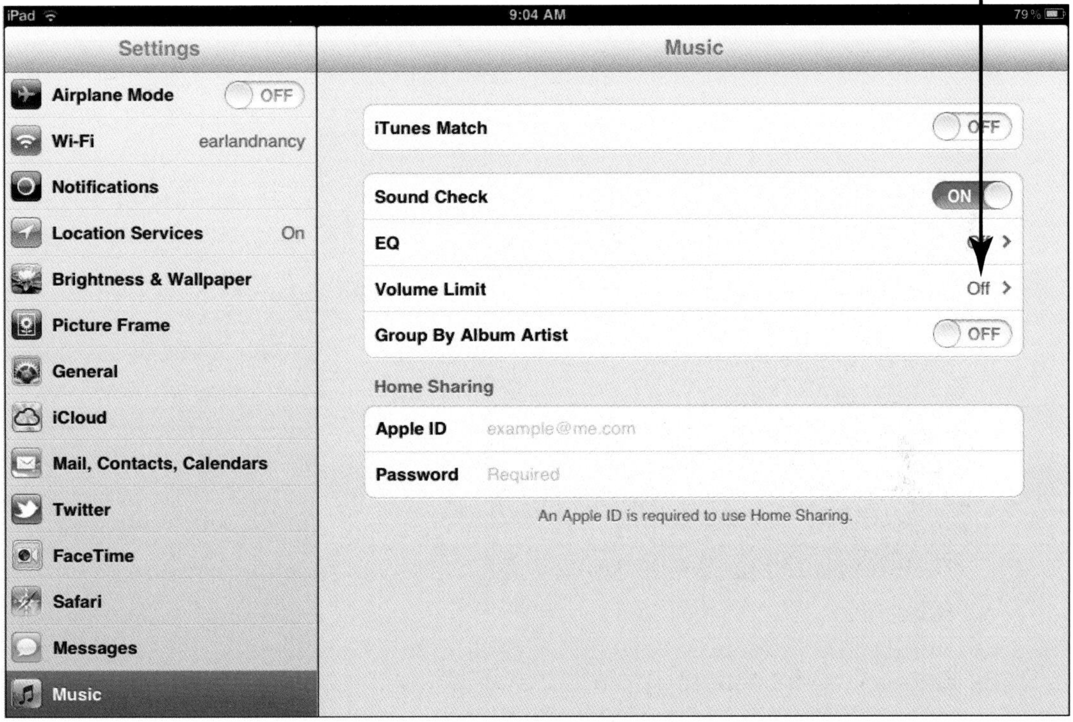

Figure 20-6

 When all else fails, reboot. This strategy worked for us — just press the Sleep/Wake button until the red slider appears. Press and drag the slider to the right. After the iPad turns off, press the Sleep/Wake button again until the Apple logo appears, and you may find yourself back in business, sound-wise.

Get Support

Apple is known for its helpful customer support, so if you're stuck, I definitely recommend that you try it out. Here are a few options you can explore for getting help:

⟶ **The Apple Store:** Go to your local Apple Store (if one is handy) to see what the folks there might know about your problem.

⟶ **The Apple support website:** It's at `www.apple.com/support/ipad` (see **Figure 20-7**). You can find online manuals, discussion forums, and downloads, and you can use the Apple Expert feature to contact a live support person by phone.

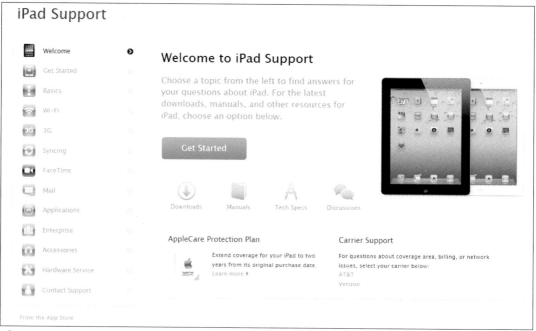

Figure 20-7

⟶ **The *iPad User Guide:*** You can use the bookmarked manual on the Safari browser to visit `http://manuals.info.apple.com/en_US/iPad_User_Guide.pdf` and open a more robust version of the user guide that comes with your iPad.

⟶ **The Apple battery replacement service:** If you need repair or service for your battery, visit `www.apple.com/batteries/replacements.html`. Note that your warranty provides free battery replacement if the battery level dips below 50 percent and won't go any higher during the first year you own it. If you purchase the AppleCare service agreement, this is extended to two years.

Apple recommends that you have your iPad battery replaced only by an Apple Authorized Service Provider.

Find a Missing iPad

You can take advantage of the FindMyiPad feature to pinpoint the location of your iPad. This feature is extremely handy if you forget where you left your iPad or someone steals it. FindMyiPad not only lets you track down the critter but also lets you wipe out the data contained in it if you have no way to get the iPad back.

Follow these steps to set up the FindMyiPad feature:

1. Tap the Settings icon on the Home screen.

2. In the Settings pane, tap iCloud.

3. In the iCloud settings that tap the On/Off button for Find My iPad to turn the feature on (see **Figure 20-8**).

MobileMe	Done
MobileMe	
Account	ipadsenior@gmail.com >
Find My iPad	ON
Allow this iPad to be shown on a map or remotely wiped.	
Delete Account	

Figure 20-8

4. From now on, if your iPad is lost or stolen, you can go to `http://iCloud.com` from your computer and enter your ID and password.

5. The Find My iPhone screen appears with your iPad's location noted on a map.

6. To wipe information from the iPad, click the Remote
Wipe button (see **Figure 20-9**). To lock the iPad from
access by others click the Remote Lock button.

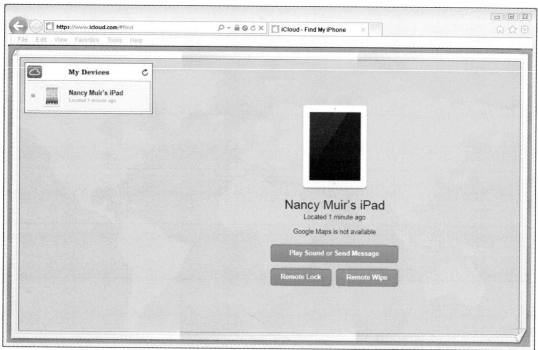

Figure 20-9

 You can also click Display a Message or Play a Sound
to send whoever has your iPad a note saying how to
return it to you — or that the police are on their way,
if it has been stolen! If you choose to play a sound, it
plays for two minutes, helping you track down
anybody holding your iPad who is within earshot.

Backup to iCloud

 You used to only be able to backup your iPad content using
iTunes, but with Apple's introduction of iCloud, you can
back up via a Wi-Fi network to your iCloud
storage. You get 5 GB of storage (not including iTunes
bought music, video, apps, and electronic books) for free or

you can pay for increased levels of storage (10 GB for $20 a year, 20 GB for $40 a year, or 50 GB for $100 a year).

1. To perform a backup to iCloud, first set up an iCloud account (see Chapter 3 for details on creating an iCloud account) and then tap Settings on the Home Screen.

2. Tap iCloud and then tap Storage & Backup (see **Figure 20-10**).

Tap this option

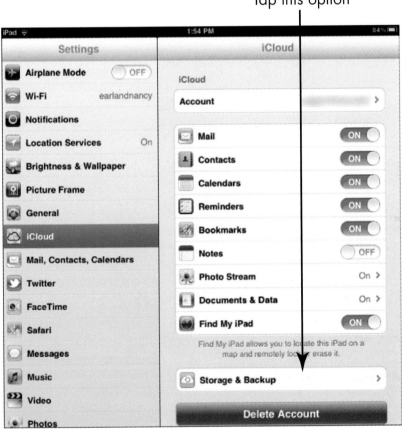

Figure 20-10

3. In the pane that appears (see **Figure 20-11**) tap the iCloud Backup On/Off switch to enable automatic backups. To perform a manual backup tap Back Up Now. A progress bar shows how your backup is moving along.

Set this to On

Figure 20-11

Index